80p

lonely planet FOOD

GOURMET TRAILS

EUROPE

INTRODUCTION

Europe is arguably the most diverse culinary continent on the planet. Centuries of occupation, migration and exploration have infused the cooking pot of virtually every country. Food traditions can be fiercely local, to the point where they're only practised in one particular medieval village, and there are recipes here that have been passed down from generation to generation for almost a millennium. But this is also a continent of pioneering and creative chefs, who are writing a new food language by fusing tradition with new cooking techniques and sustainable sourcing methods. Drinks, too, are a key part of this region's allure. This is a boozy part of the world. That means wine, of course, but also craft and heritage distilleries - all of which produce unique drinks reflecting the lands in which they were made.

This book takes you on a tour of 40 of Europe's best epicurean regions, with itineraries featuring food and drink experiences for every budget. That could mean rolling up your sleeves for a country cooking class, foraging in the woods, tasting stinky cheeses or queuing with locals for outrageously good street food. But there's also Michelin-starred dining, waterfront seafood feasting and wine-tasting odysseys on dreamy vineyard terraces. In Europe, you can have it all. Bon appétit!

CONTENTS

CENTRAL EUROPE

NORTHERN EUROPE

SOUTHERN EUROPE

EUROPE

NORWAY

OSLO ✪

22

SCOTLAND

NORTH SEA

DENMARK

COPENHAGEN ✪

15

✪ EDINBURGH

18

19

NORTHERN IRELAND

✪ BELFAST

✪ DOUGLAS

ENGLAND

11

DUBLIN ✪

IRELAND

WALES

20

✪ AMSTERDAM

NETHERLANDS

BERLIN ✪

GERMANY

21

CARDIFF ✪

✪ LONDON

✪ BRUSSELS

02

BELGIUM

LUXEM-BOURG

ENGLISH CHANNEL

PARIS ✪

06

NORTH ATLANTIC OCEAN

08

03

09

LIECH-TENSTEIN

FRANCE

BERN ✪

SWITZERLAND

24

BAY OF BISCAY

07

10

30

SAN MARINO

04

29

MONACO

26

✪

ANDORRA

05

ITALY

36

Corsica (FRANCE)

ROME ✪

37

SPAIN

✪ MADRID

BALEARIC SEA

Sardinia (ITALY)

TYRRHENIAN SEA

34

PORTUGAL

✪ LISBON

35

MEDITERRANEAN SEA

28

33

38

✪ ALGIERS

✪ TUNIS

GIBRALTAR (UK)

MADEIRA (PORTUGAL)

✪ RABAT

TUNISIA

MOROCCO

ALGERIA

TRIPOLI ✪

CANARY ISLANDS (SPAIN)

39

CENTRAL EUROPE

GET THERE

Buses and trains run from Vienna's international airport, 19km (12 miles) southwest of the city centre, into central Wien-Mitte. But the city is also well connected to the rest of Europe by rail, including a Nightjet service. Trams, S-Bahn (suburban) and U-Bahn (underground) trains take you out to the *heurigen*; most are around half an hour from the centre.

01

KLOSTERNEUBURG

08

FLORIDSDORF

07

06

05

Danube (Donau)

DÖBLING

03

04

02

OTTAKRING

INNERE
STADT ★ VIENNA

PENZING

NEUBAU

WIEDEN

HIETZING

MEIDLING

FAVORITEN

SIMMERING

01

MAUER

[Austria]

AMONG THE VINES IN VIENNA

As spring ushers in warmer days, the Viennese escape the city buzz with drowsy afternoons spent nursing a glass of zesty white wine in the capital's heurigen *taverns.*

Vienna? For wine? You must be kidding... If you had praised the city for its wine a decade ago, oenophiles would have certainly raised eyebrows in disbelief. But lately Vienna has seriously upped its viniculture game, with quality improving tenfold. Each year the city scoops international awards as vintners get increasingly experimental and focus on organic, biodynamic and vegan wines that chime with these sustainably minded times. Nature rules.

Welcome to the world's only capital city to grow significant quantities of wine within its boundaries. A quick tram or U-Bahn spin from the historic centre brings you to Vienna's 16th (Ottakring), 19th (Döbling) and 21st (Floridsdorf) districts, where the mood-lifting scene flicks suddenly from modern cityscape to hills ribbed with vines dipping gently to the Danube. This is where you'll find the city's *heurigen*, family-run taverns swirling in wine, good cheer and

history, where you can drink, eat heartily and dream the day away with on-high views of Vienna.

Deeply rooted in a wine-making tradition that dates to Roman times and now on Unesco's list of intangible cultural heritage, *heurigen* are about simple pleasures: a rustic parlour; a vine-spun courtyard; wine; generous buffets of dark bread, cured meats, cheese and pickles – the good life. White wines are the stars, from the Vienna-in-a-glass blend called Gemischter Satz, to tart Rieslings and minerally Grüner Veltliners. But juicy, spicy reds like Zweigelt are also worth a cork pop.

Most *heurigen* run from spring to autumn, announcing they are open with sprigs of fir and a sign saying *Ausg'steckt* above the door. If you want to sample the Austrian love of *gemütlichkeit* – warmth, cosiness and conviviality – there's no better place, especially as the sun sets, the wine flows and musicians bash out folk numbers on accordions and fiddles.

01 EDLMOSER

Close to Lainzer Tiergarten, a royal hunting ground turned wildlife reserve, Edlmoser is an hour's journey southwest of central Vienna, but worth the pilgrimage. Looking back on more than 600 years of family wine-growing tradition, the winery is always at the top of the class, snapping up gold at Vienna's Wiener Landessieger 2022 awards.

The *heuriger*'s vine-wreathed garden is a much-loved spot for trying wines such as rounded, floral, citrusy Maurerberg Riesling and elegantly spicy Vienna Reserve, while raiding the buffet for Austrian dishes like wild boar sausage and caraway roast pork.

Maurer-Lange-Gasse 123; https:// edlmoser.at

02 WEINSTUBE JOSEFSTADT

This delightfully old-school tavern in Vienna's artsy 8th district is a 10-minute toddle from Rathausplatz. The only sign of its existence is a metal *busch'n* (green wreath) hanging above a door. Its plant-dotted courtyard, heady with lilac in summer, is a little oasis.

Snag a table to sip your way through Vienna's vines: from Gemischter Satz, the citrusy, minerally, straw-yellow field blend for which the region is famous, to organic Rieslings and Grüner Veltliner whites. Food is simple: breads, spreads, sausages, fritters and salads, and the vibe is relaxed. Cash only.

Piaristengasse 27; www.weinstube-josefstadt.at; closed Mon

03 HEURIGER SISSI HUBER

A quick trundle on the U3 brings you to Ottakring and this *heuriger*, bringing a splash of southern flair to Vienna's vine-ribboned hills. Inside, it's rustic, with beams and terracotta tiles, but the courtyard fragrant with lavender, lemon and olive trees makes it feel as though you've been teleported to Italy – which calls for a glass of sparking rosé.

While you'll find classics like Styrian-style *backhendl* (roast chicken with pumpkin oil) and roast pork with dumplings on the menu, it also goes off-piste with light Austrian tapas. And its restaurant, Terra Rossa, dives properly into bright Mediterranean waters, with fresh fish, homemade pasta and

01 Vineyards on the outskirts of Vienna

02 A typical Austrian snack platter

03 Mayer am Pfarrplatz has been serving wine since 1683

04 Summer among the vines at Obermann

imaginative salads for drinkers to get stuck into alongside the wine. *Roterdstrasse 5; https://sissi-huber.at; closed Sun & Mon*

04 10ER MARIE

It's a 10-minute wander south to one of Vienna's oldest *heuriger*, founded by the Haimböck family in 1740. It's named after their daughter, Marie, whose ravishing beauty drew wine-loving punters from afar. Many a royal, celebrity, musician and artist has quaffed wine here over the years – Crown Prince Rudolf, Strauss and Schubert among them. The *heuriger*'s pretty country-villa looks, coupled with its tucked-away courtyard, keep it high in the popularity rankings. A glass of refreshing Gemischter Satz

pairs perfectly with buffet specials such as *kümmelbraten* (caraway roast pork), fat pork knuckles, roast chicken and vegetable strudel. *Ottakringer Strasse 224; https:// 10ermarie.at; closed Sun & Mon*

05 MAYER AM PFARRPLATZ

Beethoven felt the healing nature of vines and inspiration-boosting powers of wine at this *heuriger* when he stayed here while composing his famous 9th Symphony. A 30-minute S-Bahn ride north of 10er Marie in Döbling, this warm, woody tavern seems little touched by time and trends, and has been producing wine since 1683.

If the sun's out, sit on the cobbled, vine-draped terrace for a crisp, cooling glass of Gemischter Satz or

Riesling and a hunk of bread with toppings like dry-cured wild boar ham, pungent cave-ripened cheese and Mangalitsa pork lardo. There are also more substantial, season-driven mains, from veal goulash with herb dumplings to pumpkin risotto. Get there for around 7pm, when the accordion strikes up. *Pfarrplatz 2; www.pfarrplatz.at*

06 OBERMANN

A quick bus ride and few minutes' hike up through vines and you come to Obermann. Here, fifth generation Martin Obermann stays true to family tradition while sending the winery winging into a more sustainable future with organic methods and nature-driven principles. The welcome here is

05 Vienna's historic centre

06 Local wine-growers attend the annual VieVinum festival

to deepen your knowledge of their wines, sign up for a structured tasting session (€10 for five wines). *Amtsstrasse 10-14; www.weingut-christ.at*

08 HEURIGER WIENINGER

"The location of Vienna's vineyards – resting on marine sedimentary rocks in the foothills of the Alps – creates a unique terroir that produces wines that are as intense, lively and elegant as the Viennese themselves," enthuses vintner Fritz Wieninger at his *heuriger*, half an hour's walk north of Weingut Christ. The *heuriger* hides a vaulted cellar once run by wine-loving monks.

Now Fritz is at the helm, waving the flag for Gemischter Satz, Vienna's beloved field-blend white wine. It's made from up to 20 different grape varieties grown in the same vineyard and co-fermented. "My vision is to express Viennese character in every sip," he says. Try the Bisamberg Wiener Gemischter Satz – fresh, spicy and lightly smoky – made using sustainable biodynamic methods. The wines pair well with dishes such as potato salad, roast beef with cranberries, and schnitzel. *Stammersdorfer Strasse 78; https://heuriger-wieninger.at; closed Mon & Tue*

heartfelt and the setting lovely, especially if you come in summer when they set up tables for picnics and drinking right in the vines. Sparkling whites, Rieslings, Pinot Blancs and full-bodied Zweigelts are matched with buffet food from lentil salad to pork roast, pastrami and schnitzel. Check online for the live music line-up. *Cobenzlgasse 102; www.weinbauobermann.at; closed Mon-Wed*

07 WEINGUT CHRIST

On the other side of the Danube in Floridsdorf, the skyline fades, vines roll away and views open up. Pivoting on 400 years of family farming tradition, this is one of the city's most innovative wineries.

All of the grapes are hand-harvested at this gravity-flow winery, and pumps and motors have been removed to better retain the purity of the fruit and its flavour, which feeds through to the wines.

So far, so impressive – as is the *heuriger*, with its vine-canopied terrace, where you can try sparkling organic whites and delicately floral vegan rosés with antipasti, salads and seasonal dishes such as pumpkin-seed *spätzle* noodles and wine-grape strudel. If you want

WHERE TO STAY
HOTEL RATHAUS WEIN & DESIGN
Lodged in a handsome 19th-century townhouse, just a couple of minutes' walk from Vienna's neo-gothic Rathaus and Weinstube Josefstadt, this boutique hotel blends period features with minimalist design. The wine bar showcases a different Austrian vintner each month and breakfast (served until midday at weekends) is outstanding.
www.hotel-rathaus-wien.at

HOTEL TOPAZZ LAMEE
Central to all the sights and cathedral-topped Stephansplatz, architecturally striking Hotel Topazz Lamee has glamorous Wiener Werkstätte-inspired interiors and sells elegant organic wines from its own winery, Lenikus.
www.hoteltopazz lamee.com

WHAT TO DO
SCHLOSS BELVEDERE
Break up the vineyard hopping with a strong shot of culture in Vienna's galleries. Taking in the full sweep of the capital from its sloping statue-dotted lawns, Schloss Belvedere is a feast of baroque. Go in for *The Kiss* at the Upper Belvedere, which showcases a prized collection of Klimt's paintings.
www.belvedere.at

MUSEUMSQUARTIER
For a whirl of contemporary art in revamped royal stables, spend a couple of art-crammed hours at the MuseumsQuartier cultural centre, where the Leopold Museum presents the world's biggest collection of Schiele works.
www.mqw.at

CELEBRATIONS
GRAPE HARVEST
The *heurigen* are at their atmospheric best during September's harvest, when the vines glow gold and the Viennese get merry on *sturm* (fizzy, semi-fermented wine made with the season's first grapes).

MAY FESTIVALS
In May, the MuseumsQuartier hosts the Vienna Wine Fest, spotlighting 40 wineries, and the Hofburg (Imperial Palace) stages VieVinum, a shop window for wine growers, with tastings and School of Wine masterclasses.
www.vievinum.at

GET THERE
Ghent is just 30 minutes by train from Brussels. Its brilliant rent-a-bike system is a much better alternative to driving into the carbon-zero city centre, where getting a fine is more likely than finding a parking space.

[Belgium]

HOW GHENT DOES GOURMET

Defiantly off Belgium's classic tourist track, proudly maverick Ghent always surprises with quirky restaurants, local food specialities, craft booze and, naturally, irresistible chocolates.

Following a gourmet trail in the determinedly under-the-radar destination of Ghent is a rock 'n' roll experience. In the heart of Belgium's Flemish countryside, Ghent is often bypassed by travellers heading to the more famous neighbouring cities of Bruges and Antwerp, and the locals are quite happy with their lot. The medieval city centre with its gothic cathedral, towering belfry and fortified castle are all perfectly preserved, and nothing compares with sitting out on a sunny waterside cafe terrace sipping a craft or Trappist beer. Opulent baroque guild houses line bucolic canals and rivers, but this is no mundane museum city.

Behind the picture-postcard scenery lies a vibrant, edgy urban scene. This is the city that pioneered the idea of a day each week devoted to vegetarian food – Thursday Veggie Day. The eating out scene has a Ghent identity; gourmet but democratic in terms of affordability. It's unpretentious and essentially seasonal, with zero-kilometre cuisine served in casual, funky dining rooms that feel far removed from restaurants searching for Michelin stars.

Ghent is also a pioneer eco-destination. A city-centre carbon-zero programme promotes bikes, while an active Food Council runs sustainability initiatives such as reuse and redistribution of restaurant leftovers. Visitors should head out to the old industrial docks to discover craft beer and barista coffee. And instead of looking for the usual Belgian chocolate museum – there isn't one – track down Ghent's half-a-dozen artisan chocolatiers who create their own original pralines each morning.

01 YUZU

Belgium is synonymous with chocolate and Ghent's historic centre has all the famous names (Neuhaus, Godiva, Leonidas), but serious chocoholics track down Yuzu. Here, artisan chocolatier Nicolas Vanaise creates minimalist chocolate truffles that resemble poetic calligraphy artworks, mixing surprising combinations of flavours and textures, such as lemon and coffee or chilli, ginger and corn.

Often taking inspiration from Japan, Nicolas shies away from the modern trend of bean-to-bar. "Transforming cocoa into chocolate is a different skill and I choose to concentrate each day making and creating my chocolates here in this tiny laboratory boutique." He also makes melt-in-the-mouth pralines using local ingredients such as Ganda ham, Tierenteyn mustard, craft beer and jenever gin.
11/A Walpoorstraat; www. yuzubynicolasvanaiseandc.com; closed Sun & Mon

02 LOUSBERG MARKET

This organic market is a symbol of Ghent's sustainability ethos. Housed in a luminous old textile factory alongside a quiet canal, it's home to Ghent's own city dairy, Het Hinkelspel, and has also been transformed into a vibrant daily market. You can taste the dairy's remarkable selection of cow and goat cheeses, accompanied by a foaming glass of site-brewed Lousberg beer, while neighbouring farmers arrive to sell seasonal fruit and vegetables.

Artisan bakers bring along different kinds of bio bread, while two cooks, Stephanie and Sofie, run a canteen preparing home-cooked dishes, soups and cakes using market produce.
33 Ferdinand Lousbergskaai; www. lousbergmarkt.be; closed Sun

03 TIERENTEYN MUSTARD

Located right on the historic Groentenmarkt, Tierenteyn resembles an ancient apothecary, though the shelves are stocked with a cornucopia of mysterious stone jars filled with exotic spices and herbs, handmade pickles and candied fruit. Everyone comes here for its unique mustard, which

has been produced since the early 1800s down in the cellar using a recipe shrouded in secrecy. Made with distinctive brown mustard seeds instead of Dijon's famous yellow, Tierenteyn has a seriously sharp aroma, similar to horseradish, developing into a slightly sweet aftertaste. The Groentenmarkt square is a popular foodie address. Alongside Tierenteyn there's Ghent's oldest bakery, the best *frites* stall in town, and an organic farmers market on Fridays.
3 Groentenmarkt; www.tierenteyn-verlent.be; closed Sun

04 CONFISERIE TEMMERMAN

Over in the medieval Patershol neighbourhood, housed in a splendid baroque mansion,

Temmerman is Ghent's favourite sweetshop. Open since 1904, it's been run by five generations of the same family of artisan confectioners who make traditional *speculoos* gingerbread, liquorice, wine gums and nougat, as well as naughty *lutze peopkes* (wobbly bottom) toffees.

But what most people squeeze into this tiny treasure trove for are *cuberdons* – cone-shaped, raspberry syrup-filled jelly gums, also locally known as 'Ghent noses'. You will see *cuberdons* on sale all over town but to make sure you are buying the Temmerman's original, look for the ones that are distinguished by a carnival mask on the cone.
79 Kraanlei; www.temmerman confiserie.com; closed Sun-Tue

05 PUBLIEK

Chef Olly Ceulenaere was a high-profile founder of the innovative Flemish Foodies movement, but then opened cosy Publiek to discreetly develop his own personal cuisine. This restaurant serves a healthy, light lunchtime menu based around vegetables, then a gourmet six or seven course tasting experience in the evenings with exquisite yet simple dishes such as crunchy cabbage topped with smoked eel and pickled parsnip root, or marinated herrings smothered with baby radishes, fava beans and smoked seaweed. Ceulenaere's uncompromising philosophy has helped Publiek win a Michelin star. "We will not alter our philosophy of local, seasonal

produce; no luxury ingredients; minimal waste," he says.
39 Ham; www.publiekgent.be; closed Sun & Mon

06 VRIJDAGMARKT

Every Friday morning, most of Ghent seems to be crammed into the grand Vrijdagsplatz doing the weekly shop, weaving between fruit and vegetable sellers, cheesemongers, butchers and charcuterie stalls, bakers and pastry-makers. But the square is dominated by half-a-dozen enormous refrigerated lorries that convert themselves into noisy fishmongers selling seafood direct from the North Sea; not just sole, turbot and cod, but tasty Dutch *matjes* herrings and periwinkles, and plants such as salicorne and sea aster.

For a dose of Ghent fast food, line up at the market's *frituur*, a traditional chip stall, for a cone of crispy *frites* smothered with

mayonnaise or a soup bowl of peppery *escargots de mer* (whelks).
Vrijdagmarkt Square; every Fri morning to 1pm

07 DOK BREWING COMPANY

For the world's most famous beer nation there are surprisingly few genuine craft breweries in Belgium. Dimitri Messiaen decided that Ghent needed what he called "an action brewery", so he opened this microbrewery in a vast industrial warehouse in the old docks – an area that has since become the hottest part of town.

There are 30 beers on tap here, served alongside delicious Norwegian-style barbecue specialities. Messiaen has created 150 different brews so far – malty, hoppy, fruity, roasted, blond and dark – but each one in a single batch, never to be brewed again.

The only exceptions are the brewery's two signature ales: 13,

an award-winning Pilsner; and the Gentse Pale Ale.
Hal 16, Dok Noord; www.dok brewingcompany.be; closed Mon

08 GINDERELLA

Ghent's very own handcrafted gin is made by the eco-distilling brothers Jan and Geert Heyneman, who run fascinating botanicals-foraging tours. Depending on the season, this wild expedition takes place along Ghent's canals or in the dense undergrowth of the nearby Bourgoyen nature reserve. Geert is Ghent's chief ecology officer and knows just where to harvest Ginderella's key ingredients; invasive weeds like Japanese knotweed and lesser swinecress, as well as giant hogweed and, of course, juniper. Afterwards, there is a tasting at Jan's pop-up bar, featuring gin as well as the brothers' white and red artisan vermouths.
www.heynsquared.com/en/ ginderella

WHERE TO STAY

B&B CHAMBRE D'AMIS
Well located between the train station and town centre, this comfy, three-room B&B is run by the team behind Restaurant Alex – a popular foodie haunt for lunch and dinner, serving brunch and picnics in the garden of the townhouse that hosts the B&B.
https://alixtablejardin. be/eng/chambredamis

WHAT TO DO

SINT-JACOBS FLEA MARKET
The cobbled square outside the gothic Sint-Jacobs church, surrounded by Ghent's old-fashioned 'brown cafes', is transformed every Sunday morning into a teeming flea market brimming with tempting bargains.
www.brocantmarkt- sintjacobs-gent.be

CANAL KAYAKING
Rather than joining a touristy pleasure boat, you can now discover

Ghent's romantic canals by booking a three-hour rental to row your own kayak, an unforgettable experience.
https://en.kajaks korenlei.be

'T DREUPELKOT
Wherever you have dinner in Ghent, end the evening at this mythical hole-in-the-wall bar serving jenever gin shots in more than 200 flavours.

Try an aged jenever that is as good as a single malt whisky, a tasty lemon-flavoured glass or jenever marinated with chillies that will blow your head off.
www.druppelkot.be

CELEBRATIONS

GENTSE FEESTEN
For this 10 day festival every July, Ghent is transformed into a wild party city with live concerts, street food trucks, drinking and dancing all through the night.
https://gentsefeesten. stad.gent/en

GET THERE
Go by rail on the TGV from Paris to Strasbourg, which is 20km (12.5 miles) east of Marlenheim, the start of the Route des Vins. Or fly straight to Strasbourg or Basel-Mulhouse Airport, south of Colmar. The trail is best driven or cycled.

01

ALSACE

[France]

ALSACE'S ROUTE DES VINS

Close to the German border, this 170km wine route takes in gingerbread towns and down-to-earth vineyards.

Think of France's best regions for gastronomy and you might cite Burgundy, Bordeaux, Lille or Provence, but Alsace is the wild card the French keep quietly up their sleeve. There are few places where you can eat and drink better than on the Route des Vins d'Alsace, corkscrewing 170km (105 miles) through lyrical countryside from Marlenheim to Thann. On summer days, when sun filters through vines, lights up castles on hillsides and spills through the cobbled streets of gingerbready half-timbered towns, it is quite the country dream.

Snuggling close to Germany, this region is a one-off, cherry-picking the best of both countries to deliver flavours that are utterly unique. Specialities include *baeckeoffe* (hearty meat and potato casserole), *choucroute garnie* (sauerkraut with smoked meats) and *coq au riesling* (chicken braised in Riesling wine and herbs), best sampled under the low beams of a *winstub* (wine tavern).

Wineries here have none of the snobbishness you'll find elsewhere – they are simple, family-run affairs, with open *caves* (cellars) where you can often freely taste Grand Cru wines – zesty Riesling, elegant Sylvaner, minerally Pinot Blanc and Pinot Gris, spicy Gewürztraminer, fresh and peppery Muscat whites and full-bodied Pinot Noir reds, bursting with red fruits. Many are organic and biodynamic these days.

And these great wines go hand in hand with some of France's most accomplished cooking. Every mile on Alsace's Route des Vins seems to dazzle with another Michelin-starred gastronomic light, another restaurant capturing the poetry of the region on a plate. This is gourmet country, where a flurry of talented chefs work closely with local farmers and fishers to create sense-sharpening menus that nod to the bounty of the seasons and the beauty of the land.

OBERNAI · 01
02
ERSTEIN
LE HOHWALD · BARR
BENFELD
DAMBACH-LA-VILLE
FRANCE
CHÂTENOIS · SÉLESTAT
STE-MARIE-AUX MINES
05
03
SCHNELLENBUHL
RIBEAUVILLE · 04
RIQUEWIHR · 06
SASBACH
KAYSERSBERG · 07
GERMANY
08 · COLMAR
EGUISHEIM
BREISACH

Rhine River

01 Half-timbered Colmar has culture and good looks

02 A patchwork of vines across Alsace

03 Traditional sausages and choucroute

04 The contemporary viniculture centre of Cave de Ribeauvillé

01 SENTIER VITICOLE DU SCHENKENBERG

Obernai throws you in at the fairy-tale deep end of Alsace, with fortified ring walls and candy-coloured houses. This 1.5km (0.9 miles) *sentier* (trail) weaves gently through the vine-ribbed hills above town, whisking you through the grape-growing and wine-making process with explanatory panels.

Beginning at the hilltop cross north of town, the path twists up through the vineyards, with sensational views over the jumbled rooftops of Obernai to the plain of Alsace and Vosges mountains. In July and August, the tourist office arranges free 1½-hour guided walks, followed by tastings at a local cellar. *www.tourisme-obernai.fr*

02 LA FOURCHETTE DES DUCS

Back in the heart of Obernai, this restaurant twinkles with two Michelin stars. Here chef Nicolas Stamm puts a novel gourmet twist on fastidiously sourced regional cuisine, with a signature use of herbs. Menus swing seasonal, reviving forgotten recipes in specialities such as Alsatian pigeon with *baerewecke* (spiced fruit cake), *choucroute* (sauerkraut) with black truffle, and *baeckeoffe* casserole with Alsace black chicken.

There is a rich history simmering below the surface of this half-timbered building, too. In 1921, Ettore Bugatti (he of fast car fame) enlisted Art Nouveau artists including marquetry master Charles Spindler and jeweller René Lalique to put their stamp on the woodwork and lights in its softly lit, warmly rustic interior. *6 Rue de la Gare, Obernai; www.lafourchettedesducs.com; closed Mon*

03 L'AUBERGE DE L'ILL

An hour's drive south of Obernai, on country roads loping past vine and hill, brings you to Illhaeusern and this two-Michelin-starred *auberge* (inn), romantically reclining on the willow-brushed banks of the River Ill. It has been in the Haeberlin family for generations, but chef Marc Haeberlin elevated it to giddy gastronomic heights.

His love of nature shines in the light, dreamlike interior: a palette of soft greys and whites, with Hermès

fabrics and Murano glass, murals and floor-to-ceiling windows that perfectly frame the garden's vivid greens. The backdrop informs his astounding food: summery dishes like Breton lobster with Pinot Noir sauce and wild mushroom emulsion, salmon soufflé, and filet mignon with pea gnocchi and truffled veal gravy are spectacular. There's a separate tasting menu for vegetarians. *Hôtel des Berges, Rue de Collonges au Mont d'Or, Illhaeusern; www.auberge-de-l-ill.com; closed Mon & Tue*

04 CAVE DE RIBEAUVILLÉ

A 20-minute hop west brings you to Ribeauvillé, an instant heart-stealer with winding alleys, medieval towers and a parade of pastel-hued, half-timbered houses – as bright as a box of the town's famous macarons. But if you're into wine, seek out France's oldest wine-growers' cooperative, founded in 1895 and bringing together 40 vintners.

On the eastern fringes of town, the huge, contemporary centre harbours a viniculture museum, giving the inside scoop on the terroir. There's also a slick, backlit tasting room where you can sample its award-winning wines, made with all seven of the grape varieties grown in Alsace. On weekends it is staffed by local winegrowers. Guided visits of the cellar and vineyard can also be arranged on request. *2 Rte de Colmar, Ribeauvillé; www.vins-ribeauville.com*

05 AUBERGE DU PARC CAROLA

With a lovely terrace set up under the trees, this *auberge*, 1km north of central Ribeauvillé, entices with alfresco dining on warm days. Its quaintly timbered facade contrasts with the sleek, light-filled interior, festooned with playful contemporary art. Heading up the kitchen is dream German-French duo Michaela Peters and Laurent Pellegrini. Waving a light Mediterranean wand on regional ingredients, they create flavours that ring true in seasonal showstoppers like 64° organic Alsace egg with new potato mousseline and summer truffles, suckling pig with Alsatian honey, sesame, aubergine and courgette,

and peach tiramisu with verbena.
48 Rte de Bergheim, Ribeauvillé; https://auberge-parc-carola.com; closed Tue & Wed

06 LA TABLE DU GOURMET

A cork pop south of Ribeauvillé, rampart-wrapped, alley-woven Riquewihr looks ripe for a bedtime story. Jean-Luc Brendel is the culinary force behind this Michelin-starred restaurant, where a 16th-century, timber-beamed house has been given an avant-garde, scarlet makeover. His nature-driven menus sing with bold, seasonal flavours. "Plants and vegetables are not just garnishes – I place them at the heart of every meal," says Brendel.

Every morning he harvests edible flowers, herbs, berries, roots and shoots in his flourishing garden to go into his Éveil des Sens (Awaken the Senses) menu, which presents seven 'culinary landscapes', from

bonbon of spiced tomato to beet flower with pike and horseradish ice cream, and escargot in its natural habitat.
5 Rue de la 1E Armée, Riquewihr; www.jlbrendel.com; closed Tue & Wed

07 LA TABLE D'OLIVIER NASTI

In castle-topped, vine-rimmed Kaysersberg, 10km (6 miles) south, gourmands travel from afar to score a table at this two-Michelin-starred restaurant. The decor is a modern take on an Alsatian hunting lodge, with mocha walls, wood from surrounding forests, handcrafted furniture and stag antlers.

Chef Olivier Nasti works closely with local farmers to compose dishes that express the 'soul of Alsace': that might mean roe deer with local cherries, choucroute with black truffle and lovage jus, or Arctic char from nearby mountain lakes, cooked with beeswax and

served with a warm vinaigrette of honey and fir oil.
Hotel Le Chambard, Kaysersberg; www.lechambard.fr; closed Mon & Tue

08 JY'S

Capital of wine country, canal-laced, half-timbered Colmar has a huge number of exceptional places to eat, considering its small size. One of them is the two-Michelin-starred restaurant, JY's, in Champ de Mars park. With white linen-draped tables, trailing foliage and the promise of Champagne, the uncluttered setting is as fresh and sophisticated as the cuisine. Chef Jean-Yves Schillinger conjures explosive flavours in signature dishes like Breton lobster cooked in a Cona coffee pot with shellfish pasta and herb broth, and rack of confit pig with hay jus.
L'Esquisse Hotel, 3 Allee du Champ de Mars, Colmar; www.jean-yves-schillinger.com; closed Sun & Mon

WHERE TO STAY

A LA COUR D'ALSACE

Gathered around an ivy-swaddled courtyard, A La Cour d'Alsace harbours light, modern rooms, a spa, a gourmet restaurant and *winstub* (wine tavern) in a former manor house in Obernai. *www.cour-alsace.com*

HÔTEL DES BERGES

Astride the River Ill, five-star Hôtel des Berges in Illhaeusern ramps up the luxury, with two-Michelin-starred L'Auberge de L'Ill, luxe-rustic suites, a private fisherman's cottage and a 1970s Airstream Overlander set in beautiful gardens. *www.auberge-de-l-ill.com*

WHAT TO DO

COLMAR

Colmar has the cultural edge. It was the birthplace of Frédéric Auguste Bartholdi, of *Statue of Liberty* fame, and visitors can tour his 19th-century home, now the Musée Bartholdi. Afterwards, head to Musée Unterlinden,

which showcases the masterly late-gothic Isenheim Altarpiece, by painter Mathias Grünewald and sculptor Nicolas de Haguenau, in a Dominican cloister. *www.tourisme-colmar.com*

CHÂTEAU DU HAUT KŒNIGSBOURG

On its perch above vineyards, 900-year-old Château du Haut Kœnigsbourg near Bergheim is worth a detour for its wraparound panorama, taking in the Vosges,

the Black Forest and, on cloud-free days, the Alps. *www.haut-koenigs bourg.fr*

CELEBRATIONS

FÊTES DU VIN

Villages all over Alsace toast late summer at Fêtes du Vin (wine festivals), with tastings, vineyard walks, cellar visits, folk music and feasting. The merrymaking spills into the golden months of September and October at Fêtes des Vendanges

(grape harvest festivals), with *vin nouveau* (new wine) and *flammekueche* (local pizza-like dish). *www.vinsalsace.com*

MARCHÉ DE NOËL

Colmar twinkles festively at its Christmas market in December, which is one of France's most enchanting, bringing carols, nativity scenes, farmers markets, handicrafts and an ice rink to town. Nibble gingerbread and cinnamon *bredele* (star-shaped cookies). *https://noel-colmar.com*

GET THERE
Bordeaux is linked to Paris
in just over two hours by
high-speed TGV train, while
international visitors fly into
Bordeaux-Mérignac Airport.

[France]

NEW JOIE DE VIVRE IN BORDEAUX

France's famed wine capital is a no-brainer destination for oenophiles, but there's more to it than that – visitors can also expect a vibrant culinary scene with food markets, funky bistrots and surprising street food.

Bordeaux is booming right now. This French city, one of the globe's historic wine centres, is home to the futuristic Cité du Vin museum and has reinvented itself as Europe's latest party weekend destination, rivalling the likes of Barcelona and Berlin. Historic grand mansions and palaces that line leafy boulevards have been given an overdue facelift with centuries of dirt and grime washed away, while the rundown banks of the Garrone River have been regenerated with alternative cultural spaces, bars and foodie pop-ups, all of which mingle alongside the brilliant fountains of Le Miroir d'Eau – the world's largest reflecting pool.

This cosmopolitan city offers everything from Michelin-starred restaurants to in-vogue locavore diners. It's easy to find the traditional bistrots for entrecôte steak à la Bordelaise and Arcachon oysters, but there are also North African places to feast on couscous and tagines. Wash it all down with a hop between creative *caves à vins*, wine bars offering delicious tapas-style dishes to complement stellar wine lists.

Located on a picturesque bend of the Garonne River with access to France's Atlantic coastline, much of Bordeaux's Unesco World Heritage riverside, La Porte de la Lune, dates back to the 18th century when it was the world's busiest port after London. The exports were not just wine from the thousands of châteaux and never-ending vineyards that surround the city, but also enslaved people – a legacy that is slowly beginning to be acknowledged. And today, these sprawling old docks and vast wine warehouses have been brought back to life with dramatic housing projects, exhibition centres, music and art venues, food markets and hip hotels.

01 Bordeaux's Old Town

02 The Cité du Vin is a high-tech wine journey

03 Hop in a sidecar to get among the vines with Retro Tour Bordeaux

01 BAR DE LA MARINE

Tucked away in the old maritime Bacalan neighbourhood, the Marine's old-fashioned bistrot facade hides a host of secrets.

The dark narrow porch by the entrance suddenly opens out into lush, overgrown gardens, with vintage metal chairs and tables seating 100 diners. There are ivy-draped walls covered with kitsch flea-market mirrors, classic French *chansons* on the turntable, and a rickety wooden cabin where Bordeaux's food superstar, chef Frédéric Coiffé, personally cooks, grills and orchestrates the dance-party atmosphere.

Expect hearty, affordable comfort food: huge sharing plates of local cheeses and charcuterie, sizzling squid, steaks and veggies cooked on the grill. In winter the garden closes but the Marine's retro dining room stays open, serving from breakfast to dinner. *28 Rue Achard; www.facebook. com/bardelamarinebordeaux*

02 CITÉ DU VIN

Standing out on the Bordeaux skyline with its swirling glass and metal design is the audacious Cité du Vin, a wine museum like no other in the world. Amateur and professional wine lovers alike are swept off their feet, taken on a virtual reality journey across the world's different vineyards with wine tasting and pairing *ateliers* (workshops), digital holograms, 3D movies and sensorial challenges. The journey ends with a real-life tasting at the panoramic rooftop bar.

Although the Cité has a gourmet restaurant and brasserie, a better plan after your tasting is to walk across the road to the Halles de Bacalan, a modern covered market. The all-day *marché* spans organic vegetable stalls and artisan butchers, oyster bars and food trucks grilling juicy steaks. *134 Quai de Bacalan; www.laciteduvin.com*

03 L'ÉCOLE DU VIN DE BORDEAUX

The renowned Bordeaux Wine School has outposts in 24 countries around the world, but nothing compares to joining a course

right here in their state-of-the-art Bordeaux *atelier*. Beginners can start with the introductory workshop explaining the secrets of wine tasting and the subtle aromas of different grape varieties.

Food enthusiasts can sign up to learn about wine pairings with chocolate, cheese and even pizza, while serious wine lovers can discover the art of blending. The teachers are excellent, always ensuring there is a fun, informal atmosphere to the lessons.

After the class, pop downstairs to the elegant art deco Bar à Vin, run by the professional association governing all Bordeaux wines. It showcases tipples by the glass, with around 35 rotating producers from the 8500 Bordeaux châteaux. *3 Cours du 30 Juillet; www. ecoleduvindebordeaux.com; closed Sun*

04 RETRO TOUR BORDEAUX

There is no better way to explore the world-famous vineyards around Bordeaux than to sign up for a hair-raising adventure whizzing around in the sidecar of a vintage motorbike. Tours are aimed at wine lovers rather than serious wine connoisseurs, and guide and enthusiastic biker Alexandre Deblaere steers clear of intimidating in-depth tastings.

"We concentrate on taking deserted back routes through the vineyards, stopping off for a château tasting, but then finding a quiet spot in the vines for a relaxed picnic to enjoy the food and wine," he explains.

Choose between the renowned Châteaux Margaux in the Médoc, the medieval town and vineyards of Saint-Émilion, or the historic wineries of Sauternes, passing by the mythical Château d'Yquem. *Pick-up 12 Cours du 30 Juillet; www. retro-tour.com/en/destinations/ retro-tour-bordeaux-en*

05 LES CAPUCINS

Bordeaux has many brilliant food markets, but nothing compares to the historic Capucins, dating back to 1749. A classic iron-and-glass covered market, Les Capucins wakes up at 4am with butchers breakfasting off giant steaks while

clubbers stagger in for one last bottle of wine. You can buy foie gras and locally produced Aquitaine caviar, duck confit, or a hundred different cheeses.

The favourite market bar, Chez Jean-Mi, seethes with locals crowding the bar for a glass while tourists jostle for a table to enjoy a dozen plump oysters. One restaurant right outside the market stands out, Au Bistrot, cooking forgotten local specialities like *lamproie*, an eel-like fish from the Garonne, in a rich red wine sauce. *Place des Capucins; https:// marchedescapucins.com; closed Mon*

06 LA GUINGUETTE CHEZ ALRIQ

The French love their *guinguettes* – popular waterside cabarets whose joyous wining, dining and dancing

were immortalised by 19th-century Impressionist painters. Today they are back in vogue and the Garonne river bank is the perfect venue to experience this unique slice of local life with panoramic views across the city.

When Chez Alriq first pitched his site here in 1990, the city's Right Bank was an ugly industrial eyesore. Today it is the Parc aux Angéliques, a green corridor of landscaped promenades and flower gardens. La Guinguette Chez Alriq is Bordeaux's favourite, where from May to October the dancing goes on till late while the al fresco kitchen cooks up a storm of *steak frites* and *moules marinières*, alongside cocktails made with local botanicals. *Port Bastide, Quai des Queyries; www.laguinguettechezalriq.com; closed Mon & Tue*

07 DARWIN ECO-SYSTEME

Darwin is a vast complex of abandoned warehouses and army barracks right across the river from Bordeaux's centre, transformed from an urban wasteland into a dynamic hub spanning the arts, eco-sustainable start-ups, coworking, spectacular graffiti, skateboard parks and live music venues.

Darwin's urban farm produces permaculture vegetables and plants, but pride of place goes to Le Magasin Général, perhaps Europe's biggest organic restaurant and shop. This immense hall includes a pizzeria, a casual vegan and vegetarian diner, Darwin-brewed craft beers and natural wines. Upcoming projects include Origine, a bio bean-to-bar chocolate factory and Anatole, an organic bakery. *87 Quai des Queyries; https:// darwin.camp*

WHERE TO STAY
CENTRAL HOSTEL BORDEAUX
Right in the centre of town, this hip budget hostel offers classic dorm accommodation (six- or eight-bed) or comfortable double rooms with en-suite bathrooms. Meals using locally sourced ingredients are served in the funky Central Kitchen restaurant, while the small rooftop terrace is the perfect spot for sunset drinks.
https://centralhostel.fr

LE SAINT-JAMES
The Relais & Chateaux-affiliated Saint-James is perfect for a luxury stay. It's just 15 minutes southeast of Bordeaux city centre but feels a world away. Overlooking a vineyard, the owners have taken an 18th-century farmhouse and given it a contemporary designer revamp, adding a Michelin-starred restaurant and gourmet cooking school.
www.saintjames-bouliac.com

WHAT TO DO
BORDEAUX RIVER CRUISES
Rivers define Bordeaux. Join the daily cruise along the Garonne, the river dividing the city in two, or take a sailing excursion (April to October) to the Graves and Sauternes vineyards or famed Médoc châteaux along the Gironde's estuary.
www.bordeaux-river-cruise.com

LES BASSINS DES LUMIÈRES
Constructed during WWII by forced labour to protect Germany's submarine fleet, these immense concrete bunkers house a maze of subterranean water-filled channels that today host sensational immersive digital art exhibitions projected onto the walls and water.
www.bassins-lumieres.com

CELEBRATIONS
BORDEAUX FÊTE LE VIN
All of Bordeaux goes wine crazy for this biennial, four-day June extravaganza. Expect regional wine tastings led by the *vignerons*, plus concerts, exhibitions and nonstop partying. The next is scheduled for 2023; in alternate years there is an equally spectacular river festival.
www.bordeaux-wine-festival.com

GET THERE
Calvi Sainte-Catherine Airport is 7km (4.5 miles) south of the port. Trains run between Calvi, Bastia and Ajaccio, and the coastal train that shuttles between Calvi and L'Île-Rousse is one of France's prettiest rail journeys.

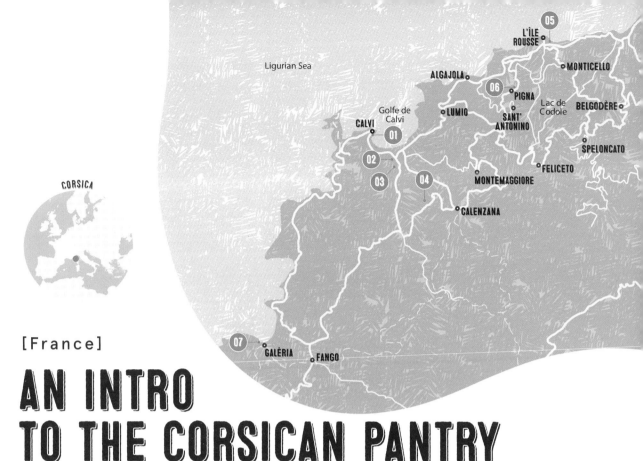

[France]

AN INTRO TO THE CORSICAN PANTRY

The Mediterranean's 'Isle of Beauty' takes the best from the land and the sea, adds a dash of French and Italian and comes up with something special.

Corsica doesn't quite feel like France. After all, this Mediterranean island was once part of the Genoese empire and the Corsican language derives from a Tuscan dialect rather than French. Centuries of invasion from pirates and other attackers meant the locals had to flee the coast into the hills, where most of them stayed. And that's where the essence of Corsican food comes from: its remote hinterland of small hilltop villages surrounded by vineyards, olive groves, orchards and mountains smothered in fragrant maquis scrubland, which flavours practically everything. Wild boar, black pigs, sheep, goats and cows all graze on rosemary, myrtle, mint, sage and juniper, which infuse meat and dairy.

Fish and seafood do figure in Corsican cuisine, especially along the coast, but they often play second fiddle to charcuterie and cheese. Calvi in the

northwest blends land and sea beautifully. Its chic quayside is lined with bars and restaurants, most of which have menus sprinkled with fish and seafood. Restaurants sit in the sands of the broad sweep of Calvi's beach, while a walk up to the 12th-century citadel reveals more restaurants down cobbled lanes. Step back from the port and there are narrow streets and tiny squares filled with more places to eat.

From Calvi you can follow the Strada di l'Artigiani (Route of Artisans) into the wider Balagne region, where local food and wine are celebrated as much as the arts and crafts. A tour of the hilltop villages of Pigna, Lumio, Calenzana, Aregno and Sant'Antonino – plus L'Île-Rousse on the northern coast and Galéria further south – will introduce you to winemakers, cheesemakers, charcuterie producers and vegetable growers, all of whose produce ends up on the plate.

02

03

01 ANNIE TRAITEUR

Annie Giaconella's *épicerie* (grocery) immediately heightens the senses – the vividness of its fresh fruit and vegetables, Corsican charcuterie dangling from the ceiling, counters brimming with local cheeses, olives, homemade quiches, pizzas, tarts, antipasti and salad ingredients.

"When you come into our shop it's the whole smell of Corsica, with the scent of herbs and the hams," says Annie Traiteur shop assistant Alex Orsini, who has known Annie and her daughter Valérie, who now runs the shop, for 30 years. Annie is officially retired, though that doesn't stop her from continuing to make many of the products herself, including jams, mustards and flavoured salts. It's the charcuterie

that flies out the shop the fastest – richly flavoured *coppa*, *panzetta*, *figatelli*, *lonzu* and *prizuttu*.
5 rue Georges Clemenceau, Calvi; www.annietraiteurcalvi.com

02 CLOS LANDRY

Since 1900, five generations of the Paolini family have been making wine in Clos Landry's 25 hectares of vineyards on the southern outskirts of Calvi. Using indigenous Corsican grapes – red nieullucciu and sciaccarellu, white vermentino and biancu gentile – they make fresh and fruity Vin de Corse Calvi, a local wine that's protected under France's Appellation d'Origine Contrôlée (AOC) scheme, which is exactly what you want to drink on the Corsican coast. The rosé

gris is especially evocative of summer days on the beach. Visit the *domaine* for a tasting in the venerable stone farmhouse and take a wander through the maquis-scented vineyards, where you can glimpse Calvi's hulking citadel.
Route de la Forêt de Bonifato; www.closlandry.com; closed Sat & Sun

03 LE RESTAURANT GASTRONOMIQUE LA SIGNORIA

One of Corsica's three restaurants with a Michelin star, La Signoria makes the most of its magical setting in a secluded 18th-century manor house south of Calvi. On a sheltered terracotta terrace in the shadow of mountains and surrounded by the lush greenery

of a Mediterranean garden, chef Romain Masset exploits Corsica's abundance – fish and langoustines straight from the coast, roasted suckling pig wrapped in pancetta from a local *charcutier*, and fruit and vegetables from the neighbouring Potager de la Signoria. Masset's championing of local producers even goes as far as sourcing honey and herbal tea from the region.
Route de la Forêt de Bonifato; www.hotel-la-signoria.com; closed early Nov-early Apr

04 STÉPHANE SHINTU FROMAGERIE DE PELLICIANI

From 3D videographer in Paris to sheep breeder and cheesemaker – not the most obvious career path,

but one that Calvi native Stéphane Shintu found himself treading when his employer closed down five years ago. Now he's happy on his farm in Calenzana tending 100 Corsican sheep and making cheeses, butter and other dairy products, depending on the season. He makes the classic Corsican fresh *brocciu* along with other soft rind cheeses and *tommes de Corse*, including one with a coating of maquis herbs.

"What I like about this job is the contact with nature and its cycles, and the hands-on aspect of it," he says. You can buy at the farm (call ahead) or look out for his cheeses at La Signoria and Annie Traiteur.
Lieu dit Pelliciani, D51, Calenzana; www.facebook.com/fromagerie depelliciani; open Tues-Thu 1-3pm

05 LE MARINELLA

This classy yet laid-back restaurant on L'Île-Rousse's town beach is the place for a lazy meal – especially if you're at one of the waterside tables where you can slide your toes into the sand. Although prices carry a bit of a premium because of the location, the quality is worth it.

Le Marinella's take on tapas would make a lunch on its own: anchovy fritters with chilli sauce, deep-fried nuggets of *brocciu*, courgette balls, Corsican *saucisson* and tapenade. The mussels come with a wonderfully rich sauce of sea urchins. The evening three-course Corsican menu is excellent value and usually

06 Pork charcuterie is a mainstay of the island, which looks inland for food inspiration

07 Corsica's own fromage de Brebis

08 Scandola Nature Reserve is a Unesco World Heritage Site

offers Corsican charcuterie and sea bream with pesto.
Promenade de la Marinella, L'Île-Rousse; www.restaurant-marinella.com

06 A MANDRIA DI PIGNA

On the land where her grandfather had been the village's last sheep farmer, chef Isabelle Volpei and her husband Loïc Refrais run A Mandria di Pigna.

Within the restaurant's cosily old-fashioned interior, covered terrace and maquis-scented gardens with mountain views, the pair put Corsica's meat and vegetables in the spotlight. Their own garden supplies the veg, and local producers come up with veal, milk-fed lamb, charcuterie and

cheese – although the restaurant isn't averse to chargrilling Scottish beef, French duck and Spanish iberico pork either.

A *tarte aux herbes* distils Corsican flavours by mixing sheep's cheese with maquis herbs and a confit of Swiss chard and leeks, and the truffle risotto is out-of-this-world creamy.
Pigna; www.restaurantpigna.com; open Apr-Jun, Sep & Oct Tue-Sun, Jul & Aug daily

07 LA CABANE DU PÊCHEUR

The fact that cows amble along Galéria's pebbly beach gives a hint of the out-of-the-way feeling that hovers around La Cabane du Pêcheur, a 40-minute drive south of Calvi. Since 2008, the

husband-and-wife team of Jérôme (fisherman) and Céline (restaurant manager) behind this seafood restaurant have been serving deceptively simple fish lunches in their nicely ramshackle wooden beach shack and terrace.

Whatever Jérôme gets from the sea that day goes into tacos, burgers, soup or just grilled fillets. The vegetables come from an organic farm nearby, and all the recycled plates and cutlery go straight back into the recycling. It's not particularly cheap, but come for the stand-out freshness and flavour.
Route du Bord de Mer, Galéria; www.facebook.com/ lacabanedupecheurgaleria; closed late Sep-early May

WHERE TO STAY
HOTEL L'ACQUALE
Completely revamped by its new owners in 2020, four-star Hotel l'Acquale is in a prime spot in Calvi, just five minutes' walk from the port. Its 44 rooms are sleek, stylish and come with balconies from which to soak up wonderful views of the bay, Calvi's citadel and the heated swimming pool. The rooftop bar with panoramic views is a sublime place for an aperitif and tapas from June to September.
www.hotelacquale.com

HOTEL LA SIGNORIA
This five-star Relais & Chateaux member has 30 elegant rooms and suites in an 18th-century countryside manor house. There's a spa and outdoor pool, and it's also home to the Michelin-starred La Signoria restaurant.
www.hotel-la-signoria.com

WHAT TO DO
SCANDOLA
NATURE RESERVE
This Unesco World Heritage Site along

Corsica's northwestern coast is a beautiful marvel. High volcanic cliffs, tiny bays and nesting ospreys are what you see when you take a boat trip – as you can't access it any other way. Several companies in Calvi's harbour offer tours of varying lengths, but the four-hour one run by Calvi Evasion is particularly good and includes a swim stop.
www.calvi-evasion.com

CELEBRATIONS
CALVI ON THE ROCKS
This five-day electronic dance music festival takes over beach bars and parts of the port in July.
www.calvionthe rocks.com

RENCONTRES DE CHANTS POLYPHONIQUES DE CALVI
Nightly concerts take place in September in Calvi's cathedral and oratory, when the sound of Corsican polyphonic singing rings throughout the citadel.
www.facebook.com/ rencontrespoly phoniquescalvi

GET THERE
Île-de-France completely
rings Paris. Most
destinations are easily
reached from the capital
city by all major modes
of transport, including
Paris regional trains.

ST-DENIS

MEAUX

LA FERTÉ
SOUS
JOUARRE

07

ST-GERMAIN-
EN-LAYE

LA DÉFENSE

01

03

PARIS

LAGNY-
SUR-MARNE

Marne

Seine

08

COULOMMIERS

VERSAILLES

02

CRÉTEIL

06

MAUREPAS

05

MASSY

VERNEUIL-
L'ÉTANG

ÉVRY

ARPAJON

04

MELUN

ÎLE-DE-FRANCE

[France]

THE RENAISSANCE OF ÎLE-DE-FRANCE

For an organic taste of France, look beyond Paris to the surrounding region's devoted farmers, food producers and re-established wine makers.

Île-de-France is often, understandably, equated with Paris. Certainly, the City of Light is Île-de-France's vital core, but it's a densely populated and heavily touristed region. Meanwhile, the stretches beyond the greater metropolitan area are delightfully pastoral and rich in outstanding edible (and quaffable) products. While Paris brings in more than 30 million tourists a year, just a fraction venture out to discover outer Île-de-France's rolling plains of wide-open farmland dotted with villages, where chefs and producers are making the most of the region's natural bounty.

The resurgent wine industry is particularly appealing. For hundreds of years, Île-de-France was the largest and most acclaimed vineyard region in France – grander than Champagne, Burgundy or

Bordeaux. But the 19th century brought a perfect storm of urbanisation, grapevine disease and an emphasis on quantity over quality that devastated the industry. Things started to look up again when a ban on commercial wine production in Île-de-France was lifted in 2016. In 2020, a PGI (Protected Geography Indication) to use the region's name on labels was granted. Today there are around 200 vineyards in Île-de-France, many organic or biodynamic, or both.

The foods of Île-de-France are hardly unknown. Brie hails from the Seine-et-Marne department, as do other creamy cheeses. Notable mustards, vinegars, honeys and jams can trace their origins here too, and this region also produces a steady supply of superior grains, fruit and vegetables. All of these goodies grace the tables of quality restaurants in Paris and beyond.

01 The royal gardens of Versailles

02 La Bouche du Roi has planted vines on the Versailles plain

03 Contemporary Le Doyenné sits within ancient chateau grounds

04 Pick-your-own veg at Cueillette du Plessis

01 CLOS MONTMARTRE

Paris' most celebrated wine-producing vineyard (there are 11 in total) lies quietly behind walls and fences in one of the city's busiest neighbourhoods. Although the present vines were first planted in 1933, the plot is evocative of the six 'clos' (walled vineyards) that flourished nearby from the 12th to 19th centuries.

Grapes harvested here are pressed into the only wine produced by the city of Paris. A popular, annual, three-day Fête des Vendanges de Montmartre (grape harvest festival) marks the occasion in mid-October. Vineyard visits are possible through the Musée de Montmartre or private tours. Paris Wine Walks specialises in Paris vineyard experiences. *Rue des Saules; www.comite desfetesdemontmartre.com; access by reservation only*

02 NATURE URBAINE

Not all roofs are created equal. The one at Pavillon 6 of the Paris Expo Porte de Versailles exhibition and conference centre is special. It is Europe's largest urban rooftop farm, spread across 14,000 sq metres (150,694 sq ft) in southwest Paris and producing up to 1000 fruits and vegetables a day. Even better, it does so using sustainable agricultural practices, such as aeroponics and hydroponics.

The farm supplies Paris-area restaurants that emphasise seasonal, local food. The farm itself can only be visited through organised tours and activities, but you can book into Le Perchoir, a chic bar/restaurant that's located on the same rooftop and uses produce from the farm. *2 avenue de la Porte de la Plaine, Paris; www.nu-paris.com; closed Nov-Apr*

03 DOMAINE LA BOUCHE DU ROI

In 2016, Adrien Pélissié, Julien Bengué and Julien Brustis planted 26 hectares of vineyards with six grape varietals here on the Versailles plain, the former hunting grounds of the kings of France. This makes La Bouche du Roi the largest wine domaine in the Île-de-France.

The first vintages were produced in 2019 and the owners have now developed a host of oenotourism packages. Throughout the year, visitors can tour the grounds, try their hands at working on the vines and enjoy wine tasting or wine-food pairings among the vines.
12 Rue Saint Jacques, Davron; www.la-bouche-du-roi.com; access by reservation only

04 LE DOYENNÉ

For Shaun Kelly and James Henry, the two Australian chef-proprietors of this farm restaurant, everything revolves around the on-site vegetable, herb and flower garden and fruit trees. Tended according to regenerative agriculture practices, this *potager* employs modern farming techniques that produce tasty ingredients while improving the health of the environment. The quality edibles that are harvested then guide the chefs in Le Doyenné's gourmet restaurant.

It's a unique dining experience, especially when complemented by other regional ingredients and natural wines. The location makes it all the more special, as the farm and restaurant are within the historical grounds of the Château de Saint-Vrain, some 40km (25 miles) south of central Paris. The restaurant is housed in a converted barn and at the time of writing the owners were adding guesthouse rooms to create a rustic, upscale farmstay feel.
5 rue Saint-Antoine, Saint-Vrain; www.ledoyennerestaurant.com

05 CUEILLETTE DU PLESSIS PICKING GARDEN

By and for true lovers of fresh produce, this 25-hectare, family-run picking garden makes 50 varieties of fruit and vegetables available to food fans who appreciate real flavour. Visitors grab a basket, ease into the accessible plots and hand-pick the ingredients for their next homemade dishes.

Du Plessis is one of 10 Île-de-France–based members of the Chapeau de Paille (www.chapeaudepaille.fr) network of picking gardens, which places an emphasis on sustainable agriculture. When fresh produce drops off in winter, the picking gardens close but the on-site market remains open year-round, selling local farm

05 Cheeses are one of Île-de-France's most prized local products

06 The walled medieval town of Provins

and production, and runs through the several varieties of Brie – Brie de Meaux is the most famous – along with similar soft regional cheeses like Coulommiers. After a visit here, a simple wedge of Brie will never be the same again.
4 rue Cécile Dumez, Jouarre; https://fromagerie-ganot.fr; tours Sat only

08 LA GUINGUETTE CHEZ GÉGÈNE

In his *Le Déjeuner des canotiers* painting, Pierre-Auguste Renoir captured the lively spirit of a *guinguette* – the outdoor, waterside taverns that gained popularity in the 18th century, initially in Paris' southeast suburbs.

Today's *guinguettes* are no less atmospheric and enjoyable, with open-air dance halls decorated with fairy lights and animated by accordion music. Traditional food and plenty of wine round out the festive appeal, making them a perfect way to balance the urban-rural allure of Île-de-France.

Chez Gégène, perched on the edge of the Marne River, is the only *guinguette* not to have ceased operation since its opening in 1918.
162bis quai des Polangis, Joinville-le-Pont; www.chez-gegene.fr; closed Mon, Tue & mid-Dec to Mar

produce as well as quality regional fare such as cheese and poultry.
Route de Lumigny D20, Lumigny; www.cueillettedelumigny.fr; closed Mon

06 DOMAINE BOIS BRILLANT

In 2013, before commercial wine production was allowed in Île-de-France, Daniel Kiszel took a leap of faith. As a self-taught would-be vintner committed to permaculture farming – an approach that follows the example of natural forces – he planted the first of his vines. No one took him seriously at the time, but today his one-hectare Domaine Bois Brillant, the region's first professional winery, produces well-respected organic, natural and/or biodynamic nectars.

His Maison de la Vigne et du Vin also lays out the history of vineyards in Île-de-France and offers vineyard visits, wine tastings and work experience in the vines.
30 rue de la brosse, Guérard; www.vigneenvie.fr; open Mon-Fri, by appointment Sat

07 FROMAGERIE GANOT

Is there any cheese more emblematic of France than Brie, the celebrated creamy cow's-milk product native to Île-de-France? Turophiles (cheese-lovers) can learn all about it at Fromagerie Ganot, the oldest Brie cheese factory, which opened its doors in 1895.

On a guided tour and tasting, a 'master ripener' explains the intricacies of Brie's palate, texture

WHERE TO STAY:

FERME D'ORSONVILLE
Tilled since 1978 by the Pellissier family, this comfortable farmstay has 120 hectares of fields planted with cereals such as wheat and barley. It is surrounded by the extensive woods and moors of Gâtinais Natural Regional Park, reachable via numerous hiking and horseback riding trails.
www.ferme-orsonville.fr

MAISON STELLA CADENTE
In Provins, a typical 19th-century mansion exterior hides the unexpected and offbeat touch of designer Stella Cadente. Each room has a special theme and refined dining can be enjoyed in the elegant salon or tree-shaded terrace.
www.stellacadente-provins.com

WHAT TO DO

VERSAILLES PALACE & GARDEN
Built by King Louis XIV between the 17th and 18th centuries, this grandiose royal estate includes vast landscaped gardens and numerous

subsidiary buildings. Its lavishly decorated royal palace is a medley of salons, halls and private apartments.
www.chateauversailles.fr

REGIONAL CASTLES
Île-de-France has its fair share of private and royal chateaus beside Versailles. A few that merit special consideration include those at Fontainebleau, Vincennes, Rambouillet, Ferrières and Vaux-le-Vicomte. Don't miss the

parklands around them, especially the extensive, trail-laced forests at Rambouillet and Fontainebleau.

MEDIEVAL CITY OF PROVINS
Provins has a stunning 12th-century keep (the Tour César), complete with heavy ramparts and a small namesake vineyard, plus fascinating Middle Age underground galleries and a lovely rose garden.
www.provins.net

CELEBRATIONS

TASTE OF PARIS
Planned for four days in mid-May, Taste showcases Paris' best cooking talent. Small pop-up restaurants fill the Grand Palais where culinary stars serve tastings, lead live cooking demonstrations and showcase a dizzying array of regional products and cuisines. Some of the chefs who attend even have Michelin stars.
www.paris.taste festivals.com

GET THERE

Regular trains link Lyon, Beaune and Dijon, but to meander away from towns you'll need a car. Lyon's international airport, Lyon-Saint-Exupéry, is well connected to the rest of Europe and speedy TGVs connect Paris to Lyon in two hours by rail.

LYON TO DIJON

08 DIJON

CÔTE D'OR

07 ABBAYE DE CITEAUX

DOLE

BEAUNE

06

05

AUTUN

FRANCHE-COMTÉ

BURGUNDY

Doubs

LE CREUSOT

CHALON-SUR-SAÔNE

04

LOUHANS

03 TOURNUS

DIGOIN

CLUNY

Saône

MÂCON

RHÔNE-ALPES

Loire

PÉROUGES

Rhône

01

02 LYON

AIX-LES-BAINS

[France]

FROM LYON TO DIJON WITH LOVE

From Unesco vineyards to France's most fabled female chefs, the culinary force of this tract of France's Vallée de la Gastronomie is heartfelt and Herculean.

Tripe, snails, fine red wine and cheese so runny it needs to be spooned: the route between Lyon and Dijon in France packs a serious punch. Epicurean nirvana ever since the wine-loving Romans settled on Lyon's sun-blessed 'hill of prayer' in 43 BCE and spread their vintner wings north into Burgundy, this urban twinset is now a highlight of the Vallée de la Gastronomie – a 600km (373-mile)-plus touring route launched in 2020 to help visitors fully explore the region's gourmet credentials. This northern snapshot focuses on the area straddling Bourgogne-Franche-Comté and the Auvergne-Rhône-Alpes.

Lyon made its indelible mark on the culinary map in the early 20th century when many of the city's bourgeois families let go of their private cooks, prompting gifted female home chefs to open their own restaurants. This era ushered in a brilliant string of *mères* ('mother' chefs) and gave birth to Lyon's down-to-earth *bouchons* (Lyonnais bistrots), known

for their hearty tripe, pork and *quenelle* (pike-perch dumpling) dishes. Mère Eugénie Brazier was the world's first chef to land six Michelin stars in 1933 and helped train Lyonnais chef and 1970s founding father of nouvelle cuisine Paul Bocuse. Her legacy lives on in the likes of Adrien Zedda (Culina Hortus), Tabata Mey (Les Apothicaires) and Younghoon Lee (Le Passe Temps) – key disruptors and innovators in Lyon's ever-evolving food scene.

Meandering north through vine-striped Beaujolais into Burgundy, road-trippers will find ecclesiastical grandeur and the bourgeoisie cuisine of a 14th-century dukedom richer and more powerful than the kingdom of France itself. This is the home of world-beating unblended Grand Crus and top-drawer Charolais beef. Riverside Mâcon has been chosen as the site of a new branch of France's Cité des Climats et Vins, opening in 2023, while Dijon remains a dashing gastronomic regional powerhouse.

01 MARCHÉ DE LA CROIX-ROUSSE

Open-air food markets pepper Lyon but it's north across the Saône, on the 'hill of work' where weavers spun silk in the 19th century, that seasonal regional produce marries so well with village vibe. Stalls stretch for a kilometre along Croix-Rousse's main boulevard, beneath a pea-green canopy of centurion planes and hackberry saplings. Inch your way past trestle tables and deli vans loaded with fruit, veg and herbs, artisan breads and bowls of creamy, chive-spiced *cervelle de canut* ('weaver's brain'; cheese spread) – the historic silk-weaver staple still going strong. At cheese and charcuterie stalls ask to taste

porky *saucisson* studded with hazelnuts, and cheeses such as straw-ripened *tomme de vache* and *beaufort d'alpage* made by summer shepherds. Bring your own basket or woven straw bag to blend in with the devoutly local crowd.
Bd de la Croix-Rousse, 4e, Lyon; closed afternoons & Mon

02 FOOD TRABOULE

This new-generation food court in Lyon's Old Town brings a dozen-odd chefs under one roof to celebrate the city's increasingly diverse food scene. "Gastronomy here is about doing good and being accessible," explains Food Traboule co-creator and chef Tabata Mey.

Pick from truffle-spiked *croques monsieur*, tacos *d'andouillette*

starring the city's gutsy tripe sausage, paper cones of *frites de quenelles* ('fries' cut from Lyonnais pike-perch dumplings) and other creative street foods. The historic setting is equally spot on: Lyon's most emblematic *traboule* (passageway or square), wrapped around a Renaissance tower nicknamed La Tour Rose after its salmon-pink facade.
22 rue du Bœuf, Lyon; foodtraboule.com

03 TWO DUDES

This innovative micro-brewery in the small, riverside abbey-town of Tournus shows the creative, contemporary side of Burgundy's food and drink scene. Alchemists Pierre and Amandine shake up

traditional gastronomy with craft beer and food pairings in a back-to-basics hangar. You can either swing by the brewery to taste and buy six different IPAs, American brown ales and lagers; linger over an *apéro* (aperitif) with homemade pickles, rillettes and crackers; or reserve a *table d'hôte* dinner with flawless beer pairings, around a shared table between beer vats. Bon appétit.
ZA du Pas Fleury, Tournus; www.twodudes-brasserie.com; closed Sun & Mon

❹ FERME AUBERGE DE LA BONARDIÈRE

For two decades Nicolas Roguet has bred France's star chicken, *poulet de Bresse*, on his intimate Burgundian farm. Few Bresse birds leave France, making lunch chez Nicolas – a hearty, homemade feast of *terrine de volaille* (a smooth, poultry pâté) followed by roast chicken or à la crème (in a creamy sauce) – all the more special. "Our family farm is small. I cook the *poulet à la crème* in the morning, but everyone mucks in at lunch," he says. The exacting rules that govern his poultry's AOP (Appellation d'Origine Protégée – a coveted quality guarantee) mean the prized chicken with blue-grey legs and punk-style red wattle pecks around freely in meadows for the first 12 weeks of life.
Les Chênes, Bouhans; www. labonardiere-pouletdebresse.fr; lunch Sat & Sun, mid-Apr to mid-Nov

❺ MOUTARDERIE FALLOT

Dijon mustard doesn't have its own protected-denomination label, meaning it can be made anywhere – but it's still best tasted at the source. Moutarderie Fallot is the last family company producing Dijon mustard. Here, mustard seeds are soaked in verjuice and ground by stone as they have been since 1840.

Tours of Fallot's old and new production sites in Beaune explain how the only mustard made from locally grown Brassica seeds today is Moutarde de Bourgogne IGP; Dijon mustard-makers otherwise rely on imported seeds from Canada. Taste both after the tour at the mustard bar in Fallot's boutique. Don't miss the rainbow of flavoured mustards laced

06 Breakfast is a serious affair at Hôtel de l'Abbaye on Lyon's Presqu'île

07 Dijon's Place de la Libération, the heart of the Old Town

with regional products, such as blackcurrants, tarragon or sublime *pain des épices* (gingerbread).
31 rue du Faubourg Bretonnière, Beaune; www.fallot.com; closed Sun

06 CÔTE D'OR

Join Bourgogne Évasion for a slow cycling tour around Côte d'Or's medieval villages, ancestral cellars and hand-groomed vines. The knowledgeable guides help unveil finer details you wouldn't otherwise see. Half-day rides, departing south from Beaune along bucolic country lanes, plunge cyclists into the Pommard, Volnay and Meursault vineyards. Tasting dry whites and delicate reds in situ – with *vignerons*, between pea-green vines or in their vat room – is the easiest way to grasp this Unesco-listed concept. Santé!
www.bourgogne-evasion.fr; closed Nov-Mar

07 ABBAYE NOTRE DAME DE CÎTEAUX

Many foodies award the accolade of 'France's smelliest cheese' to Burgundy's Époisses, others to Abbaye de Citeaux. Visitors to this region can inhale the earthy, pungent aroma of ochre-skinned Citeaux at the 11th-century abbey where it has been crafted for 500 years.

Exploring the library, cloister and other parts of the Cistercian monastery where 25 monks live and work requires a reservation. Without one, you can still visit the abbey shop where the cheeses are sold. Some 300 rounds are produced here each week by master cheesemakers Frère Frédéric and Frére Joel, using unpasteurised milk from cows grazing around the abbey.
Route de Seurre, RD996, St-Nicolas-lès-Citeaux; www. citeaux-abbaye.org; closed Sun morning & Mon

08 CITÉ DE LA GASTRONOMIE ET DU VIN DE DIJON

Sink your teeth good and proper into French gastronomy and wine at Dijon's resolutely contemporary Gastronomy and Wine City, inside a monumental 13th-century orphanage. Explore the traditional French table, kitchen and Burgundy wine in permanent exhibitions; learn the French art of *dégustation* in 45-minute tasting workshops; take a cooking or cocktail class; and shop for gingerbread macarons, rare raw-milk Soumaintrain cheese and farmhouse *crème de cassis* at gourmet boutiques in Le Village Gastronomique. Don't miss out on a meal here, be it a rooftop barbecue, quick dinner or an indulgent romp through 'vinostronomy' at refined La Table des Climats – here, your choice of wine, not food, decides the pairing.
2 rue de l'Hôpital, Dijon; www. citedelagastronomie-dijon.fr

WHERE TO STAY

L'IMPRIMERIE

Until a decade ago, etiquettes for some of Burgundy's prestigious Grand Cru wines were printed at this small printing house in Beaune. Since transforming into a stylish, eco-conscious *gîte urbain*, L'imprimerie woos gourmet guests with five B&B rooms, a coworking lounge and privileged tastings of small-production wines with local *vignerons* (winegrowers) in its hybrid coffee shop-wine bar. *www.limprimerie beaune.fr*

HÔTEL DE L'ABBAYE

Petit dej is a serious affair at boutique Abbey Hotel, in a 16th-century presbytery on Lyon's Presqu'île. Amid the breakfast feast of artisan fruit juices, cheeses, *viennoiseries* (pastries) and coffee from the tiny LaGrange roastery in Haute-Saône, a bowl of Lyonnais *cervelle de canut* (cheese spread) and a *brioche à la praline* (sweet bread bun studded with Lyon's hot-pink, sugar-almond confection) are unnegotiable. *https://hotelabbaye lyon.com*

WHAT TO DO

MUSÉE DES BEAUX-ARTS

Soak up the artistic glory assembled by the dukes of Burgundy in Dijon's outstanding fine-arts museum, occupying one wing of the ducal palace in the city's historic heart. Renaissance to modern masters aside, admire ornate, late-medieval sepulchres of dukes in the wood-panelled Salle des Gardes and animal sculptures by Burgundy sculptor François Pompon in the Pompon Room. *https://beaux-arts.dijon.fr*

CELEBRATIONS

VENTE AUX ENCHÈRES DES VINS DES HOSPICES DE BEAUNE

The grandest of Burgundy's wine-fest bounty, this three-day extravaganza over the third weekend of November climaxes with a wine auction. It's held in Burgundy's blockbuster monument – Beaune's splendiferous medieval charity hospital, Hôtel Dieu des Hospices de Beaune. Built in 1443, it's instantly recognisable by its cinematic succession of dazzling, steep-pitched roofs in polychrome ceramic tiles.

GET THERE
The easiest way to get around
Normandy is to drive, either
hiring a car in Paris or taking the
car ferry to Caen, Cherbourg or
Le Harve.

01

English Channel
(La Manche)

NORMANDY

ABBEVILLE

DIEPPE

CHERBOURG ST-VAAST-
LA-HOUGUE 03
BENOÎTVILLE

ÉTRETAT

06

LE HAVRE

ROUEN

TROUVILLE 05
COUDRAY-RABUT

ST-LÔ CAEN 04

LISIEUX

GIVERNY

ÉVREUX

NORMANDY

02

DREUX

DOMFRONT

BRITTANY

ALENÇON 01 RÉMALARD CHARTRES

LAVAL

[France]

FUSS-FREE FOOD IN NORMANDY

Normandy's traditional, salt-of-the-earth cuisine is a love letter to the region's bountiful orchards, rolling pastures and beautiful stretches of coastline.

Few French regions are as bucolic as Normandy. It might be on the doorstep of Paris, but culturally it couldn't be further removed. As you head deeper into the countryside, cities and towns become ever more sparsely scattered amid lush farmland, ancient orchards and half-timbered villages where life goes on much as it has done for centuries. Add in a smattering of rustic-chic country houses and you've got all the elements for an unforgettable long weekend of culinary exploration.

Days revolve around simple pleasures: a visit to a local market followed by walks on rugged beaches or muddy tramps across fields before hearty dinners in candlelit bistros. Only in the glitziest coastal towns or best-known villages do you feel the press of tourism.

Much to nationwide mirth, cows have been found to officially outnumber people in two of Normandy's five *départements*. The region is rightly renowned for its dairy, and sinking your teeth into slabs of soft and creamy Camembert, Pont-l'Évêque and Neufchâtel should be top of your agenda.

On the coast, see oysters shucked steps from where they're farmed. In season, plump and sweet Saint-Jacques (scallops) merit not just special menus but annual harbourside festivals. As winter approaches, Normandy's specialities become as rich as they are filling, culminating in black pudding and apple tarts devoured with *bolées* (bowls) of cider by roaring fires.

Locals might be famously renowned for their 'réponse de Normand', shorthand for giving nothing away with an ambiguous reply, but when it comes to food there's no sitting on the fence. Normands know they have some of the country's best cuisine and delight in sharing (a few of) its secrets.

01 Cherry picking in Normandy's orchards – the simple life

02 & 03 Maison Gosselin deli in the harbour village of Saint-Vaast-la-Hougue

04 Apple tarts are just one of Normandy's food specialities

01 D'UNE ÎLE

When the team behind Paris' much-acclaimed Michelin-starred restaurant Septime devise a rural escape, you know to expect something special. This beautifully restored 17th-century country house from Bertrand Grébaut and Théophile Pourriat is set in eight hectares on the edge of Parc Naturel du Perche in southern Normandy. Despite the remote feel, it's anything but a culinary backwater.

Grébaut and Pourriat have created a countryside *table d'hôte* and rooms with a difference, reflecting their ambition to establish a deep and lasting connection with the region they so love. "The entire menu is built around local ingredients from the Sarthe and Normandy", says Grébaut. Even if you don't want to stay, book for lunch, when the dishes are seasonal, sustainable and endlessly creative.

Produce is foraged, grown in their own garden or sourced from local growers and markets. That means no olive oil or citrus fruits, which would need to be shipped in from further afield, and breakfast *tartines* (open sandwiches) smothered in butter and jam direct from neighbouring farms if you stay overnight.

Wines, although not local, are a highlight: all natural and organic, often biodynamic.
Domaine de Launay, Lieu dit l'Aunay, 61110 Rémalard; www.duneile.com

02 LA FERME DU CHAMP SECRET

The Mercier family has been at the heart of Normandy's dairy farming industry for four generations. Not only were they one of the first farms to open their doors to visitors some 15 years ago, but they're also among the pioneers of organic agriculture in the region. Their 180-hectare, sustainably managed estate is as rich in biodiversity as it is natural beauty. Tours take you out into the fields or hay barns to meet the cows, then into the dairy to learn the art of Camembert production.

As well as soft, unctuous wheels of their Camembert itself, you can pick up tubs of fresh cream and pats of salty, just-churned butter to take away.

La Novere 61700 Champsecret; www.fermeduchampsecret.com; tours every Fri in summer (usually Jul & Aug) at 4pm, by reservation at other times of year

03 MAISON GOSSELIN

The pretty grey-stone harbour village of Saint-Vaast-la-Hougue, the third-largest fishing port on the Channel, is home to Normandy's most marvellous food emporium. Founded in 1889 by Clovis Gosselin and now run by the fifth generation of the same family, Maison Gosselin is a true Aladdin's cave. It includes not just an *épicerie fine* (delicatessen), stocked with towering shelves of terrines, sauces and soups, but also a coffee roastery and extensive

cellar of wine and spirits. Their celebration of local ingredients is a joy to behold: pork pâtés made with apples and Calvados, crunchy *sarasin* (buckwheat) crisps and rillettes of prawns roasted in cider are just the start.

If you pick up one thing, make it a house-made broth or stock base. "The 'Clovis' court-bouillon, a mixture of spices for cooking fish and shellfish, was created by my great-grandfather," says owner Bertrand Gosselin. "I've carefully kept this century-old recipe a secret, but I'm preparing to share it with my children Lucie and Paul, who will soon take over our family store." *27 rue de Verrue, 50550 St-Vaast-la-Hougue; www.maison-gosselin.fr; closed Mon except Jul & Aug*

04 MAISON CHRISTIAN DROUIN

When it comes to all things Calvados, the apple brandy for which Normandy is renowned, Christian Drouin is the name to know. This family-run estate has been in the same family for three generations. Tours are run from their 17th-century Norman farmhouse, a picture of half-timbered perfection in the Touques Valley. Each visit includes a behind-the-scenes look at the distillery and a tasting.

Perhaps unexpectedly, the most exciting bottles are the Drouin gins – elegant and complex spirits matured in old 225-litre Calvados casks that impart subtle apple notes and a smooth finish. The estate can arrange picnic lunches to enjoy in the grounds

05 Seafood takes pride of place in Trouville-sur-Mer markets

06 Inside the Fondation Claude Monet, Giverny

(book ahead), if you'd like to stay a little longer.
1895 Route de Trouville, 14130 Coudray-Rabut; www.calvados-drouin.com; tours Mon-Sat

05 TROUVILLE HALLE AUX POISSONS

For great seafood, there's only one rule to abide by: seek out the simplest and freshest you can find. At Trouville's covered fish market, you're buying straight from fishmongers just steps from the quay where the town's flag-bedecked fishing boats unload their daily catch. The building has even been protected as an historic monument since 1991. Lunch is an uncomplicated affair of platters laden with crab, oysters, whelks and grey prawns eaten at formica tables beside the market stalls, accompanied by frosty glasses of Chablis or Muscadet. Stroll off your half-dozen *huîtres* (oysters) exploring the surrounding streets, then wander across to explore Trouville's ritzier twin, Deauville, and its stylish boardwalk.
152 Boulevard Fernand Moureaux, 14360 Trouville-sur-Mer

06 LES TRAVAILLEURS DE L'AMER

The team behind up-and-coming brewery Les Travailleurs de l'Amer are among a new guard of entrepreneurs injecting fresh life into Normandy's traditional food scene. Their amber ales, stouts and IPAs don't just use Norman wheat and barley, but pay tribute to the unique cast of adventurers – fishers, sailors and even wreck divers – who represent the true spirit of the ocean-going communities along the Normandy coastline. You might find Félix Testi, a shellfish fisherman from Granville, pictured on the label of a bottle of blanche or the oceanographer Paul Dufour on their blonde. The specially built tasting room is in Les Pieux, 20km (12 miles) from Cherbourg, but they also have a small boutique on Quai Caligny in Cherbourg itself.
23 route de Cherbourg, Les Pieux; www.lestravailleursdelamer.com; tasting room closed Sun & Mon

WHERE TO STAY

CHATEAU LE FLEUR

Painstakingly renovated by designer Anna Bewley and filmmaker Philipp Franz, Chateau Le Fleur is a luxury B&B set in an 18th-century chateau just outside Honfleur. There are just four rooms, each furnished with French antiques and decorated with a modern twist.
www.lefleur.fr/en/

GÎTES DE FRANCE

The best way to find a rural Normandy escape all your own is to book through Gîtes de France. Choose between *chambres d'hôtes*, where breakfast and hotel amenities are laid on, bijou private barn conversions and even the occasional treehouse.
www.gites-de-france.com

WHAT TO DO

FONDATION CLAUDE MONET

Monet's house and gardens remain just as magical as when the artist painted here undisturbed for some

40 years. During his time here, Monet produced endless variations of *Les Nymphéas*, the water-lily series that went on to become his most famous work.
www.fondation-monet.com

ÉTRETAT

The majestic white cliffs of Étretat have attracted everyone from Impressionist painters to fans of the ingenious Arsène Lupin novels,

now inspiration for the eponymous Netflix series. No matter your calling to this rugged coastline, blustery strolls along clifftop walking trails are the perfect way to blow away the cobwebs.
www.lehavre-etretat-tourisme.com

CELEBRATIONS

DIEPPE HERRING AND SCALLOP FESTIVAL

Dieppe, the principal scallop-fishing port in France, has celebrated

the arrival of Saint-Jacques season with aplomb for more than 50 years. Some 100,000 people descend on the town in the third weekend of November each year to feast on butter-drenched scallop skewers and catch the parade of the Brotherhood of Herrings and Scallops.
https://uk.dieppe
tourisme.com/calendar/
herring-and-scallop-festival

GET THERE
Strasbourg (just over the
border from Baden–Baden)
is easily reached by Eurostar
and TGV. The nearest
airports are Baden–Baden
and Stuttgart. Heading
into the remote forested
wilds, the trail itself is best
covered by car.

01

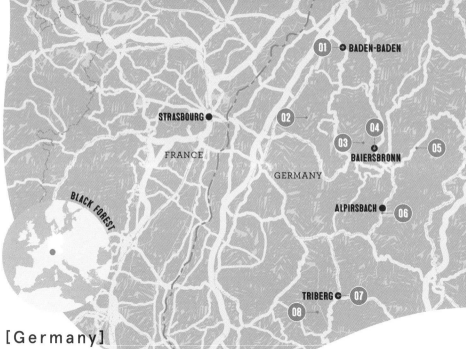

NATURAL FLAVOUR HIGHS IN THE BLACK FOREST

Staying true to its woody roots and glittering with Michelin stars, the food scene in Germany's fairy-tale forest goes far beyond its namesake cherry gateau.

As deep, dark and delicious as its famous cherry cake, the Black Forest looks as though it has been plucked straight out of a Grimm fairy tale. Hills rise steep and thickly spruce-wooded above church steeples, half-timbered villages, gigantic cuckoo clocks and a crochet of tightly woven valleys.

In tune with the great outdoors, restaurants play up season-spun, locally sourced ingredients. Nose-to-tail and farm-to-plate, organic and locavore – these approaches to food were second nature here long before they became buzzwords. Along curve after beautiful winding curve you'll see the tell-tale signs – small distilleries producing *kirsch* (cherry brandy), hills striped with pinot vines, rambling farmhouses selling smoked ham and fragrant honey, basket-wielding families foraging in the woods, and farmers markets heaving with produce.

Menus sing of the seasons: white asparagus and wild garlic in spring, chanterelles and penny bun mushrooms in late summer and early autumn, followed by the earthy delights of pumpkins and game. Hearty Swabian-style dishes such as *maultaschen* (giant pasta pockets stuffed with pork and onions), *kässpätzle* (noodles topped with cheese) and *zwiebelkuchen* (onion tart with cream and caraway seeds) will send you rolling out of beamed rural inns. And you'll never forget your first forkful of real Black Forest gateau.

If you're seeking a more gourmet experience – *herzlich wilkommen*! This region has one of Germany's highest concentrations of top tables. The village of Baiersbronn alone shimmers with six Michelin stars and tasting menus that elevate natural, integral flavours with a pinch of culinary magic and a nod to neighbouring France.

01 KAFFEESACK

Deep in the wooded folds of the northern Black Forest, the swish little spa town of Baden-Baden has always had an appetite for the finer things in life, coffee included. Where to find the perfect cup? Kaffeesack, *natürlich*. Here the barista freshly roasts coffee from all over the world, using fair-trade beans from Kenya to Brazil, India to Guatemala.

The retro-rustic cafe is a chilled spot to sip a cup of joe prepared with love and a creative flourish. They take their beans seriously here, so anything you want to know – be it the subtle nuances of aroma or the roasting process – just ask.
Hirschstrasse 6, Baden-Baden; www.kaffeesack.de; closed Sun & Mon

02 REBSTOCK WALDULM

It's an easy half-hour drive south to Kappelrodeck, where the hills are ribboned with vines and orchards. Here, Karl Hodapp mans the stove at Rebstock Waldulm, a gorgeous half-timbered, 250-year-old farmhouse full of creaky beams and rustic warmth. Karl earned his culinary stripes working in a string of Michelin-starred restaurants and this – coupled with his pride in careful, seasonal sourcing – shines through in Baden-style dishes with a nod to neighbouring Alsace.

Noble pinots from his own vineyards strike a perfect balance with dishes like cream of snail soup with wild herbs, and quail breast in a black pudding crust with plum compote. A shot of

Karl's homemade *kirsch* rounds out a memorable meal in the dark-timber, lamplit restaurant.
Kutzendorf 1, Kappelrodeck/ Waldulm; www.rebstock-waldulm.de; closed Mon & Tue

03 RESTAURANT BAREISS

Baiersbronn! The mere mention of this village sends gourmets into raptures. With a population just shy of 16,000 and a whopping six Michelin stars – including one two-star and one three-star restaurant – this is Germany's backcountry culinary capital.

Helming the kitchen at three-star Restaurant Bareiss is Claus-Peter Lumpp, who walks the culinary high-wire with his inimitable blend of ingenuity, meticulousness and

01 The Black Forest is a magnificent tumble of forested hills

02 Grimm-worthy half-timbered houses

03 Mushrooms star on menus in late summer and early autumn

04 The Black Forest's vine-flanked roads

artistic flair. Each dish sings of the seasons and tastes profoundly of its prime ingredients – be it saddle of roe deer with rosehip, Piedmont hazelnuts and wild cauliflower, or stuffed kohlrabi with ceps cooked in hay on cep purée and lemongrass.

Book well ahead, opt for the tasting menu, let sommelier Teoman Mezda pair the wines, and prepare for the meal of a lifetime. *Hermine-Bareiss-Weg 1, Baiersbronn-Mitteltal; www.bareiss.com; closed Mon & Tue*

04 WILD HERB WALKS

You need only take one look at the dark curtain of larch and spruce forest rising above Baiersbronn to imagine what rich pickings these woods hide in the way of wild herbs and mushrooms. Indeed, the entire Black Forest hums with foragers, particularly from late spring to autumn when wild herbs, berries and mushrooms – including apricot-hued chanterelles and glossy, nut-brown ceps – begin to pop up on the forest fringes and in mossy glades.

Finding them, however, is pot luck and you need to know what you're looking for. If you're a beginner, consider hooking onto one of Baiersbronn's three- to four-hour guided walks; some of which are free with a Baiersbronn guest card. See the tourist office website for dates. *Baiersbronn; www.baiersbronn.de; tours Apr-Oct*

05 PFAU SCHINKEN

When you smell the smoky aroma of Schwarzwälder Schinken, the local ham, you know you've arrived at Pfau, which gives a fascinating insight into the ham curing and smoking process on its guided tours (Tuesdays & Saturdays).

The Black Forest ham here is the real deal – we're talking seriously good charcuterie. Locally reared ham is rubbed with salt and spices, such as coriander, garlic and juniper berries, then dry-cured for four to 12 weeks, before being cold-smoked over fir wood and left to mature for a few weeks to retain its intensely woody flavour.

Pfau, a 20-minute drive east of Baiersbronn, also runs a shop for stocking up on picnic provisions;

05 Black Forest cherry gateau is the region's most famous recipe

06 Smoky Schwarzwälder – Pfau's signature product

07 The spa town of Baden-Baden makes an ideal base for exploration

besides ham, other specialities available include wild garlic, venison and kirsch-laced salami.
Alte Poststrasse 17, Herzogsweiler; www.pfau-schinken.de; closed Sun

06 ALPIRSBACHER KLOSTERBRÄU

Presided over by its former Benedictine monastery, lore has it that Alpirsbach was named after a quaffing cleric who, when a glass of beer slipped from his hand and tumbled into the river, exclaimed: *All bier ist in den bach!* (All the beer is in the stream!). Prophetically, Alpirsbacher Klosterbräu is now one of the Black Forest's finest beers, brewed from pure local spring water.

Daily guided tours whizz you through the brewing process and conclude with a beer tasting. Even if you miss the tour, it's worth heading into the shop for tipples such as the brewery's eponymous hoppy, full-bodied beer, which scooped gold at the World Beer Awards in 2020.
Marktplatz 1, Alpirsbach; https:// alpirsbacher.de; closed Sat & Sun

07 HÖHENGASTHAUS KOLMENHOF

The final steep road to Martinskapelle, topped by a medieval chapel, negotiates some pretty hairy switchbacks – but it's worth it. These steeply forested slopes, with views sprawling as far as the Alps on cloud-free days, attract walkers in summer and cross-country skiers when the flakes fall in winter.

Fitting neatly into this rustic picture is Höhengasthaus Kolmenhof, run by the third generation of the Dold family. Out front is the brook that flows into the Breg – the main source of the Danube. This accounts for the winningly fresh trout, which is served whole with almond butter and salted potatoes or poached in white wine.

Good old-fashioned Black Forest home-cooking is on the menu, playing up regional grub such as beef broth with *flädle* (pancake strips) and pork roast with buttery *spätzle* (egg noodles).
Neuweg 11, Martinskapelle; www. kolmenhof.de; closed Wed & Thu

08 CAFÉ GOLDENE KRONE

Ask any local from around these parts and they'll tell you that the best Schwarzwälder Kirschtorte (Black Forest cherry gateau) is the one their *mama* (mother) or *oma* (grandmother) makes. That's because a good Black Forest cake shouldn't just look pretty, it needs to taste of a loving, generous home.

On a high plateau in the southern Black Forest, half-an-hour's drive south of Martinskapelle, this women's cooperative cafe sits in the pretty village of St Märgen, topped off by a baroque pilgrimage church.

And the cake? The dream: a multi-layered masterpiece of moist chocolate sponge, tart morello cherries and clouds of whipped cream, with a subtle hint of *kirsch*. One forkful and you'll see why Café Goldene Krone is raved about far and wide.
Wagensteigstrasse 10, St Märgen; www.cafe-goldene-krone.de; closed Mon & Tue

WHERE TO STAY
REBSTOCK WALDULM
Producing its own wine and schnapps, family-run Rebstock Waldulm has bags of half-timbered charm and an excellent restaurant (see stop 2). *www.rebstock-waldulm.de*

HOTEL BAREISS
This Baiersbronn hotel offers every imaginable luxury – plush rooms and suites, beautiful grounds, a three Michelin-starred restaurant (see stop 3), its own wine cellar, children's club and spa. *www.bareiss.com*

HÖHENGASTHAUS KOLMENHOF
High on one of the Black Forest's loveliest hills, this family-run guesthouse has rustic-chic rooms with wood trappings and wraparound views of forests and mountains. There's a terrific network of hiking and cross-country skiing trails on the doorstep and an on-site restaurant for evenings (see stop 7). *www.kolmenhof.de*

WHAT TO DO
TRIBERG
Gawp at the world's biggest cuckoo clock at Eble Uhren-Park and hike up the seven tiers of Germany's highest (163m/535ft) waterfall, the Triberger Wasserfälle. *www.triberg.de*

BADEN-BADEN
A great launchpad for explorations. Check out the star-studded collection of modern and contemporary art at Museum Frieder Burda, and linger for a nude splash in the thermal waters of the cupola-topped Friedrichsbad. *www.baden-baden.com*

CELEBRATIONS
BLACK FOREST CAKE FESTIVAL
Rimmed by mountains, Todtnauberg delivers a feast of Black Forest gateau at this mid-April festival. Besides cake, come for the gateau-making workshops, chef demos, jam-making courses and folk music.

FASNACHT
A 500-year-old rite to banish winter with parades, feasting and late-night drinkathons. Find it in towns and villages including Rottweil, Schramberg and Elzach.

GET THERE

Geneva is the closest international airport and major rail hub for access to Valais. Depending on connection times, it takes just under two hours to reach Martigny on a very scenic journey skirting Lake Geneva. Verbier is connected to the train network by cable cars.

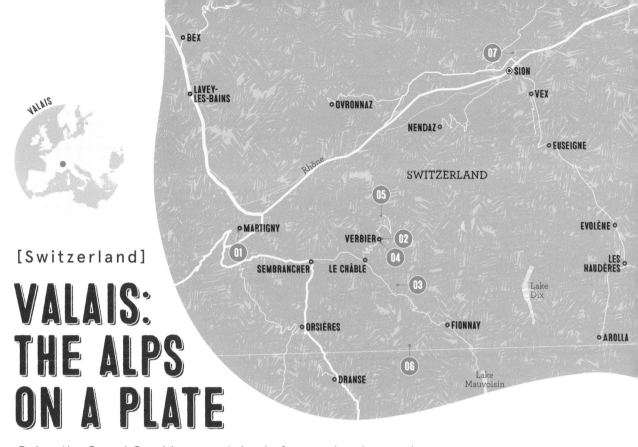

[Switzerland]

VALAIS: THE ALPS ON A PLATE

Below the Grand Combin, mountain chefs, cow-herders and Rhône Valley producers are supplying the Valais' towns and villages with slow food, speciality cheeses and little-known wines.

Though its neighbours France and Italy may get all the culinary kudos, Switzerland's Alpine regions have lots to offer the travelling gourmand. This is especially true in Valais, the canton where the Grand Combin and Matterhorn slide down to the Rhône River – a fertile strip prized for its fruit orchards. The mountain pastures of the Val de Bagnes are prime grazing territory for Switzerland's prized Herren cows, which are farmed for top-quality beef, wine-soaked charcuterie and milk that has a flowery taste thanks to the sweet grazing meadows.

The milk of the Herren cows goes into producing some of Switzerland's best cheeses too. Valais is the home of raclette – the oozy cheese dish served with potatoes and pickles – but it's also a heartland for fondue, served in fire-toasted chalet restaurants and mountain huts beloved by hikers. Recently this area has also become a slow-food destination and it's now home to Switzerland's first slow-food community, Sarreyer, which is reviving mountain food-making traditions of the 19th century. But Valais is far from stuck in the past. The Swiss are kings of invention, and food experiences are being sliced and diced in countless new ways to give visitors the full measure of Swiss flavours. Travellers can take a hiking path between restaurants for extended lunches, learn the art of raclette with local cheese-masters, or head out into the Alpine hills for foraging walks.

Valais is also Switzerland's leading wine-making region, with dozens of indigenous grapes (Petite Arvine, Completer, Cornalin) that visitors are unlikely to find on supermarket shelves back home. And vinitourism is booming, with cellar door tastings, vineyard hikes, wine museums and a new festival in Verbier giving travellers the opportunity to get to grips with the area's mineral whites and fruit-driven reds.

01 DISTILLERIE MORAND

Eau de vie (fruit brandy) is part of the fabric of Swiss life, and Distillerie Morand is the doyen of *eau de vie* in Switzerland. Founded in Martigny in 1889, it still produces some of the same recipes it launched with 130 years ago. Morand's reputation is built on the fact that it was one of the first *eau de vie* distilleries to use top-quality fruits instead of the mulch that nobody else wanted. Its 'williamine' pear version made Morand a household name and both its pear and apricot liqueurs have AOP (Protected Designation of Origin) status.

"20 years ago, people would even drink *eau de vie* at breakfast," says distillery director Fabrice Haenni. These days, however, tastes are changing and the distillery has expanded to produce creative syrups (perfect for cocktails or non-alcoholic spritzes), gin and rum. Tours include tastings of seasonal *eaux de vies* with punchy hits of quince or rhubarb, refreshing watermelon or mint syrups and absinthe. Add a cheese and charcuterie lunch in the wood-beamed bar to soak up the booze. *Place de Plaisance 2, 1920 Martigny; www.morand.ch; public tours Sat or private by arrangement*

02 LE 22

There are only 22 seats in Verbier's most inventive *table d'hotes* (fixed-price-menu restaurant), hidden behind a fake wall in the Crock No Name après-ski pub. Within an intimate speakeasy setting the chefs here are on a mission to show what can be done with fresh Alpine ingredients. Eschewing the typical mountain menu of heavy rostis, fondues and raclettes, some of Le 22's ingredients are foraged and some come from the kitchen garden; bread is bought from the bakery underneath the restaurant.

The focus is on refined cooking with a weekly changing set menu of five courses. Expect dishes such as pea and garden mint gazpacho or torched Val d'Hérens beef fillet with wild garlic and a jus made with Valais' Petite Arvine wine grapes. *Route des Creux 22, 1936 Verbier; https://crock.ch/le-22-table-dhotes/*

01 Valais' Swiss chalets are easy on the eye

02 Hill-hugging vineyards at Celliers de Sion

03 Making the most of Valais ingredients at Le 22

04 Williamine pear *eau de vie* made Morand a household name

03 CAFÉ DU MONT-FORT

Sleepy Sarreyer, Switzerland's first slow food village, is an atmospheric spot for a self-guided walk before lunch in the village square at Café du Mont-Fort. Some of its traditional wooden chalets, fragrant with trailing roses, date to the 1800s. Local residents Gaston Bess and Jean Marc Mason founded the slow food association here to show visitors how Sarreyer was once a self-sufficient hub for grain and timber production. Visit the community bakery and the old timber cutting shed for fresh apple juice, before heading to the village's Café du Mont-Fort.

As well as having a traditional absinthe fountain at the turn-of-the-century, wood-panelled bar, Mont-Fort is a champion of slow food cooking. The chefs take Alpine ingredients from the surrounding valley and imaginatively weave them into rustic dishes such as nettle gazpacho, handmade pasta with wild garlic sauce, and ice cream made with asperula, a local mountain plant, served over gin from Valais' Edelweiss Distillery. *Ch du Banderet 15, Sarreyer, 1948 Bagnes; www.facebook.com/ montfortcafe*

04 CHERRIES WALKS

Back in Verbier, book a foraging hike with local resident Cherries to find out for yourself the wealth of edibles that grow in the Alps. Heading out from central Verbier, you won't get far before you start to notice cedar-flanked verges bushy with arnica, wild thyme, violets, juniper and sunny gentian. Locals use the roots of the latter to distill a liqueur. The altitude affects what vegetation will grow and as Cherries leads you up into the mountain paths, the wild harvest will change. Pick zingy sorrel and delicate thyme for a picnic tea on the mountainside, with edible flowers to dip in chocolate raclette. *Verbier; https://cherrieswalks. com/forage-hike.html*

05 LA MARMOTTE

Named after the small mammals that scurry across the Alpine crags and pastures, this mountain chalet restaurant offers a completely different dining experience to eating

05 Valais resident
Cherries out on a
foraging walk

06 Thrilling slopes
make Verbier popular
with mountain bikers
and e-bikers

Besse and grab a front row seat on the mountain ledge in front of the hulk of the Petit Combin. *Ch-1948 Lourtier; www.verbier. ch/summer/offers/pindin- snack-restaurant-lourtier-en- summer-2826926/; open mid-Jul to mid-Sep*

07 LES CELLIERS DE SION

This giant of the Valais winemaking world was created in 1992 with the uniting of two old wine estates, Varone and Bonvin. Together they've created Valais' first oenoparc, a contemporary wine tasting and education centre just outside the medieval town of Sion. It's an architecturally striking sight, with a facade designed to mimic the texture of the dry stone walls that are a traditional feature of the steep Alpine vineyard terraces.

Visitors can take lunch on the terrace facing the foothills of the Clavau vineyards, or taste wines inside the shiny centre. From April to October, you can also climb into the vineyard terraces behind the centre on a gourmet wine walk through the vines. Along the way, charming *guerittes* – old vineyard stone huts used by winemakers to store grapes and tools – have been converted into pitstops for tastings paired with food. *Rte d'Italie 9, 1950 Sion; www.celliers.ch*

in one of Valais' towns or villages. The air may be sharp up here at almost 2000m (6562ft) but the views are divine. Rug up, grab a seat on the lively terrace and order mountain herb tea, a warming fondue or a hearty dish such as handmade tagliatelle with chicken and local morel mushrooms. It's a good place to stop after a walk along Valais' *les bisses* – man-made mountain streams dating to the 15th century, once used to irrigate Alpine farms. *Les Planards, Verbier; www. lamarmotte-verbier.com*

06 BUVETTE DE PINDIN

Each summer, when Marc Maret brings his herds of prized Herren cows up to the mountain pastures above Brunet mountain hut, he passes his time making cheese. He then sells it at a slate-roofed *buvette* (small bar) on a mountain plateau at 2300m (7546ft) that can only be reached on foot. It's a hiker's paradise: starting at Brunet (which can be reached by car or shuttle bus), a gravel trail unravels like a ball of twine between immense craggy peaks.

When you pass the stone cow sheds, hunt out the cow herder so he'll come to open the *buvette* up ahead. Order Maret's platter of seven different home-made cow's cheeses, ranking from soft and creamy up to nutty, sharp and hard. Pair it with a bottle of mineral white from a local winery such as Gérald

WHERE TO STAY
CHALET D'ADRIEN

For a traditional log cabin vibe without the burden of having to self-cater, Chalet d'Adrien is perfect. It's in Verbier, but far enough away from the centre to benefit from a terrace with panoramic views of the shard-like Alpine summits. The Michelin-recommended restaurant is another bonus for guests. *https://chalet-adrien.com*

MARTIGNY BOUTIQUE HOTEL

Marking the point where Valais' vines climb most steeply into the Alps, Martigny makes a good base for exploring the Rhône Valley's wineries. The hotel is a collaboration with the Pierre Gianadda cultural foundation; art lines the walls and the rooms are named after artists. It's also a social integration project and has trained up 30 local people with disabilities to work in the hotel. *www.martigny-hotel.ch*

WHAT TO DO
E-BIKING THE ALPS

Advances in bike technology have made it wholly possible for novice cyclists to e-bike high into the Haut Val de Bagnes on day trips. Hire a bike beside the gondola station in Le Châble and head out to the Mauvoisin dam, from where you can cycle through tunnels beneath thundering waterfalls up to the Chanrion mountain hut (2462m/8077ft). At the top, treat yourself to a well-deserved cheesy rosti, served with outstanding views.

CELEBRATIONS
VERBIER WINE FESTIVAL

This new week-long wine festival launched in 2022 to celebrate the diversity of winemaking and unique grapes of the Alpine regions. In the Valais vineyards around Verbier, many of the indigenous varieties have AOC designation but are little known outside Switzerland, and the tasting events and masterclasses at this July festival are a good place to learn about them. *www.verbierwine festival.ch/en*

NORTHERN EUROPE

GET THERE
Copenhagen Airport is
12 minutes by train from
Central Station. Metro, bus
and waterbus networks are
efficient hops, especially
if you buy a City Pass for
unlimited travel in zones 1–4.
Or download the Donkey
Republic app to pick up and
drop off inexpensive rental
bikes throughout the city.

01

[Denmark]

DELVING INTO DANISH PASTRY IN COPENHAGEN

Follow the sugar and spice through the neighbourhoods of the capital and you'll find a tradition invigorated by modern influences and culinary creativity.

Ask for a Danish pastry in Denmark and you'll get a confused look. For Danes, the swirls, folds and knots of pastry, spices, fruit, custard and *remonce* (marzipan butter) that feed the national sweet tooth are known collectively as *Wienerbrød* (Vienna bread).

Their presence in Denmark can be traced back to a time in the 19th century when Viennese pâtissiers were drafted in to replace bakers during a Danish bakers' strike. Since then, this pastry tradition has become marbled into Danish society, acting as a daily punctuation mark from breakfast boost to afternoon pick-me-up. Go to any part of Denmark today and you'll find local and regional specialities and Danish classics such as *tebirkes* (poppy seed pastries), *frøsnapper* (seeded pastry twist) and *kanelsnegle* (cinnamon snail) in bakeries and supermarkets.

Yet Copenhagen is arguably where *Wienerbrød* is at its most exciting and varied. An artisan renaissance during the noughties put premium bakeries such as Ole & Steen on the map. And now the coffee and pastry tradition is enjoying a third wave in the capital, in part propelled by the city's significant culinary confidence, including entrepreneurial Noma alumni.

Copenhagen's bakeries are both neighbourhood anchors and destination dining, with specialities that Copenhageners journey across town to buy, pedalling with focused intent down the city's busy cycle lanes. For some, that means an early morning pilgrimage to get the freshest bakes before they run out — other bakeries produce rolling batches throughout the day allowing for a spontaneous *spandauer* (open pastry filled with jam or custard) as you stroll, lured by a siren song of sugar, cinnamon and cardamom in the air.

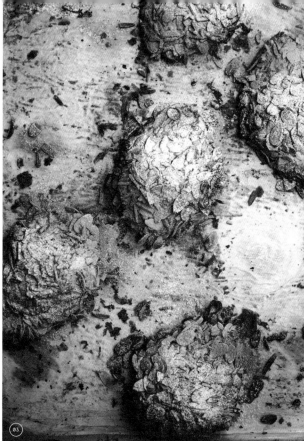

❶ COPENHAGEN COOKING CLASS

Learning to make your own Danish pastries is the best way to appreciate the sheer work that goes into their sweet splendour.

On a Nyhavn sidestreet, Copenhagen Cooking Class holds Cook and Dine classes across three industrial kitchens and a blond wood dining room. Regular *Wienerbrød* sessions for 10-12 people (book individually) take 2½ hours, half of which you'll spend coaxing a butter sheet and dough together to create the 27-layer lamination that gives the pastry its flaky texture.

It's the shapes and flavourings of the delicious pastries that really make them *Wienerbrød*, though.

You'll twist, fold and plait the dough to make circular spandauer (pastries with custard middles), kanelsnegle (cinnamon snails) and frøsnapper (seeded pastry twists). Half an hour baking and you've got a box of oven-fresh pastries to eat or take away — plus a warm glow of satisfaction.

Herluf Trolles Gade 9, 1; www.cphcookingclass.com

❷ HART HOLMEN

The Holmen islet of repurposed warehouses on the harbour's east side hides one of Copenhagen's most creative bakeries, run by a British duo – Noma alumnus Richard Hart and head pastry chef Talia Richard-Carvajal – whose focus is distinctly untraditional.

"Richard and I were conscious neither of us was Danish," says Richard-Carvajal. "So we started to play with the classics. Being foreigners it wasn't sentimental for us — we could just think, 'Oh, that tastes good'. I'm sure at first we were horribly offending people, but it gave us a way to put our spin on things and pull in new influences."

The Tardis-like display has myriad flavour surprises. "The cinnamon ham snail was a cult favourite for a while," says Richard-Carvajal. Don't miss the black sesame cookies or apple *spandauer*, worth the cycle alone for angel light pastry and locally foraged fruit done to delicate perfection.

Galionsvej 41; www.hartbageri.com

03 ANDERSEN & MAILLARD

Andersen & Maillard's
second bakery (the first is on
Nørrebrogade) occupies a high-
ceilinged space in Nordhavn, full
of muslin-hung windows and tables
ringing with tapping laptops and
animated chatter. The industrial
open kitchen aesthetic reflects
the bakery's ethos of transparency,
with coffee from micro-farmers
and an emphasis on local and
seasonal produce, sustainability
and innovation. The cube croissant
with pistachio or salted caramel
is a masterclass in pastry layering.
Wash it down with IPA beer made
from the bakery's surplus bread as
part of its zero waste goals.
*Antwerpengade 10; www.
andersenmaillard.dk*

04 JUNO

You smell the cardamom before
you even enter the small front
garden of this tiny corner bakery
in Østerbro, with tables hidden
between blackcurrant and
raspberry plants.

This paean to pastry from
another Noma alumnus, Emil
Glaser, is the place to come for a
cardamom roll, punchy with spice
that lingers in your mouth long
after you've finished.

Or take a lucky dip on the
rolling appearances of
Instagrammable creations
that come out of the kitchen
throughout the day — the lemon
cake is a staff favourite.
*Århusgade 48; @juno_the_bakery;
closed Mon & Tue*

05 COLLECTIVE BAKERY

Swing by for a coffee-to-go at
this small, no-frills spot, which is
the mothership bakery for seven
Coffee Collective coffee shops
throughout the city. Your morning
cup will be small batch java, freshly
ground, or tea weighed and steeped
according to scientific timing. If
you can coincide your visit with a
warm batch of *citronbølge* ('lemon
wave' – croissant trimmings shaped
on a skewer and painted with lemon
syrup) you've hit the jackpot.
*Nørrebrogade 176; www.collective
bakery.dk*

06 RONDO

Down the road from Collective
Bakery, Rondo is a low-key oasis of
slow pace and counter chit-chat in

a small room scattered with flour bags. "I wanted to create a real neighbourhood stop," says chef Thomas Spelling, who opened the bakery in 2021. "The fact that local people now refer to us as 'their bakery' makes me proud."

There's an emphasis on sustainability at this bakery, with organic flour used for baking and leftovers recycled through the Good to Go app. Not that you'll have anything left over from your morning bun made with cinnamon and orange zest or savoury confit tomato *spandauer*.

To really rev up your day, it's hard to beat savouring a *brunsviger* (a traditional confection of brown sugar, butter and dough from Fyn island, a pretty haven two hours west of Copenhagen) outside as the church bells across the little square peal the hour.
Sjællandsgade 7; @rondo_cph; closed Mon

07 MIRABELLE

Connected to pizza restaurant Baest, a few doors down, Mirabelle is run by ex-El Bulli/Noma chef Christian Puglisi, who creates bakery alchemy by combining Italian flair with organic Danish produce. Set in the heart of hip Nørrebro, it has a light-lunch vibe, with a deli counter and outdoor tables. The flour used is a mix of local stone-ground and an import from an organic mill in Piedmont — unsurprisingly the bread is exceptional, as is the almond croissant.
Guldbergsgade 29; www. mirabelle-bakery.dk; closed Mon

08 LILLE

At first glance you might miss Lille, with its rather ramshackle roadside decking and sunflowers in pots. Set amid the industrial waterscape of Refshaleøen, it has a distinctly end-of-the-line feel. Only the sign, propped on the floor, gives the game away. Inside, the whitewashed room with floor-to-ceiling windows, communal tables and artfully mismatched chairs is offset by serious baking.

The queue for the small counter is relentless, especially at weekends. Try the salty morning bun with butter and cheese, and open it to eat it like a Dane, before finishing with a plum *spandauer* — sharp and rich in its farm-to-table perfection.
213B Refshalevej; www.lillegrocery. com; closed Mon & Tue

WHERE TO STAY

HOTEL COCO

A short walk from Central Station, this boutique hotel is part of the Copenhagen Food Collective with 16 sister restaurants and great dining recommendations as part of its USP. Rooms blend modern and vintage vibes, while the free daily 'wine and mingle' hour fills the wine bar and ivy-clad courtyard with guests retreating from Vesterbro's bustle. *www.coco-hotel.com*

WHAT TO DO

OUR SAVIOUR'S CHURCH TOWER

Rising above the Christianshavn district like a giant pastry twist, this black and gold church tower is wound by a narrow external spiral staircase. Climbing to the top won't just burn off the *Wienerbrød* with exercise but adrenaline too — in the wind it's not for the faint-hearted, but the 360-degree view is magnificent. Book ahead and avoid walking up on the hour, when the bells ring to deafening effect. *www.vorfrelserskirke.dk*

DESIGNMUSEUM DANMARK

Arne Jacobsen's egg chair gets a plinth all to itself at Copenhagen's newest museum, but the exhibition, set in a minimalist mansion, covers much more than furniture. Take a journey through rooms, set around a courtyard, that challenge ideas of the future and how we can meet — and even redefine — it with intelligent and considered design and materials. *www.designmuseum.dk*

CELEBRATIONS

COPENHAGEN COOKING AND FOOD FESTIVAL

Celebrate new Nordic food at this 10-day food festival in August, which fills Israels Plads with more than 100 events. Don't miss the chance to make some new friends at the long-table communal dinners. *www.copenhagen cooking.com*

COPENHAGEN BEER WEEK

Craft brewers come to celebrate Danish beers in the capital, with tastings of 1000+ brews and live music over two days in mid-May at the old Danish state railways repair shop. *www.ølfestival.dk*

GET THERE

Tallinn Airport is just a 10-minute taxi ride from the city centre. The city is well connected by a vast network of buses, trams and trolleys, which are cheap and easy to use. One, three and five-day passes are available, all for under €10.

01

[Estonia]

TASTING THE SEASONS IN TALLINN

Locally grown, seasonal food has always been in favour in Estonia, but now a new generation in the capital are experimenting with booze and recipe reinventions too.

Estonia is a nation of food lovers, with a proud culinary legacy that dates back centuries. In 2022, this long established relationship with food helped attract the Michelin Guide writers, making it the first Baltic state to feature in the distinguished guide.

Tallinn's Old Town – a picturesque, Unesco-listed huddle of museums, opulent merchants' houses and churches – is still a magnificently preserved throwback to the time when the city was a prosperous waypoint on the Hanseatic League trade route. Around that period (13th-15th century), foreign spices brought in by traders began to make their way into the kitchens. Eventually they became signature components of recipes. Fast forward a few centuries and Tallinn is embracing global influences on a much larger scale. But it's also crammed with innovative chefs celebrating classic Estonian flavours in new and creative ways. To get the full feel for Tallinn you need to delve into its food, hopping between contemporary, Scandi-styled restaurants and rustic, stone-walled pubs.

Black rye bread, wild mushrooms, game, fish and forest berries are just some of the staples in Estonian cooking, but above all else it's the source of the food that counts. Estonians favour locally grown, seasonal produce and sustainable eating is a way of life rather than a climate-crisis response. Farmers markets still play a key role in this modern city.

Tallinn is also a hotbed for craft booze. Visitors can sample beer brewed in oak casks with forest botanicals or artisanal gin distilled with Estonian juniper berries. There's also a surprising repertoire of wines made with native berries, herbs and flowers, which are often overlooked by travellers.

01 CAFE MAIASMOKK

In Tallinn's medieval Old Town, Estonia's oldest operating cafe was established in 1864. Its rococo interior has remained largely unchanged for a century with its chequered floor and intricate wooden panels. Tuck into a hearty wedge of freshly baked cake or artisanal candy while watching life play out on Pikk Tänav (Long St).

Upstairs, there's a more contemporary restaurant serving homemade soup, salads and other lunch dishes. There's also a museum documenting the history of the premises and Estonia's long established tradition of decorating marzipan.

Pikk 16, 10123 Tallinn; www.kohvikmaiasmokk.ee

02 LEE

The Danish have *hygge* and the Estonians have *lee*, an archaic word that means to gather around a fireplace, exchange stories and share good food. The age-old concept is now at the centre of this fine-dining experience in Tallinn's Old Town. Here, Hiroaki Takeda and his team of ingenious chefs allow the seasons to dictate what's on the menu and classic Estonian flavours are the stars of every dish.

"When things are local they're more flavourful," explains Hiroaki. To grasp the full extent of the talent in the kitchen, opt for the 'lee experience', a surprise set menu of six courses.

Uus 31, 10111 Tallinn; www.lee resto.ee; closed Sun & Mon

03 BALTI JAAMA TURG

In Tallinn's artsy Telliskivi district, Balti Jaama Turg is home to the largest farmers market in the city, as well as street food stands and artisanal craft stores. It's been a hub for locals since its opening in 1993 and it's one of the best places to see the locally reared meats, as well as potatoes and Baltic cheeses that Estonians put on their plates.

In the meat section, find stalls catering to Tallinn's thriving ethnic Russian population with traditional beef stroganoff, dumplings and other specialities. Upstairs, go in search of local street-food success story Uulits, which sells the best burger in town.

Kopli 1, 10412 Tallinn; www.astri.ee

01 Snow-dusted rooftops in Tallinn's Unesco-listed Old Town

02 Maiasmokk is Estonia's oldest cafe

03 Food at Lee is dictated by the seasons

04 Local produce at Balti Jaama Turg

(03)

(04)

04 JUNIMPERIUM

Established in 2019 by local gin enthusiast Tarvo Jaansoo, Junimperium distillery and bar is the birthplace of several award-winning artisan gins. This includes the World Gin Awards' Best Sloe Gin, which the master mixologists here have incorporated into a zesty tipple.

This hipster bar is set inside a warehouse just opposite Balti Jaama Turg and out back is where the magic happens, in what resembles a mad scientist's lab. Estonian-grown juniper berries, with their unique tartness, form the base of each gin. The spirit is then infused with botanicals including coriander, angelica root, cape pepper and thyme, as well as citrus fruits from Estonia and beyond. Look out for limited editions such as a gin made with macerated fresh sour cherries.

Telliskivi 60m, 10149 Tallinn; www. junimperium.ee; closed Sun & Mon

05 VALGEJÕE VEINIVILLA

At Valgejõe Veinivilla in Harju County, they take wine tasting to the next level with a fully immersive experience (literally). After a tour of the cellar and learning how Estonians make their wine, you can opt to take a bath in it before heading into the forest with a glass and increasing the dopamine levels with some tree hugging. Due to the limited sunlight and cool weather conditions in Estonia, wine isn't made with the typical grapes. Instead, producers reach for berries, botanicals and other hardy fruits that can withstand the climate. Valgejõe is one of the nearest wineries to Tallinn and is a 50-minute bus ride from Tallinn Bus Station.

Valgejõe, 74712 Harju County; www.veinivilla.ee

06 HARMOONIKUM

If you like what you've been eating in Tallinn, you can prepare traditional Estonian dishes yourself at this wellness centre and cooking school housed in an old manor house. A 45-minute bus journey from Tallinn city centre, Harmoonikum offers visitors nutrition-packed cookery classes, a spa with traditional Estonian saunas, and a cafe.

Food workshops are led by Ene Lill, a trained nutritionist who has studied Estonian herbal medicine. "I have researched the science behind old traditions and how our ancestors strengthened health, prepared food and used to live," she says.

After cooking up a storm with Ene, you might like to unwind in the 'beer spa' by sinking into an oak tub filled with hops, brewer's yeast and malt, or enjoy an Estonian massage with natural aromatic oils made on-site.
Pargi tee 8, Viimsi, 74001 Harju maakond; https://harmoonikum.ee

07 PAJU VILLA

Just a 15-minute taxi drive from the Old Town is Tallinn's wealthiest district of Nõmme. Characterised by art nouveau houses and ancient pine forests, it was a summer playground for the rich during the 1920s. Standing as an emblem to that elegant era is Paju Villa. Once home to 15 families, it has retained its emphasis on gathering everybody around the table and you will feel as though you're visiting a friend's stylish townhouse for dinner.

The Michelin-recommended menu covers both international and local dishes, including steak, pike perch and seafood soup. After eating, cleanse your palate with a homemade limoncello or a passionfruit tiramisu.
Vabaduse pst 88, 11617 Tallinn; www.pajuvilla.ee

08 PÕHJALA BREWERY AND TAP ROOM

Estonians take pride in their beer as much as they do their food. Even if you're not a beer lover, a visit to Põhjala Tap Room is a must. There's a choice of 24 craft beers on tap, all of which are brewed in oak barrels with Estonian forest ingredients.

Staff run tours of the on-site brewery, but for real cultural immersion you can sign up for a cold one with a sauna session – a major part of Estonian culture. The tap room chefs also whip up Texas BBQ-themed food, which complements the big flavours of its beers.
Peetri 5, 10415 Tallinn; www. pohjalabeer.com; closed Mon

WHERE TO STAY
SCHLÖSSLE HOTEL
This romantic bolthole with just 23 rooms offers five-star luxury surrounded by medieval architecture in the heart of Tallinn's Old Town. Exposed brick walls and roaring fireplaces create a relaxed and intimate atmosphere inside, while the garden terrace is a great spot for Tallinn's long summer evenings.
www.schlosslehotel.com

RATASKAEVU BOUTIQUE LUXURY APARTMENTS
Live like a true Tallinner in a cosy, Nordic-style apartment with its own sauna – a key feature in many Estonian homes. In the heart of the Old Town, many of the city's top sights and restaurants are a stone's throw away. Shop at Balti Jaama market so you can use the fully equipped kitchen, too.
www.dreamstay.ee

WHAT TO DO
ISLAND HOPPING
Estonia has more than 2000 islands off its coast and some can be explored on a day trip from Tallinn. Take a guided tour of Prangli, Estonia's northernmost island, to cycle between quaint fishing villages and discover their unique culture. You will also learn about the pirates and robbers who once inhabited the island and whose treasure remains hidden, according to legend. Excursions leave from the tourism information office in Tallinn.
https://tallinndaytrip.com/tours/prangli-island-day-trip

CELEBRATIONS
JAANIPÄEV
Summer solstice (around 21 June) is one of the oldest events on the Estonian calendar, marking the longest day of the year. Food and drink play a central role, along with bonfires, singing and storytelling.

CHRISTMAS MARKET
Try seasonal specialities such as blood pudding, gingerbread and mulled wine at Tallinn's twinkly festive gig in December.

07

GET THERE
Trains and buses link Helsinki, Espoo, Turku, Kuopio and Joensuu, which has buses to Ilomantsi. However, a rental car opens up plenty of bonus foraging opportunities in the woods.

01

[Finland]

A FORAGING TOUR OF FINLAND

Summertime is foraging season in Finland's forests, and locals know all the best ways to enjoy nature's bounty over the dinner table.

Finns have a deep connection to the great outdoors, especially the edible landscape. During the long days of late summer, Finland's forests spill out one of the world's great free fruit feasts in the form of abundant bilberries, loganberries, raspberries, Arctic bramble berries, crowberries, forest strawberries and elusive cloudberries. Akka, the Finnish earth goddess, also provides abundant wild herbs and delectable fungi, from ceps and chanterelles to the mysterious false morel, poisonous when raw, but delicious when properly prepared.

Needless to say, foraging is a national obsession, as you'll quickly discover while exploring the sparkling lakes, dense forests and the wild-food loving restaurants of southern Finland. Foraging is protected under the *jokamiehenoikeudet* (everyman's rights) enshrined in Finnish law and visitors are

welcome to join the feast, which fills the woods with foragers from mid-July to October.

Different areas have different strengths. Bilberries are found almost everywhere and the islands of the Gulf of Bothnia are great for coastal raspberries. The mixed woodlands of the south overflow with fungi; seek out moist birch forests for chanterelles and mixed birch and oak forests for prized ceps. Wild food also encompasses wild animals; don't be surprised to see elk and reindeer on the menu.

Wild ingredients appear in everything from hearty village stews to intense menus at cutting-edge restaurants. Thanks to wild food evangelists such as award-winning chefs Sami Tallberg, Filip Langhoff and Ossi Paloneva, menus of hand-gathered berries, wild herbs and foraged fungi are popping up in some of the country's most appealing southern towns and villages.

01 KAUPPATORI

You know summer has arrived in Finland when the market stalls of the cobbled Kauppatori market square by Helsinki's South Harbour start groaning under the weight of forest-fresh berries. Locals scoop them up by the kilo to make pies, pancake toppings and *mustikkakeitto* – a delicious, cold berry soup blending bilberries, lemon zest, kosher salt and cinnamon.

As well as bilberries, lingonberries, raspberries and wild forest strawberries, look out for the cloudberry – blackberry-like and summery yellow in colour, and expensive due to its superior flavour and sparse availability. Fungi lovers can stock up on Finland's famous, maggot-free chanterelles; for preserves, fish and reindeer charcuterie, hop across to the adjacent Gamla Saluhallen market hall, built in 1889. Stalls are usually open until late afternoon.
Eteläranta, Helsinki

02 RESTAURANT GRÖN

Wild food might make you think of humble fare, but that idea goes out of the window at Restaurant Grön. The creative, Michelin-starred gastronomy of chef Toni Kostian stars a cornucopia of wild, seasonal and organic foods. "I forage wild ingredients for Grön twice a week," says Kostian. "It's the only way to make sure that we have the best possible wild ingredients on the menu." At Grön, wild food might be interpreted as spruce shoots with lemon thyme and lemon leaf, or as grilled summer berries mixed with seasonal flowers from the restaurant garden. Pick from vegan or omnivorous tasting menus of 13 courses.
Albertinkatu 36, Helsinki; www. restaurantgron.com; open Wed-Sat for dinner & Sat for lunch

03 SKUTTA

Finland has a growing number of chefs whose passion for wild food verges on religion, and Jyrki Tsutsunen is just such a chef. After honing his art in the kitchens of the Finnish Consulate in St Petersburg, Tsutsunen embarked on a mission to convert the nation to the wonders of wild food through

pop-up events fusing music, performance and foraging.

"In my work I want to combine food, space, music and art into one whole," he explains. "Nature is full of food and I want to make these unique flavours available to all people." You can sample Jyrki's culinary art at Skutta in Helsinki's Stoa arts centre, where weekday lunches feature everything from nettle mashed potatoes to bearberry salads.
Stoa, Turunlinnantie 1, Itäkeskus, Helsinki; www.skuttaan.fi; closed Sun

04 FORAGING IN FINLAND WORKSHOPS

For foraging know-how in Espoo, seek out local biologist and herbalist Anna Nyman, an enthusiastic advocate for foraged food. Her wild food workshops in northern Espoo and Nurmijärvi delve into the woods to find the best fungi and foodstuffs, targeting berries from June to August and mushrooms from August to October.
www.foraginginfinland.com

05 NUUKSIO NATIONAL PARK

Locals are raised from the cradle to take advantage of nature's bounty, but newcomers may be a bit more hesitant about grabbing any old berries or mushrooms from the forest. Fear not – help is at hand. At Nuuksio National Park, an idyllic sprawl of woods and lakes just west of Helsinki near Espoo, guided nature walks with Feel the Nature will take you deep into the forest to the prime foraging spots, where you'll learn to tell a bilberry from a crowberry, and a chanterelle from a poisonous fungus. You'll come away informed enough to go foraging on your own.
Nuuksiontie 84, Espoo; www. feelthenature.fi/en; guided foraging hikes run Jul-Oct

06 RUISSALO

Pioneering wild food chef Sami Tallberg has expanded his campaign for natural eating to include his home studio on the island of Ruissalo near Turku. Here, he hosts a fascinating range of cooking courses and dining experiences, based on forest-fresh ingredients foraged from the island's dense oak woodlands and rocky shoreline.

It's all bespoke and quite exclusive, but the menus, courses and experiences bubble over with Tallberg's enthusiasm for wild herbs and fungi.

"Foraging is a movement here in Finland," says Tallberg. "We Finns have a very strong connection to nature and we have everyman's rights, which means anyone can forage." Contact Sami in advance to discuss your options.
Ruissalo, Turku; www.samitallberg. com/en/courses

07 KOIVUMÄKI MANOR

It's a long train ride to Kuopio, but it's worth it for a trip to Koivumäki Manor. The mansion here was home to Gustav Ranin, who built an alcohol empire in the 19th century using wild forest flavours.

His historic Lignell & Piispanen distillery uses all sorts of Finnish herbs and berries in botanicals and fruit spirits. Big sellers include cloudberry and Arctic bramble liqueurs and Gustav Metsä gin, flavoured with lingonberry, birch leaf and nettle.

You can sample local dishes in the restaurant, sip spirits in the bar, tour the distillery, take wild herb tours of the grounds or join tasting tours around Kuopio. This lakeside town celebrated a year as European Gastronomic Region for 2020.
Koivumäenkuja 18, Kuopio; www.koivumaenkartano.com

08 PUUSTILA SCENIC FARM

Wild food is taken seriously in the village of Ilomantsi in lake-splashed Northern Karelia – there's even a

wild food festival here in August (see opposite page). For any foodie tour of Finland, it's well worth booking into the candy-red Puustila Scenic Farm. Farmstay guests can immerse themselves in rural Karelian life, enjoying everything from fire-pit lamb roasts to guided walks to harvest wild herbs, which are then cooked up with the owners in the farmhouse kitchen as a prelude to a wild food feast.

It's a great immersion into the foraging culture of Finland, and you'll quickly learn to differentiate between wild delicacies such as yarrow, ground elder, wood sorrel and lady's mantle.
Puustilan maisematila, Vehnävaarantie 11, Maukkula; https://en.puustilanmaisematila.fi

WHERE TO STAY

HOTEL KATAJANOKKA

This unique hotel on Katajanokka island in Helsinki was a working prison until 2002, but don't worry; you won't be sharing a cell. The expansive rooms in this 19th-century jail come with stylish bathrooms, sleek Nordic decor and framed jailhouse memorabilia. Add in a handy location close to Kauppatori market plus indoor and outdoor bars and this is somewhere you won't mind being locked up for the night.
*www.hotelkata
janokka.fi/en*

RUISSALO CAMPING

For an idyllic stay close to Turku but also in nature, try this sprawling campground on Ruissalo island. It puts you ringside next to coastal forests and gently sloping beaches. It's right at the far end of the island and there's a cafe set in a gorgeous Empire-style villa. You can camp or stay in cabins and spend your days endlessly combing the forest for wild foodstuffs.
*www.visitturku.fi/en/
ruissalo-camping_-0*

THINGS TO DO

SUOMENLINNA

After grabbing some snacks at the Kauppatori market in Helsinki, take a boat from the quayside to the fortress island of Suomenlinna, which sprawls over three interlinked isles in the harbour. The Swedes built the fortifications in the 18th century, the Russians added the church in 1854, and footpaths run to museums, historic buildings, cafes, a hostel and scenic spots along the shoreline. Locals come to picnic and swim late into the summer nights.

CELEBRATIONS

VILLIRUOKA FESTARIT

Finland's big wild food celebration is the Villiruoka Festarit (Wild Food Festival) in Ilomantsi in lake-swamped northern Karelia. Foodies, chefs and interested bystanders come together in August to explore new ways to bring the wild world into the kitchen. Expect cooking demonstrations, talks and tastings.
*www.facebook.com/
Villiruokafestarit*

GET THERE
Vilnius Train Station connects the Lithuanian capital to neighbouring capitals such as Warsaw in Poland and Riga in Latvia. Vilnius is also well connected to the rest of Europe by air, including by cheap Ryanair flights.

[Lithuania]

BALTIC REINVENTION IN VILNIUS

Lithuania's handsome capital mixes tradition with clever, contemporary takes on local food – come for overflowing markets, unique cocktails and distinctly Baltic flavours.

Lithuanian cuisine is a complex beast with a gnarly history. After a 200-year union with Poland, the Grand Duchy of Lithuania disappeared off the map in 1795 when Russia swallowed the Baltic territories. It didn't reappear as an independent country until 1918 after WWI. Many of the 'traditional' dishes that remain recycle influences from Poland and Russia, or can be traced back to peasant cuisine, which continued to thrive in backwaters during centuries of cultural repression.

Many visitors find Lithuania's classic recipes a little unusual. There's *saltibarščiai* – a cold summer beetroot soup thickened with sour cream, not too dissimilar to borscht, with a bright, paint-like lavender colour that makes it a favourite with Instagrammers. There's *cepelinai* – glutinous potato dumplings typically stuffed with minced pork, topped with a dollop of sour

cream and crispy lardons. Then there's the popular snack *kibinai*, a pastry not too dissimilar to a Cornish pasty or empanada, whose origins can be traced back to a tiny influx of Turkic Karaim people in the 14th century. Jewish communities, too, have left their mark – smoked fish is another ubiquitous local food.

As the capital city, Vilnius is the best place in the country to sample the many facets of Lithuanian cuisine. Here, farmers markets are overflowing with the staples that define the local diet: berries and mushrooms from the woods (Lithuanians are avid foragers); game, pork charcuterie and sausages; giant bricks of rye bread; and pickles galore. And beyond that? Well, there's plenty more. A new wave of local producers and chefs are peppering the medieval streets with innovative bars, restaurants and cafes – taking Lithuania's traditional flavours in new directions.

01 HALĖS TURGAVIETĖ

The area in which this lovely 1906 market hall sits is one of Vilnius' greatest regeneration successes. Just 20 years ago, the streets around Vilnius Train Station were rife with prostitutes and slums. Today the 19th-century houses surrounding Halės Market are splashed with street art, and the market itself is buzzing from morning til late at night.

Farmers and producers surrounding the capital flock to Halės to sell their fruit and vegetables, hard cheeses, huge slabs of rye bread, local honey, blueberries, walnuts and more: a stroll here is a great introduction to Lithuania's traditional diet. Beneath the wrought-iron canopy inside the hall, there's also a smattering of small bars serving market-produce plates alongside beer, wine and local spirits. Come either in the morning to see market life in full throes with shoppers, or after dark (Thursday to Saturday) when locals pile in for drinks. Youngs' Club is a favourite. *Pylimo str 58; www.hales turgaviete.lt*

02 DŽIUGAS CHEESE HOUSE

Hardly changed since the 1950s, this wood-panelled cafe serves its coffee with golden nuggets of cheese instead of biscuits. Both are strong – the name derives from a Samogitian legend about a giant warrior called Džiugas who made a powerful, large and delicious cheese on his wedding night.

Head into the shop for tasting samples of the different strength cheese, aged between 12 and 36 months. This is the Parmesan of Lithuania: its nutty, complex flavours increase with the maturing of the cheese. Afterwards, take coffee on the petite square-fronting terrace along with a cheese-stuffed *kibinine* (traditional savoury pastry pocket). Before leaving, grab the shop's speciality to go: a tangy cheese ice-cream made with local cranberries. *Aušros Vartų g 3; www.dziugashouse.lt*

03 LOKYS RESTAURANT

A short stroll away, down Vilnius' photogenic cobbled streets, Lokys is one of the capital's oldest medieval-style 'hunter' restaurants, so-called

01 A cafe hanging
over the Vilnia River

03 Global bites at
Paupio Turgus

02 Unesco lists
Vilnius Old Town for its
architectural importance

04 Smoked fish is a
staple of the traditional
Lithuanian diet

because they focus on historic hunter dishes, taking inspiration from the forests and fields of Lithuania and the food that thrives there: game (venison, wild boar), pork, mushrooms, potatoes and so on.

Menu items are marked with the century in which they originated and some of the options are unique, such as venison tartare with pickled cornichons (16th century); beaver meat stew (13th to 14th century); and creamy boletus mushroom soup with pumpkin oil (14th century). If in doubt, order Lithuania's national dish, *cepelinai* (potato dumplings with sour cream and bacon, dusted with parsley) – here, they're stuffed with game rather than the traditional pork.

To accompany your food, order a glass of the homemade *kvass*

(sweet bread lemonade), made with naturally fermented rye bread. Lokys' take on the local speciality is served cloudy and infused with caraway seeds to give it an especially aromatic kick. Be warned that it's an acquired taste.

Inside the dimly lit, woody interior there's also a local produce deli where you can stock up on goodies such as dandelion syrup, hemp flower tea, flaxseed crackers and candied pine cones.
Stiklių g 8; https://lokys.lt

04 KING & MOUSE

Although this smashing little alleyway bar is better known for its 300-strong whisky selection (possibly the largest in Lithuania) and whisky shop, it's run by the

owner of Pakruojis Manor Distillery, which specialises in spirits infused with local botanicals. The distillery is housed on a vast 18th-century estate outside Vilnius. One of the oldest distilleries in Lithuania, it was reborn in 2018 as a craft distillery with the aim of popularising and championing Lithuanian flavours.

The bar's mixologists have developed a range of cocktails to showcase the distillery's at-times unusual flavours. Park yourself outside at a standing barrel table in the skinny alleyway, or in the postage-stamp-sized bar area inside and prepare for some unique flavours. The distillery's spirits include a thyme liqueur with honey and saffron, schnapps made with horseradish or beetroot, a maple

05 Octopus at
Gastronomika

06 The 1906 facade of
Halès Turgavietė

07 Day-tripper
favourite Trakai
Castle Island

liqueur and a cherry brandy. For something unusual, try the 'Spicy and Smokey' cocktail, which mixes smoked bacon fat schnapps (a play on Lithuania's liberal use of lardons in traditional dishes) with ginger beer. *Trakų gatvė 2; https://kingand mouse.lt*

05 PAUPIO TURGUS

Skirting the edge of the Old Town along the Vilnia River, Vilnius' new Paupys district is recognised as one of the most significant regeneration projects in the Baltics. What was once an abandoned factory area, left to wrack and ruin, has been converted into a green living zone with neat rows of terrace and apartment housing grounded by this lively market.

In complete contrast to historic Halės Market nearby, Paupio Turgus is a strikingly contemporary affair, with a glass roof and living foliage – 1300 plants help create a greenhouse-like atmosphere, playing on the development's green credentials. Pumping music, wall art, four bars, grocery stores and 17 restaurant kiosks serving global food – you could spend hours noshing and drinking here. Try the Lipskio Aline bar for local craft beers chalked up on a board, washed down with a side of fried bread. *Aukštaičių g 7; www.paupioturgus.lt*

06 GASTRONOMIKA

Chef Liutauras Čeprackas is on a mission to transform perceptions of Lithuanian food and the menu at his flagship Gastronomika restaurant shows contemporary Lithuanian cuisine at its finest. Book ahead and settle in for the restaurant's gut-busting, seven-course tasting menu, presented with a big dollop of panache inside a striking glass-walled space on the Old Town's Bokštas Square.

Čeprackas trained in some of the finest restaurants in San Sebastián, Spain, which explains the skill on display in Gastronomika's menu, dish presentation and sometimes surprising flavours, mixing international influences with Lithuanian produce. That might mean fluffy dumplings with seasonal mushrooms, curd and egg yolk, or octopus with Jerusaleum artichoke and fermented cabbage.

The succulent quail kiev, with carrots, parsley and raspberries, is one of his signature dishes. The tasting menu is a steal compared with the equivalent quality in other European capitals. *Bokšto g 6; https://gastronomika.lt; closed Sun & Mon*

WHERE TO STAY

DOWNTOWN FOREST HOSTEL & CAMPING
Guests feel like they're sleeping in the woods at this peaceful spot between the Old Town and new district of Paupys. There are dorms and private rooms, as well as tree-shaded glamping pods and campervan parking in the hostel's leafy surrounds. The outdoor bar, foosball and barbecue pits promote a friendly atmosphere after dark. Look out for music nights in its sloping gardens. *https://downtownforest.lt*

ARTAGONIST
Behind the colourful facade of this 15th-century townhouse, common areas have been stripped back to create playful mural canvasses, while hotel rooms oscillate between flashes of contemporary Lithuanian art and original features. Head directly north from the hotel and you'll end up at the foot of the leafy trails that lead uphill to Gediminas Tower. *www.artagonist.lt*

WHAT TO DO

GEDIMINAS CASTLE & MUSEUM
The icon of Vilnius, Gediminas Tower is all that remains of the fabled castle that once topped the city like a thorny crown. Today, the tower hosts a branch of the National Museum of Lithuania, focused on city history. *https://lnm.lt/en/museums/gediminas-castle-tower*

TRAKAI
The picture-perfect Trakai Island Castle, built on Lake Galvė by Lithuanian dukes in the 14th century, could be straight out of a fairy tale. A popular day trip from Vilnius, it's also the home of Lithuania's favourite snack, *kibinai*, which can been traced back to Trakai's Turkic minority Karaim people. Come for a stroll around the island followed by a lunch of steaming *kibinai* at Senoji Kibinine, one of the most revered local producers.

CELEBRATIONS

CULTURE NIGHT
Dance, theatre, music, photography and dramatic installations take over the capital's streets for this annual night of revelry paying homage to Lithuanian arts. Many events are free. *www.kulturosnaktis.lt*

GET THERE

SAS and Norwegian fly
frequently to Kristiansand
and Stavanger from/via
Oslo, both with a flight time
of around 50 minutes. Much
of the coast is remote, so
driving is the way to go.

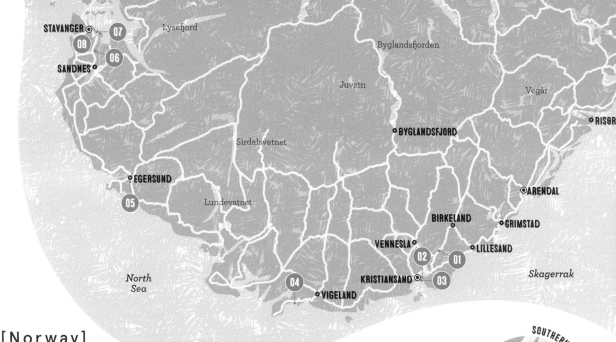

[Norway]

NATURE'S BOUNTY ON THE NORWEGIAN COAST

Chefs on Norway's southern coast champion sustainability while pushing the boundaries of culinary theatrics. In this sea-lashed land, nature always comes first.

Dipping its toes into the storm-smashed, flint-blue North Sea, southern Norway presents a painterly scene. Its coastline is a filigree of fjords, dune-flanked beaches, rocky islets and villages stacked with brightly painted timber cottages. The light is sharp, the horizons are wide and the air smells of seasalt. On bright days and under big skies, life feels utterly in tune with nature's rhythms.

It's an inspiring place for a chef to be – here among the shifting tides, sands and skies, with the seas, forests, fields and mountains on your doorstep, the landscape is ripe for fishing, foraging, hunting and picking. It is no wonder that some of Europe's most innovative, sustainably minded chefs adore this region, with its abundance of seafood, game, berries, mushrooms and herbs. Nature has done its bit – now for the culinary theatrics.

As you swing your way west up the coast from Kristiansand to Stavanger, the landscape ups the drama, shifting from lush farmland to ragged coastlines and mountains. And there are many surprises for food-loving travellers along the way. The world's largest underwater restaurant is here, but there's also more offbeat culinary delights to discover – from a former royal estate that's largely self-sufficient, to a coolly revamped school gym punching high with Nordic small plates.

Whether you're slurping oysters on a wooden pier as a fiery sunset blazes, or getting the inside scoop on how to grow gourmet mushrooms, the connection to coast and land is palpable. Even in Stavanger's Michelin-starred temples, chefs strive to capture the wilderness, bringing you back to nature and giving you a deeper understanding of what is on the plate.

01 BOEN GÅRD 1520

Magic hangs in the air at Boen Gård 1520, idyllically spread along the wooded banks of the Tovdalselva River in southern Norway. The estate looks back on a regal history: King Christian II owned its rich salmon fishery in the early 16th century, and in the 1670s it belonged to Queen Sophie Amalie of Denmark and Norway. Today, the red-timber estate buildings have been stylishly revamped and the restaurant has been elevated to giddy heights thanks to chef Tomasz Rochon. Self-sufficiency is the watchword in French-inflected menus playing up garden-harvested vegetables, apples, berries, herbs and honey, wild salmon from the river and locally farmed lamb. Dishes such as scallop tartare with trout roe and smoked mayonnaise and quail with mushroom duxelles are outstanding. *Dønnestadveien 341, Tveit; www.boengaard.no; closed Sun-Tue*

02 SMAG & BEHAG

A 20-minute drive south and a leap across the water brings you to seaside city Kristiansand and this joyous reincarnation of a late 19th-century school gymnasium. Right near the waterfront and fortress, its brick interior is quite something, with a soaring vaulted timber ceiling and soft light sifting through arched windows. Chef Hans Petter Klemmetsen's food lives up to the restaurant's name 'Taste and Please', with a menu spotlighting small dishes as intricate as they are delicious, from scallops with potato, cucumber, green strawberry and fermented asparagus sauce to glazed pork belly with fennel, yellow beet, rutabaga and apple sauce. And it's all remarkably informal. *Dronningens Gate 48a, Kristiansand; https://smag-behag.no; closed Sun & Mon*

03 FISKEBRYGGA

Where boats chug along the Gravane Canal that separates central Kristiansand from the island of Odderøya, this redeveloped fishing wharf is a visual treat of loping bridges and timber warehouses. Grab lunch to go from a takeaway fishmonger like Reinhartsen, then sit by the wooden steps in the harbour to scoff

01 Stavanger old town

02 Boen Gård serves
salmon from its rivers

03 A 19th-century gym
houses Smag & Behag

04 Under is partially
submerged beneath
the North Sea

05 Eigra's open
kitchen dishes up
seasonal small plates

langoustines, king prawns, crab claws or the day's catch from paper bags. In summer, the wharf hosts live music every Thursday.
Fiskebrygga, Kristiansand; www.reinhartsen.no

04 UNDER

Here's how to get critics talking about you: take a rocky, wave-whipped coastline, enlist Snøhetta architects to build a restaurant resembling a half-sunken periscope and submerge the glass-fronted dining room five-and-a-half metres below the icy North Sea. Toss in top-of-the-game Danish chef Nicolai Ellitsgaard and Under is absolutely deserving of its Michelin star.

Bathed in moody blues and peering out at swirling fish and storm-ruffled seas, the world's largest underwater restaurant promises to plunge you into uncharted gastro waters. And the food? Sensational. Nicolai orchestrates 18-course menus with panache in dishes boldly singing of local seafood, wild meats, mushrooms and berries. The exact menu is kept under wraps until you dive under. Want to go within the next six months? Book right now.
Båly, Lindesnes; https://under.no; closed Sun & Mon

05 EIGRA

A breezy drive of open skies, seas and skerries whisks you to Egersund, a captivating town lined with candy-coloured timber houses, each more photogenic than the last. But you're here for the food at Eigra at the Grand Hotell, where the mood is laid back and the decor stripped-back Scandi chic with parquet floors, bistro seating and backlighting.

The season-focused small plates flying out of the open kitchen are peppered with foraged finds. Expect a big hit of Nordic: blueberry soup with kefir, juniper oil and fir shoot sorbet and butter-soft, charcoal-grilled Jæren steak – all prepared with flair and thought. Warm up with a cocktail in the vintage-cool bar.
Storgaten 12, Egersund; https://eigra.no/eigra-kjokken; closed Sun

06 TOPP SOPP

Sopp is Norwegian for mushroom, and fabulous fungi are what this farm on Stavanger's southern

06 Herring and potato served with roe at Michelin-starred RE-NAA

07 Preikestolen (Pulpit Rock) is one of Norway's most photographed sights

fringes is all about. It's the baby of passionate mycophiles and ecologists Joakim and Ingrid who believe that mushrooms are the key to ecosystem survival. "We grow our mushrooms in locally sourced waste such as coffee grounds and sawdust to intensify their flavour," enthuses Ingrid. "Sustainability does not have to be a compromise."

Stop by to buy your own – perhaps some fleshy, juicy oyster mushrooms, shiitake big on umami, or coral-like lion's mane mushrooms packed with antioxidants. If you time it right, you can join one of their grow-your-own courses. *Jåttåveien 63A, Stavanger; www. toppsopp.no; closed Sat & Sun*

07 RE-NAA

"I fell in love with the nature and produce this region offers. Our hyper-seasonal menus show our connection to the ocean, fjords and mountains," says Sven Erik Renaa, head chef at two-Michelin-starred RE-NAA in Stavanger. Here everything is so casual and understated that eating meticulously composed, flawlessly cooked food feels like the most natural thing in the world.

And natural it is, with menus drawing on ingredients from the surrounding region. The dishes are bold and imaginative, sprinkled with foraged flavours, micro-herbs and edible flowers. That could mean sea urchin with shrimp and green strawberries, Rennesøy mackerel with rhubarb and wasabi, or chicken skin with lovage, pine shoot and bitter chocolate: you'll never want it to end. *Steinkargata 10; www. restaurantrenaa.no; closed Sun-Tue*

08 SABI OMAKASE

"Using Norwegian produce in dishes like sashimi with local reindeer and Wagyu and langoustine nigiri is a dream. My ethos is that simple can be extraordinary," says Roger Joya at nearby Michelin-starred Sabi Omakase. With covers for just 10 very lucky diners, scoring a seat here is like winning the lottery. Admittedly, the restaurant looks like nothing from the outside, but push open the door and you'll find yourself propped up at a long chef's table in a seductively dark, backlit, Zen-style space.

Joya, one of Norway's few sushi masters, puts Norwegian riffs on Edomae-style sushi, treating each oyster, prawn and piece of fish with reverence to enhance its natural flavour and texture for lucky diners. Watching him work is pure theatre. When he isn't cooking, he is out scouting for the best produce with divers and fishermen on the coast. *Pedersgata 38a, Stavanger; https://omakase.no; closed Sun-Wed*

WHERE TO STAY

BOEN GÅRD 1520

Wake up to the sound of rushing water at this historic, riverside hotel. The pick of the crisply rustic rooms are in a stylishly converted granary and threshing barn. It's a peaceful spot to fish for salmon, walk among ancient trees – and eat at the famed restaurant (stop 1). *www.boengaard.no*

HAVHOTELL

The Scandi-chic Havhotell in Lindesnes makes a perfect seaside base for cycling, kayaking, beach-going and dining at Under. *www.havhotellet.no*

GRAND HOTELL

Over in Egersund, the Grand Hotell mixes up 19th-century charm with minimalist rooms in whites and dove greys. *www.grand-egersund.no*

WHAT TO DO

PREIKESTOLEN (PULPIT ROCK)

From Stavanger, you can boat past rainbow-arced waterfalls and sheer

cliffs on the cyan-blue Lysefjord to reach the trailhead for Pulpit Rock, thrusting 604m (1981ft) above the fjord. *www.preikestolen 365.com*

NORWEGIAN SCENIC ROUTE – JÆREN

Swinging along the south coast, this national route detours to pale-sand, dune-fringed beaches like Borestranden and Solastranden, where surfers and kite-surfers

harness North Sea waves. Stop off at the geologically spectacular, boulder-strewn Magma Geopark, shaped by igneous rock more common on the moon than on Earth. *www.nasjonaleturist veger.no*

CELEBRATIONS

SØRLANDETS MATFESTIVAL

Kristiansand hosts Sørlandets Matfestival in July, a food festival

with tastings of regional produce, farmers markets, street food, barbecues and live music. *https://sorlandetsmat festival.no*

MANDAL SKALLDYRFESTIVALEN

Mandal delivers a feast of boat-fresh seafood at its mid-August festival, with music, art, cookery demonstrations and prawn-peeling competitions. *www.skalldyrfestivalen.no*

GET THERE

Warsaw Chopin Airport is around 25 minutes from the city centre. Many international and domestic flights stop here, however some budget airlines fly to more distant Modlin airport. FlixBus connects Warsaw with cities across Europe, including Berlin, while local and international trains stop in Warsaw Central. The city itself is well connected with a network of trams, metro and Uber.

Map labels:

Vistula

Plac Teatralny — 03

Saxon Garden

Park Kazimierzowski

ŚRÓDMIEŚCIE PÓŁNOCNE

ZA ZELAZNA BRAMA

POWIŚLE

ŚRÓDMIEŚCIE

07

04

Plac Trzech Krzyzy

02

06

ŚRÓDMIEŚCIE POLUDNIOWE

05

Plac Konstytucji

Ujazdowski Park

01

UJAZDÓW

[Poland]

WARSAW: RISING STAR OF THE EAST

Socialist-era dining houses bump shoulders with Michelin-starred restaurants in Eastern Europe's chic and evolving food capital.

While some tourists still overlook Warsaw – Poland's political and economic centre – in favour of its better-dressed cousin, Kraków, those who can see beyond the gritty exterior will be floored by a staggeringly diverse dining scene that brings to mind New York City in the 1990s.

Warsaw's Old Town was obliterated in WWII by the Nazis during the 1944 uprising. Laboriously rebuilt over five years, the city's historic centre is now a Unesco World Heritage Site and a profound symbol of Poland's determination not to have its history or identity erased. Soviet communism followed war, true independence came in 1991 and the economy has boomed since Poland gained entry to the EU in 2004.

Walking through the Old Town allows visitors to retrace the footsteps of 13th-century dukes and WWII partisans. History matters here, but just as important is what's taking place in the city's vibrant and optimistic present. Creative chefs are reimagining traditional cuisine, long-established immigrants from Vietnam are serving arguably the most authentic *pho* in Europe, and even vodka has been given the artisanal treatment as a genteel accompaniment to a well-crafted meal. As any Pole will be happy to attest, *wódka* (vodka) was invented in Poland long before Russia caught on, and can be found in as many varieties here as whisky in Scotland or wine in France.

Traditional Polish fare is weaponry against a fierce winter: potatoes, meat, bread and vodka. Socialist era milk bars - inexpensive eateries serving *pierogi*, cutlets and other classic dishes - are still plentiful. Yet today they rub shoulders with Michelin star restaurants, speakeasy-style cocktail bars, artisanal bakeries and bars where craft beer is poured by bearded hipsters.

01 HALA KOSZYKI

Opened in 1909 as a market building, Hala Koszyki has been restored and reinvented as a trendy, modern eating and drinking destination. Inside this grand and historic structure are more than a dozen restaurants and bars serving pretty much every kind of cuisine a traveller could crave.

Enjoy traditional Polish *kielbasa* (sausage) washed down with craft beer at Kiełba w Gębie, or indulge in some creamy pasta and traditional northern Italian pizza at Ristorante Semolino. Need something vegan? Try Mango Vegan Street Food, which swaps the meat for falafel in a variety of wraps and burgers. Pro tip: climb the stairs to the top floor for unflustered seating with views of the shoppers and restaurants below.
Koszykowa 63; https://koszyki.com

02 BAR BAMBINO

Milk bars are a Polish institution. These cafeterias thrived during socialist times as a way to offer cheap, nutritious meals to the working masses. The Warsaw food scene has made great strides since then, but popping into a *bar mleczny* should still be high on your agenda.

Bar Bambino is regarded by locals as one of the best and its central location makes it easy to visit. Here, you can rub shoulders with local families and bargain-hunting students, and enjoy astonishingly low prices on classics like *pierogi* (dumplings stuffed with meat, mushrooms or cottage cheese), *kotlet schabowy* (breaded pork cutlet) and *zurek* (traditional rye soup). Bambino also offers vegetarian options.
Hoża 19; https://barbambino.pl

03 ELIXIR BY DOM WODKI

Vodka is to Poland, this restaurant argues, what whisky is to Scotland or cheese is to Switzerland. Elixir is the brainchild of Dom Wodki, a Warsaw institution that celebrates Poland's six centuries of vodka distilling. Located right next to its Vodka Museum and recommended by the Michelin guide, Elixir invites diners to challenge their preconceived notions of Poland's signature spirit by pairing each

dish with a carefully chosen vodka. And the chefs inject a contemporary twist to traditional Polish fare with their menu. Try *de volaille* (chicken kiev) drenched in white truffles with Belvedere Heritage 176 vodka, or take the lighter path with herring – a Polish staple – served with beetroot puree, apple caviar and a chaser of Dwór Sieraków Superior vodka. *Pl Teatralny, ul Wierzbowa 9/11; www.domwodki.pl/en*

04 WELES BAR

After a hearty dinner, ditch Warsaw's main thoroughfares to find this fashionable cocktail den. It's deliberately well hidden. You'll head down a deserted sidestreet, before climbing the steps to what looks like a back alley service entrance. Beyond the unmarked door, descend the stairs and there's chandeliers, dark walls and Warsaw's fashionable cognoscenti sipping expertly crafted Manhattans, Martinis, Old Fashioneds and other delicious concoctions.

It's prohibition-era New York, transported to 21st-century Warsaw, and it's a drinking experience that shows off the style and creativity of the city today. Just don't tell too many people about it. *Nowogrodzka 11; www.instagram. com/welesbar; closed Sun & Mon*

05 OH MY PHO

Poland's Vietnamese population is estimated to be upwards of 50,000. Fuelled by student exchange programmes supported by their respective communist governments between the 1950s and '80s, Poland's long established Vietnamese expat community makes this one of the best places in Europe to sample a truly authentic *pho* - a steaming bowl of fragrant and spicy beef soup guaranteed to dispel even the most cloying of vodka hangovers.

Small, unimposing and as authentic as it gets, Oh My Pho offers exactly what the name implies. Knowing diners shower their soups with spicy Sriracha sauce and chase down the hot broth with a cool Saigon beer. *Wilcza 32; www.facebook.com/ ohmyphowilcza*

06 & 07 Cuda na Kiju is at the forefront of Warsaw's craft beer movement

08 Warsaw's annual beer festival promises more than 1000 different tastings

06 CIASTKO Z DZIURKĄ

Many Poles overseas will say that what they miss most about Poland is *pączki* – Polish doughnuts, filled to the brim with cream cheese, custard or sweet, rich fruit. For locals, this sweet treat represents the comfort of home. Conveniently located just down the road from Oh My Pho and a host of other restaurants, Ciastko z Dziurką has earned a reputation for selling (probably) the best *pączki* in Warsaw alongside other baked delights such as scones with red currants and white chocolate, or *jagodzianki* (rich blueberry buns),

making this the ideal spot to end an afternoon of walking and sightseeing on a high note.
Wilcza 26; www.facebook.com/ ciastkozdziurkaa; closed Mon

07 CUDA NA KIJU

Opening in the office of the former Communist Party Headquarters in 2013, Cuda na Kiju ushered in Poland's craft beer revolution. Eschewing the mass-produced lagers that previously dominated, Cuda na Kiju (which translates as 'Miracle on a Stick', a Polish expression for something unexpected and splendid)

sports multiple taps offering a constantly changing array of local and international beer, including smooth Polish session ale and tart IPAs with hops imported from as far afield as New Zealand.

The restaurant also serves lovingly made pizzas that are almost scientifically designed to facilitate beer consumption. Here the past and present mingle - outside on the terrace, hipsters sit in the shadows of the socialist-era office buildings, listening to the fountain and discussing football.
Nowy Świat 6/12; www.facebook. com/CudaNaKijuMultitapBar

WHERE TO STAY
H15 BOUTIQUE HOTEL
Inside the former Soviet Embassy, this small hotel offers 47 stylish rooms in a grand 19th-century building right in the beating heart of Warsaw. The on-site restaurant is as highly regarded as the hotel. Ask for a room with a balcony so you can breathe in the buzz of the city while getting ready for your night out. *www.h15-boutique.com*

WHAT TO DO
WARSAW OLD TOWN
Awash with medieval architecture, Warsaw's Old Town was meticulously rebuilt after WWII. From the Old Town Market Place to the Castle Square, you'll experience medieval Europe reconstructed - as much as possible with the original materials - by 20th-century crafts-people working from memory, off photographs, and even from architecture students' textbooks. The effort was completed so successfully you may have to pay close

attention to notice signs of the reconstruction and the damage that necessitated it.

POLIN MUSEUM OF THE HISTORY OF POLISH JEWS
Before the Holocaust, Poland was home to more than 1000 years of Jewish history, tradition and culture. POLIN exists to honour and celebrate "a nation murdered," though the experience is not merely grim. Here visitors learn about the dynamic Jewish culture and discover the efforts being made to keep it alive. *https://polin.pl/en*

CELEBRATIONS
WARSAW BEER FESTIVAL
First held in 2014 and taking place at various times across the year, the Warsaw Beer Festival celebrates Poland's rapidly growing love for all things craft beer. The event attracts top brewers and promises a range of more than 1000 beers. Wash them down with street food served up by enthusiastic chefs in food trucks. *https://warsawbeer festival.com*

GET THERE
Efficient trains and buses connect Gothenburg and Stockholm and other towns in southern Sweden. SJ Rail (www.sj.se) has trains to Dalarna from Stockholm, but to reach outlying locations such as Hyltebruk and Vissefjärda, you'll need to hire a car.

SOUTHERN SWEDEN

[Sweden]

SUMMER FEASTING IN SOUTHERN SWEDEN

Follow the sunshine around the south of Sweden from Gothenburg to Dalarna, sampling the foods of Midsommar and catching a glimpse of Sweden's soul.

Although fans of the 2019 hit movie *Midsommar* may associate this festival with spine-chilling horror, visitors to southern Sweden will find the real Midsommar event a time for joyful celebration. It's also an excuse for one of the year's most uninhibited feasts. The tradition of marking the longest day of the year dates back to pagan times, but these days it's all about gathering for picnics in the woods with friends and family.

Time your trip right, and you can expect to feast on Sweden's most celebrated delicacies in between swims in crystal clear lakes, hikes in silent, pristine forests and trips to the country's best beaches and unspoilt coves. Being well south of the Arctic Circle, the mixed forests and coastal waters of southern Sweden bring a cornucopia of seasonal foods to the Midsommar table during the short, warm Swedish summer.

The focus of the feast is *sill* – pickled herring, or more accurately, a wild assortment of pickled herring preparations – and smoked salmon also makes an appearance, as does cream-slathered strawberry cake and copious quantities of *snaps*, Sweden's traditional spice-infused firewater.

Celebrated on the Saturday falling between 20 and 26 June, Midsommar is just the beginning of the summertime bonanza in Sweden, which rolls right through this balmy season – a time to forage for wild bilberries, raspberries and more in the woods. Things crescendo again in August with *kräftskiva* (crayfish party) season, when families and friends gather for shell-cracking banquets of blood-red crayfish and tastings of *surströmming* (fermented herring), which is so pungent that these events always take place outside.

① FESKEKÖRKA

Gothenburg and the tiny islands that dot the Bohuslän coast are famous spots to enjoy the giddy fun of Midsommar. Even if you miss the event, it's worth swinging by in summer to browse markets stacked with seasonal treats. Pick of the catch in Gothenburg is the 'Fish Church' – a huge, chapel-like market that's a veritable cathedral to the flavours of the ocean. Browse stalls for slabs of *gravadlax* (cured salmon), pickled herring, heaped shrimp sandwiches and seafood-heavy salads, then munch your sea-seasoned spread at outdoor picnic tables with a view towards the Rosenlunds Canal.
Rosenlundsgatan, Gothenburg; www. feskekorka.se; closed Sun & Mon

② KAJUTAN

For sit-down seafood in Gothenburg that's so fresh you can almost hear the nets dripping, pay a visit to this popular restaurant at Stora Saluhallen, an attractive 19th-century indoor market piled high with summertime goodies. The brightly lit space is a fine place to enjoy delights such as Swedish caviar, shrimp on toast, crabcakes and crayfish gratin.
Kungstorget; www.kajutan saluhallen.se; closed Sun

③ STEDSANS IN THE WOODS

Midsummer is all about celebrating the rhythms of nature. One of the best places to get in touch with your inner dryad is Stedsans in the Woods in Hyltebruk, about two hours southeast of Gothenburg. In an achingly beautiful setting, ringed by trees on the edge of Hallasjön lake, this off-grid, healing retreat was founded by writer and food stylist Mette Helbæk and her husband, chef Flemming Hansen. The menu here is just-picked, which could mean foraged in the woods, gathered in the farm garden, or sourced from producers within shouting distance – you won't know what's on offer till you arrive.

"We work with the local seasons and all the little micro seasons in our gardens and the forest," explains Helbæk. "Our guests never know what they will be served – and often we don't either before we go out and harvest."

01 A Midsommar celebration spread

02 & 03 Feskekörka is Gothenburg's 'fish church'; come for seafood picnic fodder

04 Kräftor (crayfish) parties take over southern Sweden each August

Visitors stay for one or three nights in forest cabins or a campsite amid the greenery, swimming in the lake, steaming in the floating sauna, taking cooking classes and guided foraging walks, and immersing themselves deeply in nature.
Bohult 109, Hyltebruk; www.stedsans.org

04 KYRKEBY BRÄNNERI

Sweden has a rich tradition of distilling alcohol, from clear vodka-like *brännvin* to a dizzying range of *snaps* (local firewater) concoctions. The latter are typically flavoured with cumin, fennel and anise, or seasonal ingredients such as wormwood, St John's wort, yarrow, elderflower and various fruits and berries. Sadly, most of Sweden's rural distilleries were consolidated into the Absolut brewery at Åhus in 1971, but the Kyrkeby Bränneri – Sweden's oldest distillery, founded in 1771 – has risen from the ashes as a working museum.

Tours of the historic distillery are combined with tastings of the spirits produced in the old workings. "At Kyrkeby Bränneri we make traditional potato vodka like they did in the 1800s and spice it with local bog myrtle to go with crayfish in August and with local rowanberry for the Christmas smorgasbord," says manager Göran Persson.
Torggatan 30, Kyrkeby, Vissefjärda; www.kyrkeby.com; tours Apr-Oct

05 STUREHOF

No dish is more strongly associated with late summer than *kräftor* (crayfish). In August, party hats and lanterns come out, songs are sung and plenty of *snaps* is quaffed at southern Sweden's *kräftskiva* parties. But it's also easy to sample *kräftor* in the capital, Stockholm.

Elegant Sturehof is one of many local restaurants selling whole crayfish boiled with salt, dill and beer. It's upstairs in the historic Sturegallerian mall; even famous names such as Jon Bon Jovi and Bill Clinton have eaten here. Crayfish come boiled the traditional way or stuffed into satisfying crayfish sandwiches.
Sturegallerian, Stureplan 2, Stockholm; www.sturehof.com

06 ÖSTERMALMS SALUHALL

To browse Sweden's summer richness in one handy location, head to the many-spired brick building containing Östermalms Saluhall. This is Stockholm's most sophisticated marketplace. Inside, beneath a hangar-like roof, you'll find orderly rows of wooden stands selling everything from forest-fresh berry juices and Swedish cheeses to pungent *surströmming* – Baltic herring, lightly salted and fermented inside a sealed can until the metal stretches to almost bursting from the gases bubbling inside.

Östermalms is a great place to find local seafood, seasonal herbs and charcuterie made from elk and reindeer meat. Arrive hungry and curious. When you've finished browsing the market, pull up a chair at Lisa Elmqvist's restaurant for a stand-out seafood dining experience.
Östermalmstorg; https:// en.ostermalmshallen.se; closed Sun

07 MIDSOMMARFIRANDE FESTIVAL

Bordering Norway and within easy driving distance of Stockholm, lake-dotted Dalarna county slumbers quietly for much of the year, before erupting into a riot of activity for Midsommar.

On the Friday between 18 June and 26 June, a giant maypole is hoisted up in the town of Leksand on the shores of Lake Siljan, in a natural depression created during the last ice age. Vast crowds gather, garlands are strung together from wildflowers, and locals don traditional dress and fill the streets with dancing and noise.

It's a prime opportunity to sample the full bounty of Midsommar foods, washed down with plenty of local *snaps*. If you stay in a local hotel or Airbnb, your hosts will almost certainly lay on a spread.

You may also be invited to join in the dancing and hoisting (don't be surprised if this leads to being invited to a full-blown family midsummer celebration). Stock up on *snaps* before you come so you have something to bring to the party.
www.visitdalarna.se/en/ midsummer

WHERE TO STAY

DORSIA HOTEL

Fabulously flamboyant, the Dorsia in Gothenburg looks like the home of a 19th-century millionaire. There's a hint of boudoir about the lavish, fabric-filled rooms, executed in shades of crimson and purple, which drip with drapes, Damask patterns and velour. Breakfast here is an extravagant buffet and the hotel is known for its lavish afternoon teas. No doubt about it, staying at the Dorsia feels a bit like being in a cabaret in real life.
www.dorsia.se/en

VANDRARHEM AF CHAPMAN & SKEPPSHOLMEN

Proof that you don't need to spend big bucks to have a memorable stay in Stockholm, the af Chapman is a boat-turned-hostel anchored in a prime location off Skeppsholmen. This 19th-century sailing ship once plied the Atlantic, but today it has dorms below deck and amenities onshore,

including a kitchen for self-caterers. Pick up ingredients for summertime feasts at the nearby NK Saluhall food market, a short walk away across Kungsträdgården park.
www.swedishtourist association.com/ facilities/stf-stockholmaf-chapman-skeppsholmen-hostel-house

WHAT TO DO

GET IN TOUCH WITH THE EDIBLE COUNTRY

In collaboration with four Michelin-starred Swedish chefs, Visit Sweden has created the Edible Country outdoor dining concept to help visitors experience Sweden's wild food. There are 13 bookable wooden bench tables dotted around the country; the idea is

that use them to set up portable stoves and cook Michelin-class, chef-designed menus using seasonal wild foodstuffs such as meadowsweet, chanterelles and ramsons' berries (wild garlic) – all ingredients that you can forage for free in the surrounding landscape.
www.visitsweden.com/ edible-country

GET THERE

Flights arrive into Belfast International and City airports; buses run from both airports to the city centre. Stena Line runs a ferry service between Belfast and Cairnryan, Scotland (2 hours 20 minutes) and Liverpool, England (8 hours). Translink bus and train services connect Belfast with Ballycastle and Portstewart, but exploring the coast is easiest by car.

Atlantic Ocean

05 BALLYCASTLE

PORTSTEWART

06 **04**

07 COLERAINE

BALLYMONEY

LIMAVADY

North Channel

ANTRIM

LONDONDERRY

BALLYMENA

LARNE

MAGHERA

CARRICKFERGUS

TYRONE

ANTRIM

NEWTOWNABBEY

02 HOLYWOOD BANGOR

COOKSTOWN

DOWN

03 **01** NEWTOWNARDS

Lough Neagh

☆ BELFAST

ARMAGH

BELFAST & THE NORTH COAST

[Northern Ireland]

SURF & TURF IN NORTHERN IRELAND

Feast your way from Belfast through lush farming pastures to coastal villages, where a new generation of artisan producers are combining tradition with innovation.

To experience Northern Ireland's food scene, the best place to start is Belfast. Here, Michelin-starred restaurants and specialist food shops can be explored alongside the city's thriving arts scene, excellent museums and buzzing nightlife. Locals may grumble about the weather, but the north of Ireland's rainy climate is at least partially to thank for the region's vibrant green pastures.

Though farming has long been a way of life for rural communities, recently there has been a renewed value placed on quality local produce. Farms and suppliers are name-checked on the menus of Belfast's top restaurants, where talented chefs get the best flavour from the ingredients. Look out for Hannon's Himalayan-salt aged Glenarm Shorthorn Beef, Comber Earlies (a thin-skinned new potato grown near Comber in County Down), and langoustines, crab and scampi from Kilkeel and Portavogie.

From Belfast, the Antrim coastline forms a scenic route northwards, with a Norman castle, dramatic cliff walks, coastal hiking trails and surfing beaches along the way. The Causeway Coast is famous for the Giant's Causeway above all else, but it is also home to an expanding number of artisan food producers and outstanding restaurants that take advantage of high-quality local produce and seafood.

Here the catch-of-the-day might include lobster, scallops and haddock, best enjoyed in one of the area's informal beachside restaurants with views of the churning North Atlantic Ocean. Another local speciality is dulse, an edible seaweed that is often dried and eaten as a snack or used as a seasoning. Some of the best local produce can be sampled at the Naturally North Coast and Glens artisan market, which is held in different locations along the Causeway Coast from week to week.

01 ST GEORGE'S MARKET

To get a taste of some of the best local produce head to St George's Market, an elegant Victorian indoor market packed with independent traders selling artisan goods. The market operates Friday through Sunday, with slightly different traders each day, but the best time for food lovers is Saturday's food and craft market. Here you'll find stalls selling fresh seafood from Portavogie and Kilkeel, as well as produce from local farms including fruit and vegetables from Helen's Bay Organic and sausages and steak from Hillstown Farm.

If the smells from the food carts whet your appetite, head to Belfast Bap Co for a classic bap (egg, bacon and sausage piled high in a soft bread roll), filled potato bread or soda farl, all key ingredients of a traditional Ulster Fry (the local greasy breakfast and popular hangover cure). Wash it down with a flat white from Drop Hopper Coffee Roasters or stop by the Suki Tea stand to pick up some Belfast Brew, the company's signature Irish Breakfast Tea.

12-20 East Bridge St, Belfast; facebook.com/ StGeorgesMarketBelfast/; open Fri-Sun

02 MIKE'S FANCY CHEESE

The counters of Mike Thomson's small Belfast shop heave with a mouthwatering display of some 50 different cheeses, all sourced from Irish dairies except for the Italian Parmesan. At the back, the glass-fronted maturing room houses neatly stacked wheels of cheese. "Irish cheese is heavily influenced by European cheeses," Thomson explains. Gouda- and Alpine-style cheeses are sold here, as well as a handful of blue cheeses, sheep's cheese and hard and lactic-style goat's cheeses.

Many of them are from small boutique producers, such as the Carraignamuc and Sobhriste raw milk cheeses from the Lost Valley Dairy in Cork, where the five dairy cows are hand-milked. Thomson also makes his own Young Buck blue cheese. "We produce it using raw milk from Holstein Friesian cows on a farm in Newtownards. It takes three or four months to mature,

01 Cathedral Quarter in Belfast

02 St George's Market is a home for artisanal producers

03 Mike's Fancy Cheese sources from Irish dairies

04 Ursa Minor is king of the sourdough brunch

then we bring it fresh to the shop. The wheel is sold out by the end of the week," he says. Pick up some Abernethy butter (a slow-churned butter produced in County Down), a loaf of sourdough and a jar of Belfast-made chutney to take on a picnic.
41 Little Donegall St, Belfast; www. mfcheese.com; closed Sun

03 THE SUNFLOWER

Not only is this authentic Belfast pub one of the friendliest joints in town, with nightly live music, it's also a good place to sample local craft beer. Look out for stouts, lagers, pale ales and IPAs by Boundary Brewing Co, an independent East Belfast brewery, and MacIvors Armagh cider.

Soak it up with pizza from the wood-fired oven.
65 Union St, Belfast; www.sunflowerbelfast.com

04 URSA MINOR BAKEHOUSE

Dara and Ciara O'hArtghaile use only three ingredients to produce their exceptional sourdough loaves: flour, water and salt.

The key to successful sourdough bakery, according to Ursa Minor, is to allow the organic grains time to ferment in the water. Loaves are baked directly on the oven floor to achieve the perfect crust.

Above the bakehouse, the Ursa Minor cafe sells pastries and whips up brunches made with seasonal local ingredients. Check the website calendar for

the latest dates of its sourdough breadmaking classes.
45 Ann St, Ballycastle; www.ursaminorbakehouse.com; closed Sun & Mon

05 NORTH COAST SMOKEHOUSE

Ruairidh Morrison's smokehouse on the north Antrim coast is largely a one-man operation: Morrison sources, smokes and distributes the smoked salmon, trout, salt, black pepper and dulse himself.

After learning to smoke fish in New Zealand using small portable smokers, Morrison initially tried upscaling the smoking process. "We found we couldn't get the same quality, so we went back to

05 & 06 Native's
overflowing lobster roll;
the menu is dictated by
the daily catch

07 Giant Causeway's
otherwordly stacked
rock formations

using several small burners. Our products are handcrafted and labour intensive," he explains. "We use beech wood chips for hot and cold smoking and we don't use any artificial flavouring or preservatives."

The salmon he uses comes from Glenarm organic farm, less than an hour south down the coast, and Morrison guts and fillets the fish himself. The carcasses then go to a friend on Rathlin Island to be used as bait for lobster fishing, and in exchange Morrison receives dulse from the family's kelp farm. Make an appointment to visit the smokehouse and buy produce onsite.

3/61 Leyland Rd, Ballycastle; www. northcoastsmokehouse.com

06 BROUGHGAMMON FARM

On learning that most male kid goats were put down at birth, the Cole family were prompted to address what they saw as unnecessary waste by rearing male goats to produce cabrito meat on their north Antrim farm. Various cuts of goat meat, wild seasonal game and free-range rose veal charcuterie are prepared at the family's onsite artisan butchery.

Visit the farm to see the goats, peek inside the polytunnels, pick up supplies at the farm shop and taste the produce at the farm cafe. Butchery classes, wild game workshops and foraging courses are also available.

50 Straid Rd, Ballycastle; www. broughgammon.com; open Fri-Sun

07 NATIVE SEAFOOD & SCRAN

The chalkboard specials at this casual beachside seafood restaurant and fishmongers change depending on the catch of the day, which is collected directly from the fishing boats in Greencastle.

Housed in an informal corrugated iron shack so close to the sea you can taste the salt spray, Native's menu features sustainably sourced, fresh local seafood prepared with care and creativity, including Lough Foyle oysters, a signature chowder and fish tacos made with Donegal haddock. There's also a coffee and pastry counter stacked with Portuguese tarts and cookies from a nearby independent bakery.

11 The Crescent, Portstewart; www. nativeseafood.co.uk; closed Sun

WHERE TO STAY
THE HARRISON
The accommodation on offer at this boutique hotel in Belfast's Queen's Quarter is described by owner Melanie Harrison as 'chambers of distinction', a reference to the fact that the 16 rooms are each styled in honour of a different local personality. Original features in the 1879 building are offset with bohemian wallpapers, local textiles and upcycled materials.
www.chambersof distinction.com

BUSHMILLS INN HOTEL
This historic hotel offers well-appointed rooms, turf fires and even a secret library. It's located within walking distance of Bushmills whiskey distillery (open to the public for tastings and tours) and the Giant's Causeway.
www.bushmillsinn.com

WHAT TO DO
TITANIC BELFAST
Set in a gleaming, angular building overlooking the slipway from which *Titanic* was launched, this impressive multimedia museum takes visitors on a high-tech journey from the ship's design and construction right through to its ill-fated maiden voyage.
www.titanicbelfast.com

GIANT'S CAUSEWAY
The other-worldly hexagonal rock formations of the Giant's Causeway are an unmissable stop for any visitor to the north Antrim coast.
www.nationaltrust.org. uk/giants-causeway

CELEBRATIONS
OULD LAMMAS FAIR
Held annually on the last Monday and Tuesday of August, this famous Ballycastle street fair dates back some 400 years and attracts thousands of visitors. As well as live music and horse events, the Ould Lammas Fair is known as the place to buy yellowman (a hard, chewy honeycomb) and dulse (a local seaweed). The Naturally North Coast and Glens artisan market is held on Ballycastle seafront during the fair.
www.naturallynorth coastandglens.co.uk

GET THERE
There's an international airport at Newcastle, and Berwick-upon-Tweed and Newcastle are both accessible by train and long-distance bus. Local buses connect most towns; more rural areas such as Kielder Forest are best explored by car.

NORTHUMBERLAND & TYNESIDE

Farne
Islands

BERWICK-
UPON-
TWEED

01

COLDSTREAM

BAMBURGH

o SEAHOUSES

o KELSO

WOOLER

SCOTLAND

CRASTER

JEDBURGH

02

ALNWICK o

o ALNMOUTH

Northumberland
National Park

o AMBLE

ROTHBURY

03

OTTERBURN

NORTHUMBERLAND

Kielder o FALSTONE
Water

o MORPETH

BELLINGHAM

04

PONTELAND

WHITLEY
BAY

07

CHOLLERFORD
o LOW BRUNTON

TYNEMOUTH o

05

o ACOMB

06

o NEWCASTLE-
UPON-TYNE

SOUTH
SHIELDS

o HEXHAM

Tyne

SUNDERLAND

[England]

NORTHERN SOUL FOOD, REMASTERED

The rich bounty of Northeast England's coast and countryside are being elevated in new and inventive ways across Northumberland and Tyneside.

A succession of crumbling castles lines the Northeast coast – relics of a time when this was a land of violence between the old enemies of England and Scotland. There are echoes, too, of even more ancient history, in the Roman forts at Housesteads and Vindolanda, and, connecting them, the snaking ruins of Hadrian's Wall, once the very frontier of the Roman Empire.

Today, this is a place of bucolic serenity – though reminders of the past remain, and the realm of food and drink, in particular, links modern Northumberland with its history and with the bounty of the land and sea. The beloved Craster kipper is still served with pride across the region. And though the monks are long gone from Lindisfarne, the honey mead they

pioneered continues to be produced there. Where contemporary Northumbrian cuisine really comes into its own, though, is with the increasing number of chefs turning timeless local ingredients into something entirely new, creating 'foraged beers' and Michelin-starred, Scandi-infused food, for example.

Away from the table, this is an area that merits deep exploration. The remnants of Hadrian's Wall, dotted with ancient Mithraic temples and ruined settlements, make for a hiking trail like no other, while the nearby wilds of Northumberland National Park are home to diverse bird life and presided over by some of the darkest night skies in Britain. In vibrant contrast, Newcastle's galleries and concert venues are redefining the city as a cultural hotspot.

01 AUDELA

The produce of Northumberland and the Scottish Borders is raised to an art form at Audela, one of the region's finest restaurants for Modern British cuisine. This culinary movement is fast gathering pace and acclaim, as a new generation of talented chefs cast off the shackles of British food's reputation as beige and uninspiring, turning instead to dishes that celebrate the high-quality ingredients of the countryside and coast.

At Audela, in the walled Elizabethan market town of Berwick-upon-Tweed, that means wild mushroom bourguignon with pearl barley and butternut squash; beef sirloin from the Northumberland hamlet of Fenwick

Stead; and North Sea monkfish and pickled cockles. The restaurant's name also has local roots – Audela was the last boat to be built in Berwick's shipyard, back in 1979. *64 Bridge St, Berwick-upon-Tweed; http://audela.co.uk; closed Mon–Wed*

02 JOLLY FISHERMAN

For over a century, a heady aroma has hung over the coastal village of Craster: the smell of smouldering oak, emanating in white plumes from a humble stone smokehouse. This is the headquarters of L Robson & Sons, origin of the famous Craster kippers – butterflied, salted and oak-smoked herring. The smokehouse shop is open for visitors to take kippers

away (perfect for a countryside picnic), but to best enjoy them, along with the rest of the coast's sumptuous ingredients, head to the Jolly Fisherman, a gorgeous traditional pub – think oak beams, brick walls and roaring fireplaces – overlooking the sea. Here, the prized catch is reimagined in inventive ways; order the tempura monkfish or the kipper scotch egg. *Haven Hill, Craster; http://thejollyfishermancraster.co.uk*

03 NORTHERN WILDS

The woodlands of Kielder Forest are among the largest in Britain and harbour all manner of delicious wild-growing ingredients, from citrusy wood sorrel to chanterelle mushrooms. Foraging fungi in

01 Bamburgh Castle
on the Northeast coast

02 Fungi foraging with
Northern Wilds

03 First & Last
beers even attract
local wildlife

04 Hjem's food style is
Nordic-Northumbrian

particular is a dangerous game,
though, which is where expert
guides like Linus Morton and Louise
Hepworth of Northern Wilds come
in. They'll lead you through the
forest, helping you differentiate
between a deadly death cap and
a tasty hedgehog mushroom,
and giving you tips on how to
turn foraged ingredients into
meals that are not only delicious
and wholesome, but can also be
enticingly exotic – Linus's speciality
is turning local pigeon and rabbit
into a Moroccan *pastilla*, while
springtime 'sushi and seaweed'
courses will teach you how to
make Japanese-inspired food with
foraged coastal goodies.
Cottage 1, High Green, Kielder;
www.northernwilds.co.uk

04 FIRST & LAST BREWERY

Family-run, environmentally aware
and immersed in the produce and
flavours of Northumberland, there's
much to like about the First & Last
Brewery in the quiet village of
Bellingham. Their range of unusual
and delicious beers draws heavily
on native Northumbrian ingredients,
many of them gathered from nearby
countryside. Try the light, coconutty
notes of the Gorseflower Pale, a
rich Damson Porter, or a malty
Belgian beer infused with
Northumberland plums.

"They taste slightly different
each year depending on things like
sunlight and rainfall," says founder
Sam Kelly. "We wanted our beers
to have a taste of the landscape."
As the environment gives so much

to First & Last, it gives back, too.
Proceeds from the brewery's Ratty
Pale Ale go towards a local project
aimed at reintroducing water voles
to the North Tyne River, while
electricity used in the production of
the beers is green and renewable.
Foundry Yard, Bellingham; www.
firstandlastbrewery.co.uk

05 HJEM

It's been suggested that the
distinctive Geordie dialect may owe
something to a Viking influence,
and one modern local word shared
with Danish and Norwegian is *hjem*,
meaning home. This relationship
is played upon at this magnificent
restaurant, run by Northumberland-
born Ally Thompson and her
husband, Swedish chef Alex

Nietosvuori, which has earned a Michelin star for its Nordic-Northumbrian cuisine.

"You really see the seasons in the north of England and I'm able to lean on the surroundings, using the best British ingredients with Swedish techniques," says Nietosvuori. The result? A 15–18 course tasting menu with creations such as smoked eel and Doddington cheese, and Northumbrian lobster claw beignet. Food is paired with a top-class selection of wines, and the setting – English country inn with just a hint of Scandi minimalism – is perfection. *Hadrian Hotel, Wall; www. restauranthjem.co.uk; closed Sun–Tue*

06 HOUSE OF TIDES

Into Newcastle now, the beating heart of Northeast England, and the marvellous House of Tides,

the city's sole Michelin-starred establishment. Sitting pretty on Newcastle's quayside, in a handsome Grade I-listed property that was once a wealthy merchant's house, this gourmet place radiates quality as soon as you step through the door.

And the menu doesn't disappoint: dishes might include venison tartare with caviar and smoked beetroot, pork jowl with smoked eel and apple, and dark chocolate with Thai basil and lime.

Ingredients are nearly all sourced from nearby. Despite the accolades, there's a pleasantly laid-back feel to House of Tides – no strict dress code, and relaxed service – so you can just focus on enjoying the superb food. *28–30 The Close, Newcastle; www.houseoftides.co.uk; closed Sun–Tue*

07 RILEY'S FISH SHACK

The River Tyne snakes east out of Newcastle, past the terminus of Hadrian's Wall and crumbling Roman forts, and reaches the North Sea at Tynemouth. Here there's the elegant ruins of Tynemouth Priory, but the undoubted jewel in the crown is Riley's, a humble fish shack in a shipping container on Tynemouth's King Edward's Bay beach.

The menu changes with each day's haul, but reliable fixtures are Lindisfarne oysters, sole, squid and hake, all ocean-fresh and delicious. And while regional classics feature – our old friend the Craster kipper, for example – Riley's really shines in the dishes that give a creative, cosmopolitan twist to the local ingredients. The spicy bang-bang monkfish is highly recommended. *King Edward's Bay, Tynemouth; http://rileysfishshack.com; closed Tue*

WHERE TO STAY

HADRIAN HOTEL
Attached to Michelin-starred Hjem, this lovely, unpretentious hotel has 11 en-suite rooms with decor that's a modern take on the classic British country-inn aesthetic. It's ideal if you want to try Hjem's wine pairings, but also very handy for exploring Hadrian's Wall. *www.hadrianhotel.co.uk*

OLD RECTORY HOWICK
Coastal Northumberland stays don't come much more enchanting than the Old Rectory, a short stroll from the coast and less than a 10-minute drive from Craster. There are just five farmhouse-style guestrooms and the food is superb. Craster kippers are a mainstay on the breakfast menu, while evening meals (book ahead) feature local meat and vegetables. *www.oldrectory howick.co.uk*

WHAT TO DO

HADRIAN'S WALL
Once the northwestern frontier of the Roman Empire, what remains

of Hadrian's Wall is now a National Trail. Some fortifications still remain, and it's easy to walk the wall in sections from various places, including the aptly named village of Wall, also home to Hjem and the Hadrian Hotel. *www.nationaltrail. co.uk/en_GB/trails/ hadrians-wall-path*

KIELDER WATER & FOREST PARK
This vast woodland of spruce, pine and larch is home to an array of wildlife, some of which is rare in other parts of the country – half of England's red squirrel

population lives here, as well as nesting ospreys. It also includes Kielder Observatory, a wood-hewn research station built to gaze into some of the darkest night skies in Britain – a must-visit, particularly in winter. *www.visitkielder.com*

CELEBRATIONS

NEWCASTLE BEER & CIDER FESTIVAL
Each April, brewers and cider makers from across the Northeast and beyond descend on Northumbria University Students' Union in central Newcastle, showcasing the finest

in real ale, perry (pear cider) and more. *https://nclbcf-tynland. camra.org.uk/wordpress*

ALNWICK FOOD FESTIVAL
The charming market town of Alnwick, home to an impressive castle and gardens, hosts this food festival each September. Stalls sell everything from Northumberland cheese and sausages to Malaysian curry, while Lindisfarne mead – a potent honey wine originally brewed by the monks of Holy Island – is also a regular fixture. *www.visitalnwick.org.uk*

GET THERE

There are train stations at Darsham (near Southwold) and Cromer. Buses zip along the Suffolk coast, connecting through Norwich to Cromer, where you can pick up the handy Coasthopper (www. sanderscoaches.com), linking villages between Cromer and Wells-next-the-Sea. The Coastliner 36 (www.lynxbus. co.uk/bus-routes/coast-liner-36) tracks the coast between Wells and King's Lynn.

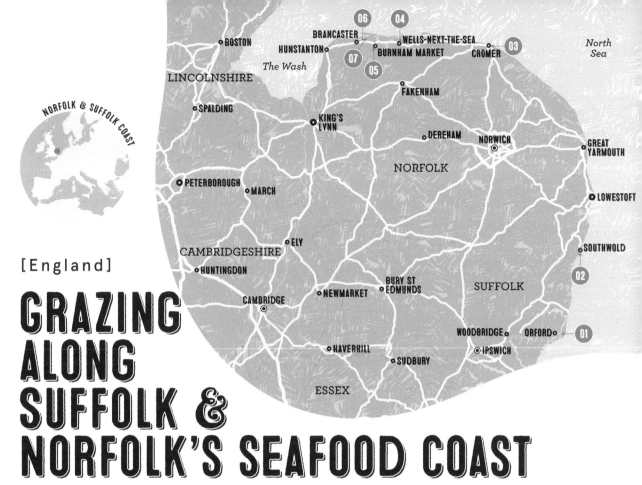

The Wash

North Sea

BOSTON

LINCOLNSHIRE

BRANCASTER 06
HUNSTANTON 04
07 WELLS-NEXT-THE-SEA
BURNHAM MARKET
05 CROMER 03

FAKENHAM

SPALDING

KING'S LYNN

DEREHAM

NORWICH

NORFOLK

GREAT YARMOUTH

PETERBOROUGH

MARCH

LOWESTOFT

ELY

CAMBRIDGESHIRE

HUNTINGDON

SOUTHWOLD

02

BURY ST EDMUNDS

SUFFOLK

CAMBRIDGE

NEWMARKET

WOODBRIDGE
ORFORD
01

HAVERHILL

IPSWICH

SUDBURY

ESSEX

NORFOLK & SUFFOLK COAST

[England]

GRAZING ALONG SUFFOLK & NORFOLK'S SEAFOOD COAST

Discover England's ancient seafood traditions, some dating back to Roman times, on the brine-scented coast of Norfolk and Suffolk.

Unbeknown to many visitors to England, this sea-ringed, seafaring island has rich seafood traditions to rival anywhere in Europe, dating back to the Romans if not before. A century ago, English menus were a varied palette of fish soups, stews, cold plates, pies and pickles, featuring everything from writhing eels, tiny sprats and plate-flat brill to oysters, cockles and mussels. The medieval church crammed the calendar with 'fish days', when fish was the only animal permitted on the dinner plate.

During WWI and WWII, hauling in the bounty of the sea became a dangerous game of roulette, and the seafood feasts that filled the nation's pubs vanished, to be replaced by a limited menu of breaded scampi and fried cod and chips. To sample Britain's traditional seafood culture today, you have to sail to the edge of East Anglia, where small inshore boats still bring home the best of the North sea on a cottage-industry scale. You'll find that fabulous seafood is a constant refrain as you drift from dainty fishing village to rolling, dune-backed beach; you'll even find it for sale in the inland waterways of the Norfolk Broads.

In the marshy waters of the Wash near King's Lynn, brown shrimp have been landed and potted (preserved in butter) since at least the Georgian era. In the flint-built villages and nostalgic Victorian seaside resorts along Norfolk's northern shores, fat, fox-red crabs are still dressed for dinner and mussels and juicy cockles are gathered, boiled and pickled, as they have been for centuries. The seafood action spills into neighbouring Suffolk, where British oysters – a favourite food for Roman emperors – are hand-reared at Orford and 'fish and chips' can mean lobster or mackerel in sunny Southwold.

⓪① PINNEY'S OF ORFORD

It might be hard to believe today but oysters were once the food of the working man, feeding marching Roman foot soldiers and the teeming Victorian slums of East London. In the sleepy Suffolk hamlet of Orford, the owners of Pinney's have been rearing oysters the old-fashioned way since the 1950s, supplying quayside fishmongers and the nearby Butley Orford Oysterage restaurant with their British seafood.

The Pinney family is involved in every step of the process, from catching and harvesting seafood on their own boats to smoking fish and pressing pâtés and fishcakes on the premises. Grab seafood to go, or dine in simple comfort at the Oysterage – either way, you're in for a wonderful fishy treat.
Market Hill, Orford; www. pinneysoforford.co.uk; Apr-Oct Wed-Sat, Nov-Mar Fri & Sat

⓪② SOLE BAY FISH COMPANY

If you're going to eat fish and chips, you might as well eat it so fresh you can still hear the smack of the catch being landed on deck. Set in a black, wooden fishing shack on the harbourside at Southwold, this fisher-owned restaurant delivers novel takes on the seaside staple – sea bass and chips, mackerel and chips, half-lobster and chips – plus more familiar variations.

They're served alongside lip-smacking platters of dressed crab, smoked sprats, crevettes, cockles, whelks and crayfish tails. "The varied coast from the Wash to the Thames estuary provides the perfect habitat for fish and shellfish," says manager Andy Wix. "This really is some of the best produce in the whole of Europe."
22E Blackshore, Southwold; www. solebayfishco.co.uk

⓪③ DAVIES FISH SHOP

Crabs are to Cromer what sole is to Dover. Offshore from this agreeably old-fashioned Victorian seaside resort in Norfolk, the fattest, creamiest brown crabs in England skulk in the briny depths.

Cromer crabs are served dozens of ways, but the best way to sample them is 'dressed' – delicately cooked and pressed back into their

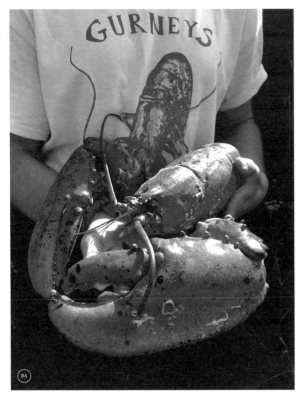

shells – at no-frills Davies Fish Shop on the road running back from the pier. If you want whistles and bells, go elsewhere. At Davies it's all about trays of ice, striped awnings and wafts of brine – and crabs, of course, caught daily on the owners' boat, the *Richard William*.
Garden Street, Cromer; closed Sun-Mon in winter

04 WELLS CRAB HOUSE

Cromer must be fuming that one of the most lauded places to try its famous crabs is just along the coast at Wells-next-the-Sea. The Wells Crab House disappoints only those foolish enough to turn up without a reservation, with a menu that trots the globe but settles, at its best, on cold platters of dressed crab, buttered Wells lobster, oak-smoked salmon and cider vinegar cockles.

It's a welcome reminder that English seafood menus were once a joyous celebration of the sea. A close relationship with local fishers ensures that everything has that fresh-off-the-boat tang, so bring an appetite, and ideally a group for sharing.
38 Freeman Street, Wells-next-the-Sea; www.wellscrabhouse. co.uk; closed Sun & Mon

05 GURNEY'S FISH SHOP

Detour slightly inland between Wells-next-the-Sea and Brancaster to reach the market town of Burnham Market, where Gurney's Fish Shop is stacked with treats from Norfolk's coast. The house delicacy is potted shrimp, a preparation of boiled-on-ship brown shrimp hauled from the Wash near King's Lynn, preserved in nutmeg-flavoured butter – a traditional preserving technique that dates back to at least the 18th century.

Fishing and shellfish harvesting continued in the Wash right through WWII, when fishing became one of the most perilous activities on the coast.
Market Place, Burnham Market; www.gurneysfishshop.co.uk; closed Sun

06 THE MUSSEL POD

The English have been eating mussels for at least as long as the Belgians. At Brancaster – where a

06 The seafood platter at The White Horse pub

07 White Horse diners among the tidal marshes

08 Norfolk's Cley Windmill, now a hotel

classic Norfolk beach sits serenely beyond the marshes – the tradition is still going strong. This is the laid-back home of the Brancaster Bay Shellfish company and the Mussel Pod, a mobile seafood van serving quirky takes on *moules frites* near the Jolly Sailors Pub in Brancaster Staithe. Here, lip-smacking mussels come cooked in mariniere sauce, garlic butter, Thai spices or English cider.

"Our family has been fishing for shellfish in Norfolk for centuries," explains owner Thomas Large. "The clean waters and the nutrients washing off the salt marshes make our mussels especially fat."
Olive House, Main Rd, Brancaster Staithe; www.facebook.com /brancasterbayshellfish; closed Tue

07 THE WHITE HORSE

The briny marsh waters that play a vital part in the life cycle of Norfolk's inshore fisheries can be seen from your table at the White Horse, an award-winning coastal pub in Brancaster Staithe famed for its platters of local seafood. Patrons gather in the rear marquee to gorge on North Sea lobster, Cromer crab, Staithe Smokehouse salmon, Brancaster mussels, oysters and cockles pickled with saffron and crevettes, fanned by coastal breezes. The seafood platter is a feast for a family. "Norfolk seafood celebrates generations of local fishermen's craft," says manager Rob Williamson. "You will not taste a better oyster. They thrive in the waters across the marsh, as Scolt Head island acts as a defence against the tides."
Main Rd, Brancaster Staithe; www.whitehorsebrancaster.co.uk

WHERE TO STAY

SUTHERLAND HOUSE

The attached seafood restaurant is almost as big a lure as the rooms at this historic guesthouse on Southwold's main drag. It once hosted dignitaries such as a young James II. Rooms have historic pargeted ceilings, exposed beams and free-standing baths. The restaurant menu runs to cod loin, Cromer crab and buttered samphire. *www.sutherland house.co.uk*

CLEY WINDMILL

One of Norfolk's most charming places to stay, this creative conversion of a once-working windmill rises beside a sea of rippling marshes in Cley-next-the-Sea in north Norfolk. Hints of the mill's working life spill into the rooms, which offer uplifting views over the marshlands. Guests can feast on Norfolk-themed tasting menus crammed with local produce including, of course, seafood. *www.cleywindmill.co.uk*

WHAT TO DO

HOLKHAM HALL

At this grand, Palladian-style stately home, you get lavish interiors, gorgeous grounds and one of Norfolk's best beaches thrown in for good measure. It was built to house the Grand Tour treasures gathered by the first Earl of Leicester, and the estate is fronted by the dune-backed Holkham National Nature Reserve. *www.holkham.co.uk*

CELEBRATIONS

CROMER CRAB & LOBSTER FESTIVAL

Cromer's celebrated crustaceans get the fanfare they deserve at this anuual seafood festival, which hops between Cromer and Sheringham in Norfolk. There's live music, cookery demonstrations, a street market and all sorts of meal deals on the festival's Scrumptious Seafood trail. *www.crabandlobster festival.co.uk*

GET THERE
South Pembrokeshire is a 145km (90-mile) drive west of Cardiff and its airport. A car reaches the region's remotest corners, but there are decent public transport connections between towns and major villages, including coastal buses. Trains run between Haverfordwest and London's Paddington (4½ hours) roughly every two hours.

01

[Wales]

RISING TIDES IN PEMBROKESHIRE

The pull of the coast is irresistible in this corner of Wales. Here, the food scene is booming like the Atlantic surf, with producers and chefs playing up foraged flavours.

On Wales' southwest coast, things have recently taken a culinary turn for the wilder, with chefs drawn to the rich pickings of Pembrokeshire's rock pool-splashed coves, cliff-wrapped bays, lush hedgerows and heather-cloaked hills. The views of sky and fizzing surf are uplifting and chefs are trying to capture them on the plate, with hyper-local produce and a pinch of imagination. Some are discreetly shooting for Michelin stars. On these expansive shores, anything feels possible and there's the freedom to experiment.

There is a timelessness to this landscape, whether you are hoofing over cliff and stile on the coast path or wandering across hills strewn with prehistoric standing stones. And this deep connection to the past, to the pulse of seasons and tides, to the offerings of land and sea, reverberates in the kitchen. Here

producers and chefs are often friends and neighbours, and menus are rooted in place and tradition. Each year brings a wave of exciting new producers – from chilli farms to craft breweries. And a good meal can be as simple as a boat-fresh crab sandwich on the beach or as intricate as a wild-food tasting menu.

Tripping from Pembrokeshire's south to north coast, this trail spotlights the region's chefs and producers and their love of nature and reinvention. Where food and drink is made and served matters here – be it an old boat shack where seafood comes with a view of wave-ruffled shores, a converted cow shed where vermouth is distilled using hand-harvested botanicals, a meadow-rimmed farm where edible insects star on menus, or a revamped potting shed where a chef blows minds with a feast of foraged flavours.

01 THE STONE CRAB

Whipped by the waves of the Celtic Sea, south coast Saundersfoot is just the kind of place you would expect to find excellent seafood. And it doesn't get better than at this stone shack next to the clanking boats in the harbour. Fish identification charts and nautical knick-knacks line the walls in the rustic, blue-splashed interior. And the menu is whatever the boats bring in: whole lobster; smoked mackerel with chilli-lime pâté; crab with samphire-white wine spaghetti. The huge sharing platter for two – with scallops, king prawns, mussels and calamari – is the dream.

The Harbour, Saundersfoot; https:// stonecrab.co.uk; closed Mon

02 STILL WILD

"Pembrokeshire is a forager's dream. Sea wormwood from the estuary or botanicals from the cliffs – we're spoilt with the varied flavours that go into our vermouth," enthuses James Harrison-Allen.

Blink and you'll miss his micro-distillery in a converted cowshed in the village of Kilgetty, 5km (3 miles) north of Saundersfoot. James swapped his life as a House of Commons researcher to follow his dream: moving to Pembrokeshire to spend days at one with nature and create spirits that sing of the place that stole his heart. Hogweed, rock samphire, bog myrtle and elderberry all go into his award-winning vermouths. Try floral, herbal dry vermouth or bittersweet rosso vermouth with an orange twist in the courtyard bar (open Thursdays). Tanked with botanicals like seaweed, gorse and sea buckthorn, the coastal gin is delicious too.

Cresselly House, Kilgetty; https:// stillwilddrinks.com; reservations required

03 FERNERY AT THE GROVE

A 10km (6 mile) drive north brings you to this fantasy country manor, which is like a Jane Austen novel come to life on a summer afternoon, when the lawns swirl with wildflowers and butterflies. But the Grove is more than just a looker – it has serious culinary credentials. Its gourmet restaurant, Fernery, is romance in a nutshell,

with white-linen draped tables, candlelight, artfully arranged ferns and a hushed vibe. Chefs big up garden-grown veggies and herbs, foraged finds and sustainably sourced local fish and meat in ingredient-led menus that wow with dishes such as squab with celeriac, cherry and nasturtium, and smoked potato with dashi, asparagus and bottarga.
Molleston, Narberth; https:// ferneryrestaurant.co.uk; closed Sun-Tue

04 ANNWN

"Everything about Pembrokeshire inspires me: its plants, berries, soil, trees, flowers and grasses. Here, fine dining is rooted in conservation. Ecosystems are being destroyed and

we need to get back to nature," says chef-forager and fisherman Matt Powell, who trained in Michelin-starred kitchens before taking his talent back to the wilds of Wales.

By day, he wears wellies and lugs a bucket as he roams Pembrokeshire's rocky shores and hedgerows. By night, he's at the stove in the old potting shed on the Lawrenny Estate, southwest of Narberth. Score a table and you're in for a 10-course feast, with the likes of wild garlic preserved in its lifecycle, aged kelp broth with siphon weed emulsification, oyster leaf and scurvy grass, and duck-egg yolk with hedgerow plants. It's ingenious cooking you'll never forget.
The Little Retreat, Lawrenny; www. annwnrestaurant.co.uk; closed Mon-Wed

05 CAFÉ MÔR

Where Wales slings its southern hook out to sea, the surf-smashed Angle Peninsula lures beachgoers to a quirkily revamped boat that bills itself as the world's first solar-powered seaweed kitchen. At the helm is forager and seaweed evangelist Jonathan Williams, who ditched his nine-to-five office job to comb Pembrokeshire's shores for seaweeds to pep up the takeaway dishes at Café Môr. This is beach food at its finest, whether you go for a breakfast bap with laverbread, homemade pickles and seaweed-chilli sauce, or a lobster roll slathered in seaweed butter. For more seafood, including local Atlantic Edge oysters sustainably harvested by marine biologist

Andy Woolmer, pop into the Old Point House next door.
Old Point House, Angle; https://beachfood.co.uk; closed Mon & Tue

06 WILD ABOUT PEMBROKESHIRE

"All the world's problems can be solved by seaweed. Aches and pains, arthritis and iodine deficiency. Biofuels for the aviation industry. Global hunger. You name it," says John Mansfield, who calls the ravishing coast of St Davids home. Together with his wife, Julia, he runs eye-opening seashore foraging walks, which soon teach you to tell your bladderwrack from your sea lettuce.

Afterwards, nip into their coolly designed art deco cafe in the heart of St Davids, the Really Wild Emporium, for coffee and a seaweed brownie, or dinner spotlighting forage-focused dishes like carrot and hogweed pakora, slow-cooked Gwaun Valley lamb with wild garlic buds, and meadowsweet and lemon posset.
24 High Street, St Davids; https://reallywildemporium.co.uk; closed Mon & Tue

07 GRUB KITCHEN

"Bugs aren't disgusting, they are the key to a more sustainable future," enthuses entomologist, ecologist and farmer Dr Sarah Beynon – the heart and soul of the Bug Farm in St Davids.

After getting an insight into the beauty of insects in the farm's bughouse and on its surrounding meadow trails, book a table for lunch at the Grub Kitchen, where Sarah's husband, Andy Holcroft, cooks terrific grub in the truest sense of the expression.

You might begin your meal with spicy crickets, followed by a signature bug burger with polenta fries. If you don't fancy bugs, there are plant-based dishes and local seafood to try, such as Solva crab on toasted sugar kelp focaccia with fennel slaw and nursery salad. Grab a box of choc-chip cricket cookies before you leave.
Lower Harglodd Farm, St Davids; www.thebugfarm.co.uk; closed Mon

08 LLYS MEDDYG

In the cheerful seaside village of Newport, this handsome Georgian coaching inn, reborn as a boutique hotel and restaurant, has carved out a sensational reputation for food championing foraged, fermented, home-smoked and garden-grown ingredients. Shunning food miles, the menu is lightly creative, with dishes such as hot-smoked salmon (from their own smokehouse) with horseradish espuma and kohlrabi salad, and Welsh lamb tortellini with spiced yoghurt and sea greens. With reclaimed wood, low ceilings and soft lighting, the restaurant is a mix of coastal cool and rustic mountain chalet in look and feel. There's a lovely garden for summer dining.
East St, Newport; www.llys meddyg.com

WHERE TO STAY

THE LITTLE RETREAT

To cover Pembrokeshire's large area, consider more than one base. On the same site as Annwn (see stop 4), on the Lawrenny Estate, you can glamp on the wooded shores of the Cleddau Estuary at this retreat. Luxury domes have wood-fired hot tubs and stargazing tents come with outdoor bathtubs. *www.littleretreats.co.uk*

THE GROVE

This country manor in the Narberth hills is a class act with its lavish Arts and Crafts interior and food led by what's in season in the kitchen garden. *https://grovenarberth. co.uk*

WHAT TO DO

PEMBROKESHIRE COAST PATH

Work off the food with a brisk walk along this 300km (186 mile) long coast path, which rambles up and over gorse-clad cliffs and through kissing gates to one gorgeous castaway bay and Iron Age hill fort after the next. St Davids, birthplace of Wales' patron saint and home to its most impressive medieval cathedral, is a good starting point. *www.pembrokeshire coast.wales/coast-path*

CELEBRATIONS

Summer and autumn bring a sprinkling of food festivals to the coast of Pembrokeshire. In June, Tenby's South Beach throws its street food festival and Pembrokeshire Fish Week (held at multiple locations) reels in seafood fans, with tastings, cookery workshops, demonstrations, foraging sessions and all-round fishy feasting. The food-loving town of Narberth holds its food festival on the last weekend in September, a mix of live music, chef demonstrations, street food and stalls selling everything from Welsh cheese to chorizo, beer and preserves.

GET THERE
Skye is five hours by car from its
nearest international airports,
Glasgow and Edinburgh. Inverness
Airport serves regional flights
– travel by train from there to
mainland station Kyle of Lochalsh
for onward local bus connections
with the island's capital, and useful
base, Portree.

ISLE OF SKYE

STAFFIN
UIG
05 STEIN
Rona
08
EDINBANE
COLBOST
DUNVEGAN 04
Isle of
Skye
Raasay
03 PORTREE
02
BRACADALE COILLORE
07
TALISKER CARBOST SLIGACHAN Scalpay
01
BROADFORD
Sea of the
Hebrides
GLENBRITTLE
ELGOL ISLEORNSAY
08

[Scotland]

ELEMENTAL EATING ON SKYE

This mythical Hebridean island produces some of Scotland's finest foods, which talented local chefs use to create dishes inspired by the epic landscapes.

Skye is having a culinary moment – and long may it continue. Located in the northwest of Scotland, this is the largest island of the Inner Hebrides and arguably the region's finest source of local produce. Skye's dark, jagged shores are hugged by the UK's clearest seas, making it ideal for hand-dived scallops and oyster farming in particular. Thousands of wild red deer also roam freely, while its temperate climate and sheltered lochs allow for foraging of wild garlic and seaweed.

While there's long been a fine dining undertone on Skye, a new wave of no-frills sheds, trucks and restaurants slinging oysters, pizzas and pastries keep it affordable for most, with dining establishments often headed up by local people, for local people. You'll often find restaurateurs who've never left the island relying on their childhood friends, multi-generational

fishermen, to supply produce, while distillers craft small batch spirits inspired by the nature around them.

Skye is made less remote by its own road bridge, which allows year-round access and gives it an edge over other Scottish islands. Locals have largely benefitted from the bridge, which opened in 1995, as connections continue and businesses can remain open, should they choose to, outside of the traditional peak tourism season of March to October.

Its dramatic landscape and mysticism often dominate travel itineraries. No surprise: this is an enchanting island where fairies and dinosaurs roamed, or at least the dinosaur footprints at An Corran Beach prove the latter. Today, the self-proclaimed Misty Isle is a real food destination with visitors the world over making a bee-line for Skye on self-led food tours that sample the best of its regional Scottish cuisine.

01 RED SKYE

Found just a couple of miles over the Skye Bridge from mainland Scotland, Red Skye naturally acts as a culinary introduction to the island for many visitors. Head chef John Brown has spent more than 35 years cooking on Scotland's west coast and his experience shines through in the locally inspired menu. Lobster, scallops and venison all feature.

Red Skye's set-up within a former primary schoolhouse is relaxed, with no frills and a competitively priced menu. It's no surprise that this place gets booked up quickly.

Breakish; www.redskye restaurant.co.uk; closed Sun

02 ISLE OF SKYE BAKING COMPANY

Who doesn't like the smell of oven-fresh loaves? This delightful shop in Portree's Old Woolen Mill ticks all the boxes – from bread to poppy cakes, and then some.

It's on an industrial estate a short walk from the harbour, but the location doesn't deter fans. Quirky products such as Raasay gin-flavoured shortbread and Talisker whisky chocolate spread are often on sale. Opening hours can change during the summer because the team pop up at Scottish markets and events, so check online before visiting

The Old Woolen Mill, Dunvegan Rd, Portree; www.isleofskyebakingcom pany.co.uk; closed Tue, Sat & Sun

03 ISLE OF SKYE DISTILLERS

Scotland's islands shape the story and taste of its world-famous spirits, and Skye is no stranger to distilling. New kid on the block Isle of Skye Distillers produces the award-winning Misty Isle gin, featuring fresh water from the Storr Lochs and botanicals unique to the topographic elevation of Skye.

On Wednesdays and Fridays join expert distillers at their Gin School to concoct a unique bottle of gin, yours to take home. From selecting the botanicals to labelling the bottle, every step of the process is covered in this three-hour session, which also includes a bonus 10% off in the shop afterwards.

Rathad na Slignich, Portree; www.isleofskyedistillers.com

01 Showing off Skye's
local speciality

02 The colourful village
of Portree

03 Three Chimneys
weaves Skye bounty
into its menus

04 Torched scallop at
Edinbane Lodge

04 EDINBANE LODGE

Housed within a building dating back to 1543, Edinbane Lodge is the only restaurant in the Highlands to be awarded Four AA Rosettes. Chef patron Calum Montgomery, a Skye local, takes full advantage of his close relationship with island fishermen and crofters, some of whom are even childhood friends.

His seasonal menu features local oysters, mussels and wagyu as staples, and the unique mileage menu is another welcome addition to this fine-dining establishment. With zero miles on the clock for many items, farm-to-table really is put into practice here.

Old Dunvegan Road, Edinbane;
www.edinbanelodge.com; closed
Sun-Tue

05 LOCH BAY

Established in 2016 by renowned chef Michael White, Loch Bay sits in a row of whitewashed cottages overlooking the Waternish Peninsula. The crofting township of Stein may feel like an odd spot for Skye's only Michelin star, but it is worth persisting with the single track road.

Just twenty covers make up this intimate Scottish-French restaurant whose sole menu offering is Fruits de Mer – prawns are caught at the jetty opposite; it doesn't get fresher than that. A real log fire and Harris Tweed furnishings complete the cosy experience, while Skye's oldest pub, The Stein Inn, is next door.

1 Macleods Terrace, Stein;
www.lochbay-restaurant.co.uk;
closed Sun & Mon

06 THE THREE CHIMNEYS

The Three Chimneys is up there as Skye's most acclaimed restaurant, so it should come as no surprise that its tables are some of the UK's most sought after. Book well ahead to dine in this gorgeously secluded spot on the bonnie banks of Loch Dunvegan.

Head chef Scott Davies weaves Skye's bountiful produce found on land, sea and 'Skye' through his menus, stuffed with the island's rich seafood and game heritage. Loch Dunvegan crab is a must, as are the double-dived Sconser scallops. For a special treat, book the chef's table, then stay in one of its six adjoining luxury guest rooms.

Colbost, Dunvegan;
www.threechimneys.co.uk

05 Oysters waiting
to be shucked at The
Oyster Shed

06 Oatmeal oyster
at Michelin-starred
Loch Bay

07 Skye's bracing
Fairy Pools

07 THE OYSTER SHED

Skye local Paul McGlynn inherited his oyster farm from his father in 1981 and has carried it on, almost losing it all in 2011 when a bacterial virus wiped out 1.75 million oysters. Fortunately, his business survived and in 2012 McGlynn set up The Oyster Shed as a place to sell local produce direct to customers. Later, it sprouted as this unassuming hillside seafood shack with a rustic lean-to overlooking the hills.

Locally caught crab, langoustine and scallops also feature on the menu at this year-round spot, popular with both locals and tourists. An oyster stop here makes an ideal amuse-bouche before a wee dram at the world-famous Talisker distillery at the foot of the hill.
Carbost Beag; www.theoysterman. co.uk; closed Sun

08 AN CRÙBH

An Crùbh, meaning 'the hub' in Scottish Gaelic, is a community general store, cafe and event space that supports reintegrated crofting through its stocking of local produce. Skye honey, seafood, meats, vegetables and ales make up just a handful of its regional specialities for sale, while gifts from island crafters and artists can also be purchased. Add in views across the Sound of Sleat and it's definitely worth the drive off the well-trodden track to get here – especially when timed with stand-up comedy nights, table-top sales, or a *cèilidh* (Scottish gathering with dancing and Gaelic folk music).
Sleat; www.ancrubh.com; closed Mon & Tue

WHERE TO STAY
KINLOCH LODGE
Once a 17th-century farmhouse, Kinloch Lodge later becoming a shooting lodge and family home before a hotel conversion in 1972. Little else but the hills, the sea and abundant wildlife surround this boutique lodging, and its unique guest rooms reflect the sheer beauty of its location. Its restaurant is also an experience: dine here for a real taste of Skye's larder.
www.kinloch-lodge. co.uk

BROADFORD HOTEL
Skye's history is everywhere to be seen, and the Broadford Hotel's liqueur-soaked past is a celebrated part of it. Drambuie, Skye's firewater, was first batched in this very hotel bar during the late 19th century. Today, the hotel is a four-star retreat with cosy bedrooms, sea views, hearty food and that famous island welcome.
www.broadford hotel.co.uk

07

WHAT TO DO
OLD MAN OF STORR
This hulking, pointy rock formation, which can be seen for miles around, is Skye's most photographed spot. It's arguably best tackled under dramatic skies – the moody weather only accentuates the landscape. Summit views cross the Sound of Raasay over to the mainland beyond.

THE FAIRY POOLS
Brave swimmers should head for this famed cluster of waterfalls and pools near Carbost. Scottish waters are bracing all year round, so pack a wetsuit for a deep dive into these natural, crystal clear pools. If it's too crowded, you could try the lesser-known Marble Pools at Torrin as an equally lovely alternative.

CELEBRATIONS
SKYE HIGHLAND GAMES
Each August, this authentic Highland tradition continues with thousands watching participants compete in events such as tossing the caber, piping and dancing. The longstanding tradition has taken place every August since 1877, bar the war years and the Covid pandemic.

SOUTHERN EUROPE

GET THERE

Tirana International Airport, also known as Rinas International, has direct connections with much of Europe. Buses from neighbouring countries including North Macedonia (Skopje) and Greece (Thessaloniki) arrive at the International Bus Station about 30 minutes' walk from the centre. Tirana is small enough to navigate mostly on foot.

01

[Albania]

TIRANA CALLING

Welcome to the most dynamic dining scene in the Balkans – here in Albania's graceful capital, locals are looking to the future while respecting their complex past.

Shepherds sipping *raki* on misted mountains passable only on horseback. Fishers emerging from the Mediterranean, salt residue staining their hands white. Towering mosques in one of Europe's few majority-Muslim countries. Some 173,000 nuclear bunkers — the legacy of Cold War paranoia, dotting the landscape. These are just some sketches of Albania, long neglected, easily misunderstood, and overwhelmingly deserving of a spot on any European gastronomic itinerary.

In this small country of fewer than three million people, the best and most varied dining (and drinking) experiences are to be found in the capital, Tirana. Here, BMW-driving political elite sip expertly crafted cocktails, tourists seek out some of Europe's finest seafood, and intrepid-minded foodies brave local delicacies such as *kokë qengji* — lamb's head

traditionally served to an honoured guest and available at several well-regarded restaurants. Wandering the streets you smell the spiced aroma of *byrek* (filled pastries often stuffed with spinach) and *qofte* (meatballs), available at kiosks for loose change.

Through four centuries of Ottoman rule, Albania maintained a fiercely simmering national identity symbolised by the warrior-hero Skanderbeg, who lends his name to Tirana's spacious and atmospheric central square. The 20th century saw invasion by Italy and then the hyper-Stalinist rule of homegrown dictator Enver Hoxha. Since the end of the Cold War, democratic Albania has been slowly rebuilding.

In recent years, tourists have started to take note of the country's stunning natural beauty and the warm hospitality of the inviting capital, but its deliciously complex food is still largely underrated.

01 ODA

Start your trip by paying homage to Albanian cuisine at its most traditional and rural. Inside a converted old-style Albanian house, Oda is decorated with artefacts dating to the Middle Ages. Its menu is as traditional as the decor, which means heavy on the mutton but also vegetarian options such as roasted bell peppers and stuffed aubergine, with warm homemade bread.
Rruga Luigj Gurakuqi; www.facebook.com/people/ODA-Restorant/100063520124785/

02 PAZARI I RI

After a hearty feast at Oda, wander just a hundred or so metres away to Pazari i Ri (New Bazaar) — follow the shouts of shopkeepers haggling with grandmothers over everything from fresh vegetables at the Green Market to fish straight out of the ocean at the venerable Ergi Fish store.

Grab a coffee at Ardi Caffe served by Ardian, the restaurant's warm and passionate owner, and watch the life of the city unfurl at the market's 150+ stalls.
Rruga Shemsi Haka; www.pazariiri.com

03 SALT RESTAURANT

Located in Blloku, Tirana's upscale dining and eating district, Salt is the antidote to the heaviness of traditional local fare. Since 2016, this sleek and classy restaurant has been serving fresh sushi with salmon sashimi, soft and buttery octopus, and Mediterranean-inspired classics such as fried feta cheese.

Brunch opening hours (on weekends) combined with an irresistible cocktail menu make Salt a tempting and popular option at any time of the day.
Rruga Pjetër Bogdani; https://salt.al

04 TARTUF SHOP RESTAURANT

On a gorgeous pedestrianised street near the pre-13th-century Fortress of Justinian (also known as Tirana Castle) lies the fantasy of all truffle lovers. Waiters will be happy to explain that the restaurant owner's dad lives in the mountains and keeps specially trained dogs who scour the soil for truffles.

01 Skanderbeg Square, named for an Albanian warrior-hero

02 Traditional coffee, Turkish-style

03 Tirana's skyline, framed by mountains

04 Dajti Ekspres skimming the forests beyond Tirana

This luxurious gourmet gold is then brought back to the restaurant to be richly heaped onto everything from spaghetti carbonara to hamburgers and even fried eggs during breakfast time.

Order the restaurant's signature negroni cocktail and let the sweetness of the drink mellow the intensely sharp truffle flavour that saturates the entire menu. *Kalaja Tiranes, Shëtitorja Murat Toptani; www.facebook.com/ tartufshop*

05 ARTIGIANO AT VILA

With an interior almost scientifically designed to set diners at ease, with leaves overhanging wooden seats in the lush, tranquil garden and indoor decorations that change with the seasons, Artigiano wins over locals and travellers alike.

Here, homemade olive oil made from olives grown on Albania's south coast is drizzled over lovingly produced pizzas topped with the freshest of burrata mozzarella.

Bring a book and enjoy the total experience of calm as the flames of the woodfired oven fill the air with the scent of the deliciousness set to arrive on your plate. *Rruga Papa Gjon Pali II 9; www. facebook.com/Artigiano.Tirane*

06 KOMITETI - KAFE MUZEUM

Part bar, part cafe, part museum, entering Komiteti feels like paying a visit to a wise and eccentric relative who has spent decades hoarding all manner of artefacts – Cold-War era phones, Ottoman-style shisha pipes and all manner of carvings decorate this place. It also happens to have 18 types of *raki* on hand. This pungent spirit made of grapes and frequently clocking in at over 40% alcohol is something of a rite of passage for visitors to the Balkans. Beware: the local belief that *raki* seldom leaves a hangover should be treated with suspicion. *Rruga Fatmir Haxhiu; www. facebook.com/komiteti. kafemuzeum/*

07 COLONIAL COCKTAILS ACADEMY

Just across the block from the house of former dictator Enver Hoxha sits one of the original bars of Tirana's now trendy Blloku

05 & 06 Salt
restaurant shows the
cool, contemporary
side of Tirana; sushi is
one of its specialities

07 BUNK'ART is housed
inside a defunct nuclear
bunker

district. For more than 10 years,
Colonial Cocktails Academy has
treated visitors to passionately
crafted cocktails of the highest
quality, including a tart Old
Fashioned, a lethal Long Island
Iced Tea, and all manner of its own
original creations and twists. Try
the Margarita Calabrese with white
tequila, mango, orange liqueur, red
pepper and fresh lemon juice. The
enchanting atmosphere and warm
service make this a perfect place to
end your day.
Rruga Pjetër Bogdani 3;
www.colonialtirana.com

WHERE TO STAY
PADAM BOUTIQUE HOTEL
Located in a classic Albanian villa and just a short walk from highlights such as Tirana Castle and Skanderbeg Square, this boutique hotel offers modern and comfortable lodgings. There's a restaurant on-site and many rooms come with balconies that overlook the villa's carefully tended garden.
https://padam.al

WHAT TO DO
BUNK'ART
Paranoid communist dictator Enver Hoxha is the reason why the Albanian landscape is pockmarked with more than 170,000 nuclear bunkers. Many are smaller than backyard sheds and gather dust in people's gardens, but the bunker in which BUNK'ART now resides was a serious installation with multiple layers, tunnels, communication rooms and other infrastructure. Now a contemporary art exhibition, it's a great place to experience the

juxtaposition of Albania's fearful communist past and its creative, outward-looking present.
*Rruga Fadil Deliu;
www.bunkart.al*

DAJTI EKSPRES
A short stroll away from BUNK'ART, this modern cable car lets visitors swap the underground for the mountain tops. The Dajti Ekspres claims to be Albania's most popular tourist attraction, and it's certainly a diverting way to spend an afternoon as you ascend the 1613m (5292ft) Dajti Mountain in picturesque comfort. A decent enough restaurant awaits you at the top, along with walking trails and even an 18-hole mini golf course.
*Stacioni i poshtem i teleferikut, Komuna Linze; https://
dajtiekspres.com*

CELEBRATIONS
KORCA BEER FESTIVAL
A three-hour drive from Tirana, the city of Korçë earns its place on tourists' maps thanks to its famous beer festival. Some 100,000 visitors descend on the city every year (typically in August) for several days of beer drinking, live music and general rowdy celebration.
https://festaebirres.com

GET THERE
The nearest Croatian airport is in Pula, but it has a limited flight schedule. Ljubljana (Slovenia) and Trieste (Italy) are within a two-hour drive and have car-rental desks.

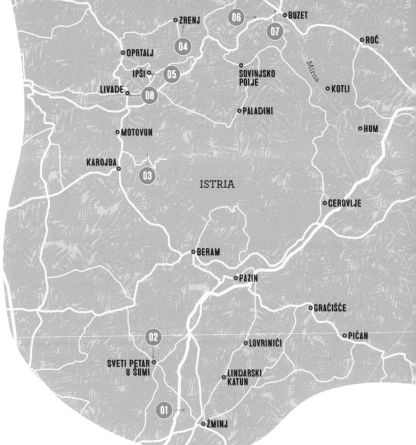

[Croatia]

ISTRIA'S EARTHLY DELIGHTS

Wine, olive oil, truffles and cheese – underrated Istria has an abundance of classy produce, made the traditional way on one of Croatia's most beautiful peninsulas.

This little corner of Croatia has changed nationality so many times you'd think it might have an identity crisis. In the last 100 years alone, it's swapped hands between Austria, Italy and Yugoslavia. Yet Istria has clung on to its local character throughout its tumultuous history, and food has played an enormous part in that.

Small, family-run farms remain the dominant feature in a bucolic landscape of rolling hills swathed in ancient woodland. Tractors are often the main traffic on the winding country lanes, puttering between orchard, field, olive grove and vineyard. Those forests and fields sweep up to medieval hilltop towns, their higgledy-piggledy stone houses home to gourmet produce shops and restaurants. And there's barely a village here without a *konoba* (pub) rustling up meals from goods harvested locally.

Makers are keen to share the story of their produce and their region with visitors. Days can be filled calling in to local farms, with endless samples enthusiastically brought out to try. There's enough variety and quality here to build a fine picnic – olive oil, cheeses, sausages, hams, all kinds of fruit and fruit brandy, and wine produced using grapes unfamiliar to most.

There's also the chance to find your own ingredients. Alongside Italy, Istria is the only place in the world where you can find the white truffle. The locations where they grow are well guarded, but it's possible to join trackers and their dogs to unearth both white and the more common black truffle. In autumn, the prime hunting season, there will be some sort of truffle dish on every menu, from the most upscale restaurants to down-home *agriturismos*. Come with a half-empty suitcase – you'll be taking a lot of produce home.

01 MLJEKARA LATUS

Mljekara Latus offers a snapshot of everything good about the Istrian food scene. The family-run dairy, in a small village surrounded by pastures, clings hard to tradition. Owner Sandi Orbanić first made cheese with his grandmother as a child, and the recipes he uses today haven't changed. But he has an eye on the future, too, with a modern cheese and milk bar now part of the story. Here, visitors can try all the spoils of the dairy through guided tastings – from aged, hard Žminj cheese and fat balls of mozzarella to soft truffle cheese.

Gornji Orbanići 12/D, Žminj; www.mljekaralatus.hr; closed Sun

02 PRŠUTANA JELENIĆ

Framed awards fill the walls of the tasting room of Pršutana Jelenić – testament to the quality of the produce made here by brothers Luka and Paolo. That produce is pig, with *pršut* (dry-cured ham) a speciality at this local producer, alongside pork loin and sausages. Plentiful samples are dished up to visitors, the ham delicately carved by one of the brothers and accompanied by a glass of white wine. They also explain the process, taking guests to a curing room stuffed to the rafters with dangling ham legs and salamis.

Pazinska cesta 2c, Žminj; www.istarskiprsut.hr; closed Sat & Sun

03 BENVENUTI VINA

It feels wrong to call Benvenuti a business when running it is such a passion for Nikola and his brother Albert. "I'm completely addicted to wine-growing," says Nikola, only half joking. The Benvenuti brothers produce wines from seven grape varieties they grow in vineyards surrounding the hilltop town of Motovun. Each can be tasted alongside platters of local cheese and meat at the tasting room of their farmhouse, and there's a chance to tour the winery too. It's a great place to get to grips with less familiar wines, including smoky red Teran, crisp white Malvazijas and sweet Muškats.

Kaldir 7, Motovun; www.benvenuti vina.com; closed Sun

01 The picturesque patchwork of Istria's vineyards, olive groves and terracotta roofs

02 A ham tasting at Pršutana Jelenić

03 Sunrise in Oprtalj

04 Sample top-notch olive oils at Ipša

04 AGROTURIZAM TONČIĆ

Half the pleasure of the Tončić experience is finding it – it's a lovely drive through the hills to reach the *agriturismo*. Just when you think you must have taken a wrong turning and are hopelessly lost, there it is – a pretty cluster of farm buildings looking out over the fields and vineyards.

Hyper-local is the focus here. The food on the menu is either home-made, foraged or sourced from nearby producers in Istria.

The menu changes according to the season, but might include dishes such as mushroom ravioli or chicken stew. In summer, guests can enjoy them on the shaded terrace with lush views of olive groves and the Mirna River Valley;

in winter, hunker down by the fire in the stone-walled dining room. *Čabarnica 42, Zrenj, Oprtalj; Fri–Sun 12.30–11pm; www. agroturizam-toncic.com*

05 IPŠA

Come for the terrific views over the forests, vineyards and hilltop towns of the Mirna Valley below, and stay for some of world's finest extra-virgin olive oil. Irene Ipša and her family have been growing olives in groves dotted around northern Istria since 1998, turning them into the golden oil in a handsome white building high on a plateau near Oprtalj.

Here, they offer tours of the olive mill, sharing stories of their family, farming and the Istrian

peninsula. The tour ends with a sampling of the four oils they produce, enjoyed in a beautifully designed tasting room or out on the terrace beneath the vines. *Ipši 10, Livade; www.ipsa-maslinovaulja.com*

06 NATURA TARTUFI

"Truffles are in my blood," says Daniela Puh. She is the sixth generation of her family to hunt for the tubers, often joining her mother and their dogs to root for them in the Buzeština forests of northern Istria.

Their finds are packed up and shipped to the world's top restaurants – and are available to taste and buy in their shop. Visitors can also join the family

05

on a truffle hunt in their own
private woodland. Keep a special
eye out for the rare and prized
white truffle, in season between
September and January; a
specimen sold at auction for
€103,000 in 2021.
Srnegla 21, Mala Huba;
www.pietroandpietro.com

07 AURA PROIZVODI

The fruit that hangs heavy from
the trees in orchards across
northern Istria is put to excellent
use at the Aura Proizvodi, a
distillery at the foot of the lovely
hilltop town of Buzet. It produces
22 types of oak-aged brandy, as
well as fruit liqueurs and jams.

Alongside pear, plum and
apple, there are plenty of
unexpected flavours, such as
carob or white mistletoe, much
of it made from wild, foraged
ingredients. All are available to
try and buy in the shop and tasting
room, an atmospheric place
with thick stone walls and heavy
wooden beams.
Istarske Brigade 2/1, Buzet;
www.aura.hr

08 RESTAURANT ZIGANTE

In the foyer of Zigante is a model
of the world's largest truffle
(weighing in at 1.31kg/2.9lbs),
unearthed right here in Istria.
It's an early marker of the

establishment's complete devotion
to the tuber – having declared
itself Croatia's only specialist
truffle restaurant, it is undoubtedly
the place to come in Istria to
try truffles in every which
way possible.

Zigante has a formal atmosphere
and diners are served by suited
waiters at tables with starched
white tablecloths – consider this
a special occasion restaurant
and enjoy the wine-paired tasting
menus, where the stars of the
show are dishes such as shrimp
ravioli with truffle, and truffle
ice-cream.
Livade 7, Livade;
www.restaurantzigante.com

WHERE TO STAY
PALAZZO ANGELICA
At the edge of the hilltop village of Oprtalj, this boutique hotel is in a handsome, pink 19th-century villa. There are terrific views over the village or the surrounding forest from its eight spacious rooms and suites. The spa and pool are welcome additions after a day exploring (and feasting), as is the chance to have a brandy by the fire in the lounge.
www.palazzo angelica.com

ROXANICH DESIGN HOTEL
An unexpected find in so traditional a region, the striking interiors of the Roxanich would be just as at home in a modern urban hotel as in one found in Motovun in rural Croatia. Rooms come with playful wallpaper and furnishings, while social spaces have a slightly more industrial feel. Sealing the deal are an excellent restaurant, infinity pool and spa.
www.roxanich.com

WHAT TO DO
HILLTOP VILLAGE TOUR
Often built on sites first inhabited by the Romans, with fortifications added later by Venetian rulers, Istria's medieval hilltop towns are remarkably atmospheric places for a wander. Hours can be lost ambling their narrow cobbled streets, admiring ancient stone houses and popping out at thick defensive walls for magnificent views across the countryside. Try Motovun, Oprtalj, Buje, Grožnjan, Buzet, Završje and Hum for starters.

CELEBRATIONS
Istria is so in love with truffles it has an entire festival devoted to the area's magnificent tuber. Truffle Days runs throughout October, with special menus in restaurants, a truffle fair and cooking demonstrations. The town of Buzet also makes a giant omelette each year, using 10kg (22lbs) of truffles and more than 2000 eggs.
www.trufflefair.com

GET THERE

Abruzzo is easily accessed by bus or train from Rome and the contiguous regions of Lazio, Le Marche, Molise and Campania. Sulmona, L'Aquila and Pescara are the main cities and transport hubs. Pescara has an international airport as well as train, bus and ferry links.

01

Adriatic
Sea

ABRUZZO

PENNE

PESCARA

06

ASSERGI

01

05

SANTO
STEFANO DI
SESSANIO

CHIETI

L'AQUILA

NOCCIANO

02

07

GUARDIAGRELE

ABRUZZO

POPOLI

VASTO

CASOLI

SULMONA

03

Lago di
Bomba

AVEZZANO

COCULLO

04

SCANNO

[Italy]

ABRUZZO: THE REAL DOLCE VITA

Italy's Abruzzo region is a land of ancient beech forests and lofty mountain massifs, with a food pantry that includes saffron, lamb and lentils – here, tradition rules.

Choosing Italy's finest food region is like choosing your favourite Ferrari. They're all ridiculously good. But a case should be made for Abruzzo, the oft-overlooked tract of mountains and coastline in the central-east of the peninsula that has so far evaded tourist inundation, despite its proximity to Rome. You can dine in rustic heaven here, from a mossy mountain village to a traditional *trabucco* (fishing platform) beside the Adriatic.

Sheep farming has ancient roots in Abruzzo, and in days of yore the subsistence food of roaming shepherds was lamb, skewered and grilled over charcoal. Today, these juicy snacks are known as *arrosticini* and are staples in many local restaurants.

Lentils, sometimes called the 'meat of the poor', are another Abruzzese mountain food. The gourmet lentils of the Gran Sasso region thrive between 1000m (3280ft) and 1600m (5249ft) and inspire an annual festival in the medieval village of Santo Stefano di Sessanio. Not far away, the Navelli region produces some of the world's finest saffron, used in aromatic pasta dishes such as *cannarozzetti allo zafferano*.

Every Italian region has its speciality pasta. Abruzzo's version is *chitarra*, a thick square-cut spaghetti made using a unique stringed instrument resembling a guitar. For fish, head to the Costa dei Trabocchi, a 70km (43.5-mile) coastal strip between Ortona and San Salvo known for its distinctive sea-jutting fishing platforms, many of which are now atmospheric restaurants.

And of course there's wine. In this region, the story begins and ends with Montepulciano d'Abruzzo. The rustic, peppery tipple gained international clout in the early 21st century and enjoys a longstanding friendship with *arrosticini* and local pasta dishes.

① ARROSTICINI DIVINI

This casual restaurant in the revived centre of L'Aquila is part of a small franchise, but still feels distinctly Abruzzese. Its obligatory menu item is the region's favourite street food: *arrosticini* – charcoal-grilled lamb skewers seasoned with rosemary. Marbled meat is first threaded onto wooden skewers before being delivered to your table in colourful ceramic pitchers.

Arrosticini's best *amici* (friends) are *pane 'onde* (toasted bread soaked in olive oil) and a glass of Montepulciano d'Abruzzo wine. If you're particularly ravenous, add the rich tomato bruschetta or a saffron-laced pasta dish *Via Castello 13/15, L'Aquila; www.arrosticinidivini.it*

② SANTO STEFANO DI SESSANIO

Certified as an endangered heritage food by Italy's Slow Food Presidium, Santo Stefano di Sessanio's lentils have been cultivated by hand on the plateaus of the nearby Gran Sasso mountains for over 1000 years. Today, 12 local farmers continue to faithfully nurture the crop around this medieval hill town.

Known for their nutty mint flavour and cholesterol-lowering properties, the *lenticchie* are simmered in a simple soup served with meat skewers and fried bread. Most of Santo Stefano's restaurants can rustle up an authentic *zuppa* (soup). If you can, come for the annual lentil harvest, the Sagra della Lenticchia, in the first week of September.

③ MERCATO SULMONA

Sulmona's Piazza Garibaldi is one of central Italy's understated beauties – an expansive Gothic-Renaissance square bordered on one side by the noble arches of a 13th-century aqueduct and overlooked on the other by the brooding Morrone Mountains. Every Saturday and Wednesday, the square is given extra life with a market plying everything from cheap shoes to expensive cheese underneath a huddle of white awnings.

You'll see old *nonnas* (grandmas) selling shiny courgettes and local farmers plying red garlic from the Valle Peligna. After touring the stalls, head for the food trucks. The highlight snack is a panini filled with *porchetta abruzzese* (moist, slow-

01 The medieval village of Villa Santa Maria

02 Santo Stefano di Sessanio is famous for its local lentils

03 Traditional skewered *arrosticini* lamb

04 *Confetti* – sugared almonds – in Sulmona

roasted pork stuffed with herbs and fennel), which you can savour sitting on the steps next to the aqueduct. *Piazza Garibaldi, Sulmona; www. facebook.com/mercatosulmona*

04 MUSEO CONFETTI PELINO

Sulmona is synonymous with *confetti* (sugar-covered almonds) and *confetti* is synonymous with Mario Pelino who founded his legendary sweet-making business in the city in 1783. The Pelinos are members of Henokiens, an exclusive association of companies that have been run by the same family for more than 200 years.

These brightly coloured sugar-covered almonds are traditionally presented to guests at weddings, baptisms and communions. They

are usually sold in pretty, decorated gift bags called *bomboniere*. A walk along Sulmona's Corso Ovidio will reveal numerous shops offering them in artistic packages. For the ultimate insight, call by the Pelino factory where a compact museum divulges the history of this long-standing confectionary art. *Via Stazione Introdacqua 55, Sulmona; http://confetti mariopelino.com; closed Sun*

05 NESTORE BOSCO WINERY

For an immersive oenological experience head to Nestore Bosco, one of Abruzzo's oldest wineries. It was founded in Pescara in 1897 by Giovanni Bosco and is now run by the fifth generation of the same family. The business moved inland in

1983 to the village of Nocciano in the foothills of the Majella Mountains, where a cooler microclimate yields more concentrated wines. Tours take in the vineyard, the tunnelled cellars, a small museum and the obligatory tastings. "Visiting Nestore Bosco is an immersion in the story of Abruzzo thanks to the museum itinerary installed in the underground tunnels of the winery," says Nestore Bosco customer care manager Giovanna Colecchia.

Tours take in the vineyard as well as the museum, and finish with tastings. Visitors get to try Nestore Bosco's iconic ruby red Montepulciano, which has a tannic vanilla-berry flavour, plus a couple of high quality, aged *riservas* loaded with more spicy, peppery notes.

"A special wine to taste is the PAN Montepulciano d'Abruzzo, whose label is a piece of art by the Master Pietro Cascella," Colecchia adds. *Contrada Casali 147, Nocciano; www.nestorebosco.com/en*

06 LA CUCINERIA

While the port and seaside town of Pescara is well-known for its fish, it also showcases excellent executions of Abruzzo's emblematic pasta, *chitarra*. The thick noodles with a soft, sticky texture come in multiple renditions in La Cucineria, a modern version of a trattoria in Pescara's pedestrianised town centre. *Sapori tipici abruzzesi* (typical Abruzzo flavours) are the focus here.

There's *chitarrone* in a carbonara sauce with truffles, *chitarrina* in a creamy courgette sauce with pine nuts, and *chitarra alla teramana con le pallottine*, which to the unversed outsider is spaghetti in a tangy tomato sauce typical of Teramo province served with tiny meatballs. The latter is an Abruzzo classic and a good choice if you're vacillating on what to order. *Via Clemente de Cesaris 26, Pescara; www. lacucineriapescara.it*

07 TRABUCCO TRIMALCIONE

Trabocchi (singular *trabucco*) are historic fishing platforms mostly found in Abruzzo, Molise and Puglia whose origins are thought to date back to the Phoenicians. Invariably made of wood, they are accessible from the shore and distinctive because of their long antennae that stretch above the water, supporting large fishing nets.

Half way along Abruzzo's 'trabocchi coast' just north of the town of Vasto, this small restaurant inhabits a traditional *trabucco* overlooking the Adriatic and rimmed by a golden sweep of beach at Punta Penna. It's a small, authentic family-run place with just three tables – be sure to book in advance.

The food is as fabulous as the sunset views. Bank on Prosecco to start, a classic *brodetto* (fish stew), followed by baked fish and, of course, dessert. There's no printed menu. Instead, you'll be treated to whatever's available on any given day. *Porto di Punta Penna, Vasto; www. traboccotrimalcione.it; closed Mon*

WHERE TO STAY
LA FATTORIA DI MORGANA
Rustic, traditional and salt-of-the-earth in true Abruzzese fashion, this *agriturismo* occupies a small farm below the stunning village of Opi in the Abruzzo, Lazio and Molise National Park. Surrounded by mountains and beechwoods, you'll be sharing digs with a menagerie of free-roaming ducks, goats, pigs, horses and Abruzzo sheepdogs. The homemade meals are a major highlight.
www.facebook.com/ lafattoriadimorgana

SEXTANTIO
Welcome to a charming *albergo diffuso* (dispersed hotel) with 28 distinctive rooms and suites scattered throughout the small village of Santo Stefano di Sessanio. Helping to reinvigorate one of Italy's lesser-known settlements, the hotel marries handmade bedding and rustic furniture with underfloor heating, mood lighting and standalone baths. The affiliated restaurant, Locanda Sotto Gli Archi, serves all the regional specialities (including lentils) in a 16th-century dining room.
www.sextantio.it/en/ santostefano/abruzzo

WHAT TO DO
SENTIERO DELLA LIBERTÀ
Combine hill walking with historical insight on the legendary Freedom Trail, an erstwhile escape route used by Allied POWs and Italian freedom fighters escaping from Nazi-occupied Sulmona during WWII. The route has been turned into a 60km (37-mile)-long hiking trail, starting just outside Sulmona and zigzagging across the mountains of Majella National Park.
www.parcomajella.it/ Il-Sentiero-della-Liberta.htm

CELEBRATIONS
GIOSTRA CAVALLERESCA DI SULMONA
Translating as the 'knightly joust', this revived Renaissance festival transforms Sulmona's Piazza Garibaldi into a medieval parade ground where competing horse-riders display their equine skills amid much pageantry. It's held on the last weekend in July.
www.giostrasulmona.it

GET THERE
Bologna's Guglielmo
Marconi Airport is well-
connected with flights
throughout Europe; Bologna
Central station sits on Italy's
high-speed rail line. From
there, the region is best
explored by car.

01

[Italy]

FEASTING IN BOLOGNA & BEYOND

Emilia-Romagna is arguably Italy's culinary cradle, home to gastronomic traditions dating to the Middle Ages and a cavalcade of icons of Italian cuisine.

Bologna has been an anchor of European intellectualism, invention, arts and progressive thinking for centuries. Home to the oldest continually operating university in the world, it's no coincidence that this medieval hotbed of knowledge facilitated one of Italy's richest agriculture regions. Emilia-Romagna farms alone account for 5.8% of Italy's GDP and practice world standard-setting innovation and quality control – this region was the first in Italy to adopt specific rules regarding the production of quality-controlled foods and laws on food traceability.

Emilia-Romagna has more than 44 DOP (*Denominazione di Origine Protetta*) and IGP (*Indicazione Geografica Protetta*) products – the Holy Grails of speciality European food items. Every meal here is a journey through the epicurean echelons

of the world's most famous cuisine. In short, Emilia-Romagna is one of the most wonderful places to eat.

The region's culinary pedigree is centred on some of Italy's most famous staples: meat-based sauces (*ragù*, often misnamed as Bolognese sauce), egg-based pastas (tagliatelle, lasagne, garganelli), stuffed pastas (tortellini, tortelloni) and copious swine products (mortadella, lard, sausage and salumi).

The region's ancient traditions of winemaking (Sangiovese, Lambrusco), balsamic vinegar production (*aceto balsamico*) and cheesemaking (*Parmigiano-Reggiano*, *Grana Padano*) evolved as natural accompaniments from centuries-old techniques and recipes; in many cases these products have overtaken main dishes to become the stars of the table. Those in search of spaghetti Bolognese will be disappointed, but otherwise eating in Emilia-Romagna knows no rival.

01 LE SFOGLINE

Nearly every restaurant in Bologna serves the city's classic lasagne recipe: dollops of rich *ragù* and creamy béchamel between rows of layered egg pasta (the spinach-laced green version is most traditional). No ham, no ricotta, no mozzarella – no nonsense! At Le Sfogline, sisters Daniela and Monica toil away daily inside their takeaway fresh pasta shop, hand-rolling the pasta for some of Bologna's best lasagne, tortellini, tortelloni and much more.

Pasta here is sold prepared but uncooked, so you'll need cooking facilities at your accommodation: it's worth getting in the kitchen for this emblematic meal.
Via Belvedere 7B, Bologna; www. lesfogline.it; closed Sun

02 ACETAIA PEDRONI

Fresh off a lottery win, cowherd Giuseppe Pedroni opened a tavern in an outbuilding of a 15th-century Benedictine monastery near Modena in 1862. But what to do with the discarded chestnut wood barrels that held marsala wine for customers? The answer, of course, was to start a battery of traditional balsamic vinegar.

Today, sixth generation owner Giuseppe Pedroni III manages the centuries-old battery and tavern, where you can indulge in – with reservations – award-winning Modena Balsamic Vinegar IGP (the more affordable version you might see in foreign supermarkets) and Traditional Balsamic Vinegar DOP (a prized, far more expensive

nectar aged for at least 12 years that will change your life forever). "The best way to taste balsamic is to add it to what is in front of you," says Pedroni. "No special preparation is needed to open a bottle of 25-year-old Traditional, no need for a 5-star recipe. Balsamic is so versatile that it can marry anyone."
Via Risaia 6, Rubbiara di Nonantola; www.acetaiapedroni.it; closed Tue

03 FRATELLI GALLONI

Parma's two gourmet delights elicit such foodgasmic cries worldwide that the city has been named a Unesco Creative City of Gastronomy. While *Parmigiano-Reggiano* (Parmesan cheese) production casts a wider net across

01 Emilia-Romagna's farming riches are sold at Bologna markets

02 Bologna's Old Town

03 Stuffed tortellini are a regional speciality

04 Prized Parma hams hang in a shop window

05 Emilia-Romagna is the heartland of Parmesan cheesemaking

the region between Parma and Bologna, *prosciutto di Parma* (dry-cured Parma ham) has been made Parma-adjacent only at least as far back as 100 BCE, when Roman senator Cato the Censor raved about the sweet, delicate ham produced here.

The Galloni family hasn't been at it *that* long, but they have been ageing some of the world's best prime Italian Heavy Pig legs for over 60 years at their base 21km (13 miles) south of Parma. A visit here – reserve ahead – provides the opportunity to tour normally off-limit facilities and then pair exquisite prosciutto with fine countryside views.
Via Roma 85, Langhirano; www.galloniprosciutto.it; closed Sat & Sun

04 TRATTORIA DA AMERIGO

Deep in Emilia-Romagna truffle territory, 30km west of Bologna, the small village of Savigno is home to the single most memorable menu in all of Emilia-Romagna. The Michelin-starred Trattoria da Amerigo isn't terribly expensive or whatsoever pretentious; instead, it lets seasonal ingredients and regional traditions take all the credit.

"Our valley is particularly rich in good, healthy raw materials that sum up, in just a few miles, the best of what an entire region has to offer, in a landscape that alternates between farms and crops and unexpected buildings and historic sites," says owner Alberto Bettini. His grandparents started the

restaurant in 1934 as a tavern to drink wine and play card games.
Via Guglielmo Marconi 14/16, Savigno; www.amerigo1934.com; closed Mon & Tue

05 TERRA DI BRISIGHELLA

A gaggle of distinctly petrol pump-like machines lining the back wall dispense local Sangiovese wine for €2/litre at this gourmet shop. It's run by Brisighella's agricultural cooperative, C.A.B (*Cooperativa Agricola Brisighellese*), which was set up in this postcard-perfect medieval village in 1962 to promote local commodities.

Brisighella's limited-production extra virgin olive oil, Brisighello DOP, was one of the first Italian olive oils to achieve the European Union's

05 Emilia-Romagna's traditional *ragù* is a world away from spaghetti Bolognese

06 The Path of the Gods hiking trail meanders from Bologna to Florence

rinds creates a beautiful contrast in the *piadina* – a contrast that is both territorial and indigenous," she says.
Piazzale John Fitzgerald Kennedy 2, Rimini; www.dallalella.it

07 TRATTORIA BERTOZZI

It's only fitting that your food tour should end back in Bologna. In a city where you can't toss a *tortellino* blindly without hitting a fantastic restaurant, Bertozzi manages to stand out.

Often touted as the city's best traditional restaurant by in-the-know culinarians, this unassuming trattoria is both a rousing good time (it becomes superfan HQ on Bologna FC game days) and a deeply serious dive into Bologna's famed specialities. Dare we say the city's best *tagliatelle al ragù*? But meatballs with peas, *gramigna* pasta with saffron, *guanciale* (cured pork cheeks) and courgette (zucchini) and a Sangiovese-braised beef shank are all knockouts as well. Reserve ahead.
Via Andrea Costa 84, Bologna; www.trattoriabertozzibologna.it; closed Sun

most important local product protection status.

Brisighella is also special because the local artichoke *carciofo Moretto* (Moretto artichoke) grows nowhere else in the world but here every April/May. In season, the artichokes are served in fresh pastas around town, but you can visit the Terra di Brisighella any time of year to pick up *carciofo Moretto sott'olio* (Moretto artichokes in oil), which marries the town's two prized products, alongside other local gourmet provisions.
Via Strada 2, Brisighella; www.terradibrisighella.it

06 LELLA AL MARE

Iconic green-and-white kiosks serving *piadina*, a Romagnolo-born, griddle-cooked flatbread made with lard or olive oil and stuffed with myriad combinations of cheeses, cold cuts and veggies, pepper Romagna's coast. It doesn't take long to realise this tasty treat is the snack of choice along the Riviera Romagnola, and Lella Al Mare in Rimini has become a benchmark destination for the area's favourite beach-strolling snack.

Here the *piadine* are served slightly gussied up in sit-down restaurant surrounds. The menu is chock-full of tempting variations, though Lella Al Mare owner Marina Nanni can't tear herself away from Cavallo di Battaglia: prosciutto, *squacquerone* cheese and caramelised figs.

"The sweet citrus from the fig

WHERE TO STAY

CASA MARIA LUIGIA
Celebrated Italian chef Massimo Bottura and his American wife Lara Gilmore transformed this Emilian countryside villa just outside Modena into a food- and art-focused B&B in 2019. A bed here also nets you a guaranteed table at Osteria Francescana, Bottura's palate-changing 3-star Michelin destination restaurant in Modena.
www.casamarialuigia.com

WHAT TO DO

THE PATH OF THE GODS
The ancient 130km (81 miles) Via degli Dei connecting Bologna and Florence was once walked by Etruscans and Romans, but then remained largely lost until 1979. Now this route through the Tuscan-Emilian Apennines can be covered on foot (five to eight days) or bike (two to three days). It takes in landscapes including centuries-old chestnut groves, dramatic rock formations at Riserva Naturale Contrafforte Pliocenico in Emilia-Romagna, and the olive tree-draped hillsides of Tuscany. Naturally, there's an abundance of traditional osterias and trattorias along the route.

06

CELEBRATIONS

TOUR-TLEN
'Tour-Tlen' means 'tortellini' in Bolognese dialect, and this culinary extravaganza held in October features two dozen or so local chefs reinterpreting the traditional *tortellini in brodo* (pork-stuffed pasta in broth) recipe.
www.tour-tlen.it

FESTIVAL DEL PROSCUITTO DI PARMA
Held over two days each September, Parma goes all out in celebration of its prized prosciutto, serving up gastronomic entertainment and cultural events in the city.
www.festivaldel prosciuttodiparma.com

SAGRA DEL CARCIOFO MORETTO
Brisighella's artichoke festival, usually held over a week mid-May, features music and food stands dedicated to the village's most famed culinary autochthon.

GET THERE

High-speed trains connect Naples to other major Italian cities, while non-stop flights reach Italian and European destinations, as well as Dubai. Public buses, funiculars and metro trains serve the city, though central Naples is easily explored on foot.

01

[Italy]

THE EXCESSES OF NAPLES & ITS ISLANDS

Bewitching, gregarious and perpetually peckish, Naples serves up a belt-busting spread, from basil-splotched pizzas and regal ragù *to lazy island lunches.*

Overshadowed by the fearsome volcano of Mt Vesuvius, Naples has an insatiable, almost fatalistic lust for life. The Neapolitans are masters of passion and pleasure, and nowhere is this more evident than at the Neapolitan table. Whether you're tucking into a humble plate of chilli-spiked *spaghetti alle vongole* (spaghetti with clams) or a decadent *casatiello* (Easter bread laced with Neapolitan salami, pancetta, pecorino and provolone), the city's dishes burst with an intensity matched only by their settings in boisterous pizzerias and markets, scruffy, sun-bleached marinas and fin-de-siècle cafes.

Naples is the capital city of southern Italy's fertile Campania region, one that famously produces sweet San Marzano tomatoes, creamy buffalo-milk mozzarella and artisan pasta from Gragnano. Naples itself claims *spaghetti alla puttanesca* (tomato passata, garlic,

capers, chilli and Gaeta olives) and *pasta alla genovese* (in a rich sauce of slow-cooked onions).

Fuelling the city's inimitable street life is some of the country's best and cheapest street food, including Naples' signature *pizza fritta* (fried pizza). Then there is Naples' world-famous pizza margherita (tomato, fior di latte and fresh basil), invented in 1899 by *pizzaiolo* Raffaele Esposito to appease a visiting Queen Margherita reputedly bored with fussy French nosh.

Not that Naples is a stranger to Gallic influence. French chefs working in local court kitchens shaped some of its most elaborate specialities, among them *sartù di riso*, a baked rice timbale (casserole-like pie) with meatballs, pork sausage, eggs, mozzarella, peas and *ragù* fit for a Bourbon royal. Come curious, come famished and leave your diet at the door. As the ancient Pompeiians would say, life is short – live it up.

01 PINTAURO

This cinnamon-scented pastry shop is so iconic that it has its own Neapolitan saying: 'Tène folla Pintauro!' (There's a queue at Pintauro!), wryly used to describe those who are preciously 'busy'. Pintauro itself has reason to feel important. After all, it was right here that 19th-century innkeeper Pasquale Pintauro first introduced Naples to the city's defining pastry, the *sfogliatella*, inspired by a dessert created at the Monastero Santa Rosa on the Amalfi Coast.

There are two versions – *frolla* (shortcrust) and *riccia* (filo) – both filled with sweet ricotta, semolina and candied citrus. Whichever you choose, devour it while strolling glorious Galleria Umberto I across the street.

Via Toledo 275, Naples; closed Tue

02 GRAN CAFFÈ GAMBRINUS

Once you've sipped a Neapolitan espresso, coffee elsewhere in Italy will leave you scoffing '*acqua sporca*' (dirty water). Dense and sinewy, *caffè* here is in a league of its own, a sucker-punch brew served in scalding cups.

Naples' most atmospheric coffee pit stop is Gran Caffè Gambrinus, a Belle-Époque whirl of mirrors, reliefs and Posillipo School paintings that has hosted everyone from Oscar Wilde to wartime anti-fascists.

Leave the outdoor tables to the tourists and sip with locals at the counter. Drink the complimentary glass of water first, to cleanse your palate.

Via Chiaia 1-2, Naples; www.grancaffegambrinus.com

03 LA PIGNASECCA

The city's oldest street market is in the heart of working-class Naples. Stalls heave with Piennolo cherry tomatoes, artichokes, aubergines (eggplants) and just-caught mackerel, squid and clams.

Local chefs, like Raffaele Denis, like to shop here. "Market deli Ai Monti Lattari is great for local cheeses", says Denis. Try the deli's house provola, then head to Friggitoria Fiorenzano to grab some *crocchè* (cheese-stuffed potato croquettes), or settle in at

Antica Pizzeria e Trattoria al 22 for aubergine parmigiana, woodfired in terracotta ramekins.
Via Pignasecca, Naples

04 LA MASARDONA

Technically translated as 'fried pizza', *pizza fritta* is more like a flash-fried calzone, classically stuffed with salami, pork scratchings, tomatoes, provola and ricotta. Surprisingly light, the best is made at Enzo Piccirillo's La Masardona, tucked away in a raffish side street south of the central train station. Made fresh to order, most regulars order theirs *senza ricotta* (without ricotta). To keep things traditional, wash it down with a small glass of Marsala wine.
Via Giulio Cesare Capaccio 27, Naples; closed Sun & Aug

05 TANDEM

In Naples, the hero dish at Sunday family lunch is *ragù napoletano*, a luxurious meat-and-tomato sauce simmered gently for at least six hours. If you don't have a Neapolitan mamma to make it for you, find solace at Tandem, the first eatery dedicated to the city's best-loved comfort dish.

Devour it atop bruschetta, mixed through pasta, or on its own with bread for mopping up the sauce (known as *fare la scarpetta*). The fact that Neapolitans – notoriously critical of each other's *ragù* – flock here attests to its excellence. Opening times can vary weekly, so call ahead.
Via G Paladino 51, Naples; www.tandemnapoli.it

06 IL FOCOLARE

You'll need to catch the hydrofoil from Naples to the nearby island of Ischia, then take a bus or taxi to reach this trattoria nestled in the hills between Casamicciola and Fiaiano. It's worth the effort to savour what is the finest iteration of the island's celebrated speciality – a stew made with rabbits reared in traditional pits and slow cooked in clay pots.

You'll need to request Il Focolare's *coniglio all'ischitana* in advance; the same morning is usually fine. At the helm of the restaurant is the d'Ambra family, well-known local Slow Food champions and the kind of hosts who'll invite you into the wine cellar for a limoncello and a chat

about food, wine and family.
*Via Cretajo al Crocefisso 3,
Barano d'Ischia, Ischia; www.
trattoriailfocolare.it; dinner only
except weekends, closed Feb &
Wed Nov–May*

07 PIZZERIA STARITA

In Vittorio De Sica's classic 1954 film
L'Oro di Napoli (The Gold of Naples),
Sophia Loren plays an unfaithful
wife who peddles *pizza fritta* from
her *basso* (street-level apartment).
The ones used on set were made by
this veteran pizzeria, and the giant
fork and ladle used by the star hang
proudly on its walls. While *pizza
fritta* is still served, it's the bubbling,

wood-fired pizzas you're here for.
Creative toppings include radicchio
with gorgonzola, though there's
much to be said for the sublime
simplicity of a true Neapolitan
marinara, topped with tomato
sauce, garlic, basil, olive oil – and
no seafood.
*Via Materdei 28, Naples;
www.pizzeriestarita.it; closed Mon*

08 DA MARIANO

An easy hydrofoil trip from both
Ischia and Naples, the sleepy
island of Procida is home to this
acclaimed, family-run waterfront
restaurant. In warmer weather,
reserve a table on the patio to

savour flawless seafood dishes
like spaghetti with anchovies
and pecorino cheese, swordfish
and aubergine *polpette* (patties)
and charred octopus on *friarielli*
(broccoli rabe).

If it's on the menu, don't miss
the *caprese al cioccolato bianco
e limone di Procida*, a joyous twist
on Capri's famous cake, made with
white chocolate and Procida's
prized lemons. Across the island,
the pastel-hued fishing village of
Marina Corricella famously appears
in Michael Radford's 1994 film *Il
Postino* (The Postman).
*Piazza Marina Chiaiolella, Marina
Chiaiolella, Procida*

WHERE TO STAY

ATELIER INÈS ARTS & SUITES

A stylishly idiosyncratic B&B showcasing whimsical art and furniture created by late Neapolitan designer/sculptor Annibale Oste and his son Vincenzo. Thoughtfully curated breakfasts include fresh local pastries and fruits from the tranquil courtyard.
www.atelierines gallery.com

MAGMA HOME

Spread across two floors of an 18th-century *palazzo*, each of the rooms at this simple, cultured B&B are designed by local artists who have used upcycled materials, specially commissioned artworks and Italian design classics to create unique spaces.
magma.kross.travel

WHAT TO DO

CERTOSA E MUSEO DI SAN MARTINO

What began life as a 14th-century Carthusian monastery is now a trove of Neapolitan art,

created by some of Italy's mightiest creatives. The Certosa's hilltop position affords paradisiacal views of Naples, its bay and Mt Vesuvius.
www.beniculturali. it/luogo/certosa-e- museo-di-san-martino

MUSEO ARCHEOLOGICO NAZIONALE

Decorative cycles depicting wine, fruit and fish are among the wealth of Greco-Roman

frescoes, mosaics, statues and artefacts housed in what is one of the world's great repositories of ancient art.
mann-napoli.it

CELEBRATIONS

PIZZA VILLAGE

Taking over the *lungomare* (seafront) in June, this 10-night tribute to Neapolitan pie includes a pizza championship, masterclasses, concerts

and pop-up stalls peddling Naples' most famous culinary export.
www.pizzavillage.it

WINE & THE CITY

Food, vino, art and design conspire at Naples' foremost culinary festival. Held over several weeks in May or June, events include wine tastings, aperitivo sessions, dinners, exhibitions and performances.
www.wineandthecity.it

GET THERE

Palermo is connected to several mainland Italian ports by ferry, while regular non-stop flights connect Palermo to major Italian cities and numerous other European destinations. Central Palermo is relatively compact and walkable.

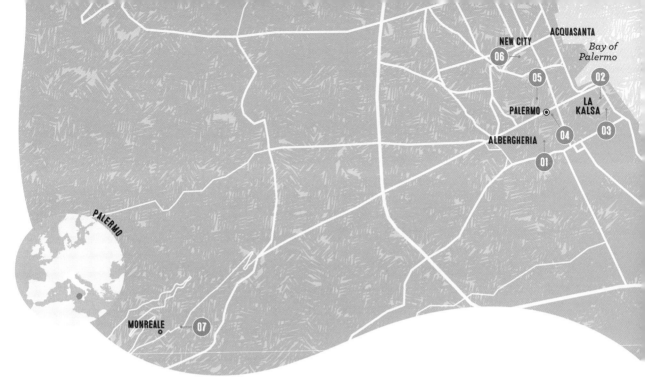

[Italy]

A BITE OF PALERMO

Sicily's capital revels in its crossroads status between Europe and Africa, with souk-like markets, daring street food and brightly coloured sweets.

Closer to Tunis than to Rome, it is sometimes joked that Palermo is the most European of North African cities. One glimpse of its date palms and qubba-crowned churches and you'll understand why. Conquered by the Saracens in 831, Palermo was the capital of the Emirate of Sicily until 1091, a gilded age in which the city became one of the most cosmopolitan centres of the Muslim world. But over millennia, everyone from the Greeks, Carthaginians and Romans, to the Germans, French and Spanish have left their mark.

This cultural *caponata* has shaped one of Italy's most unique cuisines, a sweet-and-sour fusion in which pasta, couscous and the freshest of local seafood are flavoured with almonds, pistachios, pine nuts, sultanas and the bounty of vegetables and citrus fruits grown in Sicilian soil. While fine-dining exists, Palermo's most memorable food experiences await in the humblest and most unexpected places: retro backstreet trattorias, kaleidoscopic markets, convent kitchens, and even private *palazzi* linked to literary greats.

Like Cairo and Marrakesh, Palermo is also one of the world's great street-food cities. Here, *friggitorie* (fried-food vendors), street-corner carts and battered vans peddle a cornucopia of moreish Sicilian snacks, from *arancini* (fried rice balls filled with countless combinations), *panelle* (chickpea fritters) and *sfincione* (Sicilian focaccia), to the acquired taste of *pani câ meusa* (spleen sandwich). The latter has its origins in Palermo's 15th-century Jewish community.

Just leave room for the city's Arab-rooted sweets. Should you opt for ricotta-filled *cannoli*, *cassata* or artful *frutta martorana* (fruit- or veg-shaped marzipan sweets)? The answer, of course, is to try them all.

01 MERCATO DI BALLARÒ

Palermo's Arab blood is thickest at this earthy, ancient market, snaking its way through the dusty, crumbling Albergheria quarter. Roguish vendors bellow the praises of their fresh island wares – buxom aubergines, peppers and fennel, sweet apricots and Grappolo tomatoes, olives, silvery sardines, rustic *salsiccie* (sausages), pecorino Siciliano DOP, prized Bronte pistachios and tangy capers from windswept Pantelleria.

According to acclaimed chef and market regular Carmelo Trentacosti: "A true Palermitan never buys without tasting first, so politely ask for '*un assaggino per favore*' (a taste please). In the market square of Piazza del Carmine, stop to try the *polpo bollito* (boiled octopus), *crocchè* (potato croquettes) or *stigghiole*, skewered intestines wrapped around onions or leeks and cooked on makeshift barbecues."
Via Ballarò; Mon-Sat 7.30am-8pm, Sun 7.30am-3pm

02 COOKING WITH THE DUCHESS

No ordinary kitchen class, Cooking with the Duchess will have you chopping and stirring in the very palace in which Giuseppe Tomasi di Lampedusa penned one of Italy's great modern novels, *Il Gattopardo* (The Leopard). Classes are run by the writer's daughter-in-law, the Duchess Nicoletta Polo Lanza Tomasi, whose wicked sense of humour is matched by her passion for the island's cuisine.

After a morning shopping trip to the local Capo market, organic herbs are picked in the palace garden before Nicoletta and her protégés cook their multicourse Sicilian feast. After lunch, guests are treated to a private tour of the 18th-century seafront *palazzo*, with a sneak peek at the original, handwritten manuscript for *The Leopard*.
Via Butera 28; www.butera28.it

03 FRIGGITORIA CHILUZZO

Opened in 1943 by Michele Biondo, known by locals as 'Micheluzzo', and still run by his family, this Kalsa district *friggitoria* (fried-food kiosk)

01 Palermo's palm trees give a whiff of Africa

02 Local produce at Mercato di Ballarò

03 Cooking with the Duchess

04 I Segreti del Chiostro is famous for its convent sweets

remains a favourite meeting spot for locals, who gather at its plastic tables to chow street-food staples like *pane e panelle* (chickpea fritters in a sesame bun).

The kiosk is famous for its *panino allo sgombro* (mackerel and salad sandwich), but local artist and regular Loredana Lo Verde says, "The *verdure in pastella* (tempura-style vegetables) are also very good. And at 6pm, a queue forms outside the adjoining greengrocer for the family's garlic-and-parsley *babbaluci* – boiled snails cooked in copper pots." Belly full, check out the epic street-art murals on nearby Via dello Spasimo.
Piazza della Kalsa 11; closed Sun

04 I SEGRETI DEL CHIOSTRO

Gluttony is one sin overlooked at the Monastero di Santa Caterina d'Alessandria. A 15th-century Dominican convent, its kitchen has found fame by reviving historic desserts from convents across Sicily. Daily production is limited, so head in early to score rare treats like *couscous dolce* (semolina couscous with almonds, pistachios, walnuts, candied fruit and chocolate) and heavenly *fedde del cancelliere* (shell-shaped marzipan filled with apricot jam and cream).

Leave room for the spectacular *cannoli*, arguably the best in town. The proverbial cherry is the mammoth complex itself, home to a magnificent maiolica-tiled cloister, panoramic rooftop terraces and a baroque church crowned with frescoes by Filippo Randazzo.
Piazza Bellini 1; www.isegreti delchiostro.com

05 TRATTORIA AL VECCHIO CLUB ROSANERO

Food and football collide at homely Al Vecchio Club Rosanero, squeezed into a tiny back alley. 'Rosanero' (Pink-Black) refers to the team colours of the city's beloved Palermo FC and its players and paraphernalia adorn the trattoria's old stone walls. The kitchen itself pumps out no-nonsense Sicilian *cucina casareccia* (homestyle cooking). It's the kind of coaxing grub that makes locals yearn for their grandmothers, such as *spaghetti al nero di seppia* (squid-

05 The cloisters of Palermo's Cattedrale di Monreale

06 Ciambra serves creative, contemporary Sicilian cuisine

07 Vintage maiolica decorates the rooms of Stanze al Genio

ink spaghetti), *sarde a beccafico* (sardines stuffed with pine nuts and sultanas) and *caponata e pesce spada* (sweet-and-sour vegetables with swordfish).

In typical nonna style, servings are generous. Opt for a *mezza porzione* (half portion) of the *primi* (first courses) to leave room for a *secondo* (second course) and *dolce* (dessert).

Vicolo Caldomai 18; lunch only, Mon-Wed, closed Sun

06 I CUOCHINI

Despite its discreet location in a courtyard off Via Ruggiero Settimo, retro takeaway I Cuochini is always busy thanks to its moreish Sicilian street snacks. But the term 'snacks' is a loose one here; just a few of these morsels and you've got

a bargain meal. Try the luscious *arancinette* (little *ragù*-filled rice balls), buttery *timballetti* (casserole-like pies) and *panzerotti* (fried dough pockets) stuffed with combinations such as ricotta and mint.

Trading since 1826, I Cuochini's oldest staple is the *pasticcino*, a baked disc of sweet, shortcrust pastry filled with minced meat, tomato and spices. A short walk away is Italy's largest opera house, Teatro Massimo, featured in the bloody final scene of Francis Ford Coppola's *The Godfather Part III*.

Via Ruggiero Settimo 68; www.icuochini.com; closed Sun

07 CIAMBRA

A 30-minute bus trip from central Palermo, the town of Monreale is famous for its Unesco World

Heritage-listed cathedral. But gastronomes also know it for this polished seafood restaurant. While Ciambra breaks from traditional recipes, it loses none of Sicily's reverence for prime, seasonal ingredients, prepared to showcase their natural flavours. The result is inspired, contemporary creations such as a tartare of sweet *gambero rosso* (red prawn) with strawberries and stracciatella cheese, or fettuccine dressed in amberjack *ragù* and toasted almonds.

For a blissful epilogue, finish with Ciambra's *croccante di mandorle*, an almond *torrone* (nougat) paired with a ricotta and pistachio mousse. In the warmer months, call ahead to request an outdoor table.

Via d'Acquisto 18, Monreale; www. ciambrarestaurant.it; closed Wed

WHERE TO STAY

BUTERA 28

Aside from hosting
Cooking with the
Duchess, Palazzo Lanza
Tomasi offers a range
of tastefully appointed
apartments with private
kitchens (perfect for
cooking up your own
Sicilian storm). Most
sleep a family of four or
more, and apartment
nine comes with its own
grand piano.
www.butera28.it

STANZE AL GENIO

Upstairs from a fabulous
house-museum
dedicated to Italian
maiolica tiles lies this
atmospheric, LGBTQIA+
friendly B&B. All four
rooms are generously
proportioned, with high
ceilings, antiques and
vintage maiolica. Three of
them are adorned with
19th-century frescoes.
www.stanzealgeniobnb.it

WHAT TO DO

PALAZZO DEI NORMANNI

Palermo's Unesco World
Heritage-listed Palace of
the Normans, also called
Palazzo Reale, houses
the Cappella Palatina,

an extraordinary royal
chapel designed by Roger
II in 1130. It's awash
with dazzling Byzantine
mosaics, inlaid marble
and an Islamic-style
carved *muqarnas* ceiling.
*www.federico
secondo.org*

CATTEDRALE DI MONREALE

A vision of the Virgin
(and possibly his ego)
propelled Roger II's
ambitious grandson
William II to commission
the Cattedrale di
Monreale in Palermo.
Considered Sicily's
finest example of
Norman architecture,
the cathedral's interiors
are a glittering feast of
12th-century mosaics
depicting biblical dramas
in astonishing detail.
www.monrealeduomo.it

CELEBRATIONS

FESTINO DI SANTA ROSALIA

On the evening of 14 July,
the relics of Palermo's
plague-busting patron
saint are paraded aboard
a grand chariot from the
Cattedrale di Palermo to
the seafront. Fireworks
light up the sky and street
stalls serve everything
from grilled fish to
babbaluci (boiled snails).

GET THERE
Turin is linked by high-speed trains to Europe and Italy's other major cities; its Caselle Airport also has a small number of international flights.

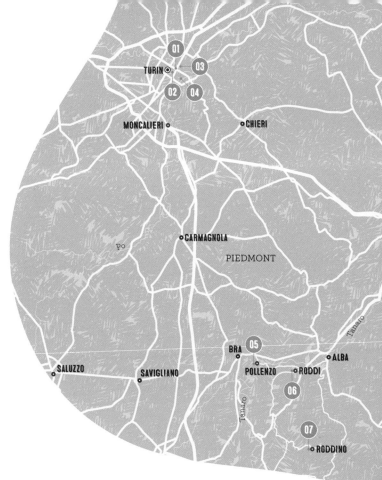

[Italy]

TAKING IT SLOW IN TURIN & PIEDMONT

Turin and Piedmont make the perfect city-country pairing, with wine, truffles and slow food on the menu in neighbourhood trattorie and rural boltholes.

Sitting in the foothills of the towering Alps, close to the French border, Piedmont is fiercely independent, with its own distinctive language, culture, cuisine and wines. Turin, the region's capital, symbolises this fresh originality. The first capital of unified Italy, official residence of the Savoy royal family and the post-war industrial engine room that created modern Italy, the city has reinvented itself as a creative capital of food, design and cinema, with old factories and warehouses now housing dynamic artistic initiatives. Yet Turin remains far less touristy and overcrowded than Venice, Florence or Rome.

It is no coincidence that the Slow Food movement is based in Piedmont – this is a region made for genuine slow travel. Stay in rustic *agriturismo* farmhouses or cosy winemaker B&Bs tasting the latest vintages in the evening. Drive or bike around the picture perfect vine-clad hills and castles that characterise the rural landscape, pausing to feast on simple but delicious Piedmontese cooking in an old-fashioned osteria. Or splash out for a gourmet meal where delicate homemade fresh pasta is topped with aromatic white truffle shavings, accompanied either by an affordable bottle of Dolcetto or a memorable vintage Barolo.

The Piedmont countryside is perfect for vineyard wine and food discoveries, with possible bases including a number of ancient towns. Alba, with its grand piazzas and noisy Saturday street market, is one of Italy's gourmet capitals. Or try Bra, an important Roman settlement that was transformed into a royal city in the 18th century with a series of lavish baroque churches and *palazzi*. More recently, it's become famous as the home of Slow Food.

01 The rolling Piedmont vineyards around Alba

02 Turin's Consorzio restaurant pays homage to offal

03 Local produce at Mercato di Porta Palazzo

04 Museo Lavazza romps through over a century of local coffee history

05 La Drogheria serves contemporary cocktails with its aperitivi nibbles

01 MERCATO DI PORTA PALAZZO

Filling Turin's entire Piazza della Repubblica with some 800 stalls, this is Europe's largest market. It's a brilliant assault on the senses from the moment you step foot in the teeming square. Raucous Torinese fishmongers compete with North African fruit and vegetable traders, bantering in Piedmont dialect as they sell the cheapest seasonal fruit and vegetables imaginable; fragrant fennel and artichokes, purple broccoli and blood red oranges.

The old covered market, Antica Tettoia dell'Orologio, is the place to discover the region's cheeses and salami. Continue through the back to a hidden secret, the outdoor farmer's market, where *contadini* (farmers) smallholders sell heritage vegetables and rare herbs fresh from their fields. From autumn, there's a cornucopia of wild mushrooms and, of course, freshly foraged white truffles.
Piazza della Repubblica, Turin; https://scopriportapalazzo.com; closed Sun

02 RISTORANTE CONSORZIO

Piedmont's traditional cuisine is essentially *cucina povera* (peasant cuisine), with dishes that use the often underrated *quinto quarto* (fifth quarter, aka offal). Consorzio is a temple to this distinctive Torinese bistronomy. Liver, kidneys and tongue are just the tip of the iceberg; the menu also proposes pasta with lamb tripe or heart *ragù*, roasted sweetbreads and beef marrow daringly paired with creamy codfish, chard and a tart anchovy parsley sauce. Look out for the ravioli stuffed with Turin's famous 15th-century recipe La Finanziera – an exotic stew including unusual but delicious ingredients such as veal brain, cock crests, wattles and testicles.

The kitchen is overseen by innovative chef Valentina Chiaramonte, who keeps everyone happy by also creating offbeat vegetarian dishes using seasonal heritage vegetables like the wonderfully named *cardo gobbo* (hunchback cardoon).
Via Monte di Pietà 23, Turin; https://ristoranteconsorzio.it; closed Sun & Mon lunch

03 MUSEO LAVAZZA

The big local coffee roaster here is Lavazza, a global brand but a genuine family-run business fiercely committed to ethical sustainability. Museo Lavazza takes the visitor through five multimedia galleries illustrating its 130-year history, from early production to retro mobile coffee vans, espresso and moka to today's ubiquitous metal capsule, and a look back at iconic graphic posters. The tasting bar even offers the chance to try Lavazza Espresso Martini.

The museum is part of what is known as Nuvola Lavazza, the Lavazza Cloud. Located in an old industrial quarter, this eco-friendly piazza houses the company's futuristic headquarters, exhibition space, a botanical garden and Condividere, an all-glass restaurant conceived by superstar Spanish chef Ferran Adrià.
Via Bologna 32, Turin; www.lavazza.com/en/lavazza-museum.html; closed Mon & Tue

04 LA DROGHERIA

Located on the monumental Piazza Vittorio Veneto, La Drogheria is not just Turin's hippest bar, but a veritable bazaar, stocking every possible cocktail ingredient and mixing tool for the amateur barman. Turin is capital of the aperitivo, home of world famous vermouths and bitters like Martini Rosso, Campari and Antica Carpano. The Drogheria style, though, contrasts with the city's opulent 19th-century salons where white jacketed bar staff prepare classic cocktails.

Here, the fashionable mixologist, accompanied by a DJ, conjures up contemporary cocktails such as Wabi-Sabi; sake, bitter umami and house-fermented black tea kombucha. But some traditions remain – La Drogheria still accompanies its aperitivi with complimentary *stuzzichini* – nibbles of salami and prosciutto, cheese, pasta, pizza and salads.
Piazza Vittorio Veneto 18/d, Turin; www.la-drogheria.it; closed Mon

05 BANCA DEL VINO

Piedmont is synonymous with Slow Food, and the headquarters of this pioneering activist global food

06 White truffles
are native to the
Piedmont region

07 A patchwork of
Barolo vines surround
Falletti Castle, home
to WIMU

07 OSTERIA DA GEMMA

This historic osteria sits at the entrance of Roddino, a typical medieval Piedmontese winemaking village clustered atop a vine-clad hill. On a clear day, the panoramic views stretch to the Alps. A meal at Da Gemma is to experience the ultimate expression of traditional Piedmont cuisine. Magazines may refer to Gemma Boeri as the Queen of Piedmont gastronomy, but this humble lady is definitely more a *cucina casalinga* (home cooking) legend than gourmet chef.

At her no-frills wooden table osteria, everyone is served the same menu – a gargantuan feast of never-ending courses at a fixed price of €31. Homemade bread accompanies artisan salami, *vitello tonnato* (cold sliced veal with a creamy sauce), hand-diced *carne cruda* (raw steak) and creamy *insalata russa* (Italian-style coleslaw), followed by copious helpings of handmade *tajarin* pasta smothered with *ragù* and minuscule *plin* ravioli in a buttery rosemary sauce.

And there's more: take a short pause to prepare for the rich beef stew followed by *bunet* (creamy chocolate and amaretti) flan and panna cotta.

Via Marconi, Roddino; www.face book.com/Osteria-Da-Gemma -141283035919485/; closed Mon & Tues

movement are found in the bustling burg of Bra, on the outskirts of the vineyards of the Langhe and Roero.

But the most impressive place to visit is actually just outside Bra, where the sleepy hamlet of Pollenzo is dominated by its colossal Unesco World Heritage-listed castle. Today, this red-brick royal residence houses Slow's Gastronomic University, cooking schools and, above all, La Banca del Vino. Founded in 2001, the Wine Bank's vaults house 100,000 precious bottles from vineyards across the whole of Italy. You can opt to taste a selection of wines from across the peninsula or join an educational cellar tour covering topics such as native grapes or sparkling wines.

Piazza Vittorio Emanuele II 13, Pollenzo, Bra; www.bancadel vino.it; closed Sun

06 LA CROTA

Chef Danilo Lorusso runs cooking courses at his gourmet restaurant just outside Alba. In the kitchen, he uses handed-down family recipes, giving lessons in making, folding and filling traditional *agnolotti di plin* (tiny ravioli), then cutting and recutting *tajarin* pasta until it becomes whispy strands. Guests learn to make hearty meat *ragù* and a lighter blend of butter and sage for the *plin*.

Antipasti are seasonal, say stuffed porcini mushrooms or crunchy asparagus wrapped in smoky pancetta. For dessert, it'll be a delicious cake made from local hazelnuts. Lorusso also organises vineyard trips and tastings, as well as truffle-seeking forest treks with a hunter and his dog.

Via Fontana 7, Roddi di Alba; https://ristorantelacrotalanghe. com/esperienze/; closed Mon

WHERE TO STAY

**B&B FORESTERIA
DEGLI ARTISTI**

Turin has great homestay options but it's difficult to beat Signora Anna, who has been welcoming guests since 2005 to her cosy apartment under the rooftop of an historic *palazzo*. There's a fully equipped kitchen, so you can go market shopping and cook for yourself.
*www.foresteria
degliartisti.it*

HOTEL CASTELLO
DI SINIO

This stunning 12th-century castle has been lovingly restored to create a dream resort in the heart of Piedmont's vineyards. It's the home of longtime resident American Denise Pardini, who is also a San Francisco-trained chef. Pardini oversees the restaurant, runs cooking classes and is an expert at organising winemaker visits and truffle-hunting expeditions.
*www.hotelcastello
disinio.com*

WHAT TO DO

WIMU

The fortress-like medieval castle dominating Barolo houses a fascinating multimedia museum dedicated to wine, spread across four floors. After your visit, head down into the 15th-century cellars for tastings.
www.wimubarolo.it

PINACOTECA AGNELLI

Fiat's iconic Turin Lingotto factory has undergone a transformation since car production ended. Above a shopping mall, cinema and restaurants lies a museum showcasing the masterpieces of the Agnelli collection. On the roof, the mythical Ferrari racing test track is now open to the public with a landscaped garden filled with thousands of flowers, plants and herbs.
*www.pinacoteca-
agnelli.it*

CELEBRATIONS

**ALBA WHITE
TRUFFLE FAIR**

Alba, home of Nutella and Kinder chocolate, is also the white truffle capital of the world. The precious aromatic Tuber Magnatum sells for around a mind-boggling €3500 a kilo and it's celebrated with a festive extravaganza in Alba each weekend during the peak truffle hunting season (October to December). Expect to see medieval pageants, concerts, a Miss Tartufo competition, cooking shows and coveted white truffle tastings all over town.
www.fieradeltartufo.org

GET THERE
Flights arrive at Marco Polo
Airport. While public bus
5 takes travellers to the
city itself, the Alilaguna
boat service has ferries
to Murano, Burano and
Torcello islands as well as
the Lido and Treporti.

01

VENICE LAGOON

MESTRE

02 Mazzorbo
03 Burano
LIO PICCOLO

Murano Sant'Erasmo
01 VENICE 05 TREPORTI
04 PUNTA SABBIONI

MALCONTENTA

FUSINA

LIDO DI VENEZIA

MALAMOCCO

Venetian Lagoon 06

Pellestrina

Gulf of Venice

07
CHIOGGIA SOTTOMARINA

[Italy]

THE ESSENCE OF VENETIAN LAGOON LIFE

Travel beyond Venice and food lovers will find lesser-visited villages with fishing, farming, winemaking and romantic waterside trattorie.

There is so much to see in Venice, and so many crowds to negotiate, that it is easy to forget that the Serenissima, as it is known, is just one of 34 islands in a vast lagoon covering more than 518 sq km (200 sq miles), separated from the Adriatic by a slim littoral of sand dunes, fishing villages and smallholder farms. Once you leave Venice behind and take to the waters, you enter another world. The fragile ecosystem of the *barene* wetlands and mud flats, forever shifting with the tide, is alive with swooping flocks of birds, fishers casting giant nets to catch squids, and locals gliding silently through the still waters in narrow wooden boats, rowing upright gondolier-style in training for the fiercely contested island regattas.

Each island has its own attraction; a hidden vineyard producing salty lagoon wine; a seafood trattoria serving plump prawns and mussels, razor clams, wriggling eels and spiky spider crabs just unloaded from fishing smacks on the quayside; an osteria cooking artichokes freshly picked from their garden with roast wild duck brought in by lagoon hunters; or a wild, isolated sandy beach where you can picnic with crusty bread, tasty salami and cheeses bought at the local market.

The lagoon is well connected by the impeccable public ferry system, which stretches to the well-known islands of Burano and Murano, over to the Lido then farther afield to Cavallino, Pellestrina and Chioggia, right at the southern point of the lagoon. Once you disembark the ferries, you can explore using public bus, bike rentals or by hiking. And then there's always the trusty vaporetto boat service waiting to slowly chug back to Venice.

01 OSTERIA AI CACCIATORI

Murano's Fondamenta dei Vetrai is the glass-making island's main tourist drag, lined with glitzy showrooms and artisan furnaces. But one hidden jewel most visitors walk straight past is this venerable 150-year-old osteria, where locals pack the tables, noisily talking football or playing cards. Glass-blowers troop in for their midday *menu operai* (working man's lunch), so visitors will need to get in quick. "I am happy to serve the daily pasta to tourists – if we are not sold out," says owner Enrico Regazzi.

Alternatively, try the osteria's famous Raboso wine with *cicheti* – traditional Venetian snacks. That might mean delicious *carrozza* (deep-fried mozzarella) with anchovies, bite-sized *polpette* (meatballs), or delicate *tramezzini* (finger sandwiches) filled with radicchio and smoky speck ham.
Fondamenta dei Vetrai 69, Murano; closed Sun

02 VENISSA

Mazzorbo is one of Venice's tiniest islands, a peaceful oasis home to barely 50 inhabitants and this ambitious project, offering travellers a genuine alternative to staying in Venice itself. Fifteen years ago the Bisol family, legendary Prosecco producers, created the Venissa vineyard here, planting an ancient lagoon grape called Dorona. Over the years they have transformed an old manor house into a wine resort, cultivated a sustainable vegetable garden that the public is free to explore and created a Michelin-starred restaurant.

Visit to discover rare lagoon specialities such as *castraùre* (baby artichokes), *zizzole* (jujube berries), *schie* (tiny shrimps), a risotto of tasty *gò* (a lagoon fish), and *bisatò* (roasted eel).
Fondamenta Santa Caterina 3, Mazzorbo; www.venissa.it

03 BURANO

The lagoon's most colourful island, often photographed for its brightly painted cottages, is still home to a small band of fishers. For a memorable experience, join local guide Luisella Romeo on a day out

Ø3

with Buranello *pescatore* Domenico Rossi. Romeo is passionate about sharing Venetian daily life and the trip involves sailing through *valli* fishing parks, shallow wetland channels and the canals of Torcello on Rossi's *bragozzo* boat.

Eventually you reach Rossi's wooden *cason* (cabin), where he explains the traditional methods of lagoon fishing, his special tools, nets and rickety wooden boxes, used to breed highly prized *moeche* (soft-shelled crabs). Once the catch of the day is hauled in, there is time for a traditional *bussolà* biscuit with a glass of Prosecco before heading back. *www.seevenice.it/en/fishermen-in-burano-and-the-venetian-lagoon/; book ahead*

04 ORTO DI VENEZIA

Sant'Erasmo is Venice's garden, a bucolic island of farms and orchards that has supplied the Serenissima's markets for centuries. Orto means vegetable garden, and when French media mogul Michel Thoulouze decided to change career, plant vines and make his own wine here, he thought Orto was the perfect name. He's since built a state-of-the art modern winery, which is open for tastings and vineyard tours.

Thoulouze only produces 15,000 bottles of his exceptionally high-quality white Malvasia wine, which has a unique saline taste because of the salty, sandy soil. It is even sold in the Parisian restaurant of superstar chef Alain Ducasse. After

a tasting, take a short walk through the island's vegetable plots to the quiet beach and waterside Al Bacan trattoria. *Via delle Motte 1, Sant'Erasmo; https://ortodivenezia.com/english. html; by appointment*

05 AL NOTTURNO

Cavallino and Treporti form a 20km (12.5 miles) littoral between the Adriatic beaches and Venice's lagoon, an unspoilt natural paradise and haven for wild birds. A 10km (6 mile) bike path leads across the water to Lio Piccolo, an idyllic hamlet on a slim archipelago of salt marshes and horticultural fields, hidden away in the wetlands.

Although inhabited since Roman times, it now has just 20 residents.

(04)

And at the end of the road, there's Al Notturno – a romantic, rustic restaurant whose waterside terrace offers spectacular sunsets.

Run by the Ballarin family for generations, everyone is served the same zero-kilometre five-course menu, starring simple, delicious fresh seafood from the lagoon, vegetables grown in their garden, and Prosecco from a nearby vineyard.
26 Via di Lio Piccolo, Cavallino-Treporti; www.facebook.com/ pages/category/Diner/Al-Notturno-1652773578305902; closed Tue

06 AGRITURISMO LE VALLI
Disembark the Lido ferry at Pellestrina and walk straight to this friendly homestay. Their 'Valli' is a fish farm for sea bass, bream, clams, and mussels, served in their popular *cucina casalinga* (home cooking) restaurant. Based

here, you can discover the rest of Pellestrina, a remarkable island just 12km (7.5 miles) long and barely 500 metres (1640ft) wide, with deserted beaches and the isolated Ca'Roman nature reserve.

Most inhabitants are fishers, but food lovers come from miles to eat on the romantic lagoon terrace of the island's famed seafood restaurant Da Celeste. Alternatively, the modest Trattoria Laguna has no view but is where the fisherman themselves have lunch – you won't eat a fresher *spaghetti alle vongole* (garlicky spaghetti with clams).
Via dei Murazzi 1d, Santa Maria del Mare, Pellestrina; https://m.facebook.com/profile. php?id=174759292582339

07 CHIOGGIA FISH MARKET
Although Chioggia is linked to Venice by bus, the dramatic way to arrive in this bustling port is by

the lagoon ferry from Pellestrina. Although it is often called Little Venice because of its canals, medieval churches and ornate palaces, Chioggia is defined by its fish market – one of the most important in Italy.

While the wholesale market is for professionals, the daily Pescheria al Minuto is open to the public and it's a feast for all the senses. Squeezed between the 14th-century Palazzo Granaio and the narrow Vena canal, more than 30 colourful fishmonger stalls, known as *mògnoli*, display the Adriatic's freshest catch of sea bass, anchovies and bream, octopus and squids, clams, mussels and mantis shrimp offloaded from the boats at 4am.
Calle Doria 953, Chioggia; www.chioggiapesca.it/en/ mercato-ittico-al-minuto-di-chioggia; closed Mon

WHERE TO STAY

CAMPING CA'SAVIO

Unspoilt sandy beaches stretch along Cavallino, where the family-run Camping Ca'Savio supports sustainable eco-initiatives ranging from water and energy saving to dune and flora protection. You can also stay in a hip silver airstream caravan or cosy chalet.
www.casavio.com

CASA BURANO

Staying overnight in Burano is an unforgettable experience as the island magically empties of all its day-trippers after dusk. The owners of Venissa have restored several canal-side fishermen's houses to create designer B&B accommodation.
www.casaburano.it

WHAT TO DO

TORCELLO BASILICA

The first lagoon settlements were here in Torcello, long before Venice, and this 7th-century Byzantine cathedral is decorated with exquisite mosaics

05

SAN MICHELE CEMETERY

This tranquil walled island cemetery sitting between Murano and Venice is filled with ornate tombs including those of famous visitors such as Ezra Pound, Diaghilev and Stravinsky. Be sure to explore the elegant 15th-century

Renaissance San Michele church and cloisters.

CELEBRATIONS

SANT'ERASMO FESTIVALS

Sant'Erasmo hosts two popular festivals. La Festa del Carciofo Violetto celebrates locally renowned

violet artichokes over two Sundays in May, while October's Festa del Mosto is the time to watch an island rowing regatta as you sip *torbolino* (cloudy grape juice beginning to ferment), traditionally paired with roasted chestnuts.

Thirasia

Palia Kameni
Nea Kameni

Aspronisi

01
02 OIA
FINIKIA

Tinos

Santorini (Thira)

FIRA

Santorini (Thira)

MONOLITHOS

MESSARIA

EXO GONIA
05

Aegean Sea

MEGALOHORI
04
03
KAMARI

AKROTIRI
EMPORIO
PERISSA

GET THERE

Santorini's airport has daily
services to Athens and
direct flights to European
cities in summer. It's four
hours to Tinos by boat
from Santorini; book with
Golden Star Ferries or
Minoan Lines (ferries.gr).
Peak services run in July and
August. Winter services are
reduced or nonexistent on
some routes.

01

KOLIMBITHRA

ISTERNIA

KARDIANI

07

KOMI

Tinos

VOLAX

06

MYRSINI

AGIOS
RUMANOS

Tinos

TRIANTAROS

KIONIA

Santorini
(Thira)

HORA
(TINOS)

08

PORTO

CYCLADES

[Greece]

ISLAND HOPPING IN THE CYCLADES

Jump between glittering Santorini and rustic Tinos to discover island delicacies, gastronomy temples and wines as unique as the Cyclades themselves.

Greece's Cyclades Islands are the stuff of dreams and bucket lists: azure seas, sparkling shores, sugar-cube houses stacking the hillsides. And across these exquisite islands, as the terrain and communities change, the cuisine changes too. Ubiquitous foods like calamari and grilled fish may have been staples of local diets for millennia, but the Cyclades is also home to unique delicacies based on the climate, soil and traditions of each island.

An exploration of these islands will take in traditional tavernas, cobbled villages, wineries and vaunted gastro-temples. You'll sample salty cheeses like crumbly soft myzithra and firmly wedged graviera. In Andros there's *fourtalia* – a type of frittata made with sausage and potatoes. Milos is known for its cheese pies, a summertime watermelon pie, and a spoon sweet made out of white pumpkin and honey.

For this microcosm of a tour, start in Santorini where caldera views, infinity pools and black-sand beaches entertain foodies, drawn to the island by excellent wine and one of the best dining scenes in Greece. Edible offerings include taverna dishes made using traditional family recipes with only local ingredients, as well as fusion food by internationally renowned chefs. Seek out Michelin-starred chef Ettore Botrini at Selene or Botrini's, or seafood luminary Lefteris Lazarou, who opened Varoulko Santorini in 2022.

And for contrast there's sweet Tinos island, a sleeper hit of natural beauty, dotted with more than 40 marble-ornamented villages in hidden bays, on terraced hillsides and atop misty mountains. While the scene here is of a mellow sort, the food, made from local produce (cheeses, sausage, tomatoes and wild artichokes), is some of the best you'll find in Greece.

01 Santorini's sugar-cube caldera houses

02 Estate Argyros, Santorini's top winery

03 Lauda creates theatre with local ingredients

(02)

01 TO KRINAKI

If you approach Santorini (officially called Thira in Greek) from the water, it's hard not to be awed by the sheer cliffs that soar above a turquoise sea; by the fact that you're sailing in an immense crater of a drowned volcano; and that before you lies an island shaped by an ancient eruption that was cataclysmic beyond imagining. Indeed, Santorini's traditional food draws heavily on its unique volcanic soil, which gives its vegetables unique qualities.

All-fresh, all-local ingredients, such as wild greens, white aubergine, hand-crushed fava (yellow split peas), caper leaves and wild asparagus go into top-notch taverna dishes at To Krinaki,

a homey spot in tiny Finikia, just east of Oia. Other typical dishes to try include tomato fritters and *skordomakarona* (homemade pasta with Santorini tomatoes, garlic, olive oil and salt). Then there's *apochti* (spiced pork carpaccio) which has Byzantine roots, and takes days to prepare with salt, vinegar and sun-dried cinnamon, pepper and parsley. Pair the food with local beer or wine made from grape varieties grown in Santorini since antiquity, while enjoying the sea view.
Finikia; www.krinaki.gr

02 LAUDA

In peak season, Santorini becomes a playground for the very wealthy, which has resulted in an abundance

of high-concept restaurants where refined presentation mixes with exquisite ingredients and creativity.

One of the top fine-dining experiences in Santorini is Lauda, which has morphed from Oia's humble first restaurant into a renowned caldera-perched destination in its own right. Chef Emmanuel Renaut uses international cooking techniques on Thiran ingredients, producing grand results.
Oía, Santorini; www.lauda restaurant.com

03 ESTATE ARGYROS WINERY

Not only is Santorini blessed with a dry volcanic microclimate that results in some of the best wine in Greece, but its vines are also Europe's oldest, impervious to the

phylloxera bug that wiped out most of Europe's vines in the late 19th century. Grapes are grown close to the ground, in a *kouloura* (nest) of vines to make the most of the moisture and protect the grapes from fierce winds.

Santorini's most lauded wines are the crisp, dry white Assyrtiko and the amber-coloured, unfortified dessert wine known as Vinsanto, both made with the heritage-protected, indigenous Assyrtiko grape variety. Assyrtiko grapes are grown across the Cyclades, but Santorini's stand out for their unique flavour. Assyrtiko is also a dominant grape in Nykteri, another Santorini wine, which was traditionally made by pressing the grapes the night after harvest.

The full-bodied Mavrotragano and medium-bodied Mandilaria reds are other specialities.

You can't go wrong sampling these wines at Estate Argyros, Santorini's most acclaimed winery. The price of tastings in the sleek wine bar includes a tour of the vineyard. *Messaria–Kamari Rd, Santorini; www.estateargyros.com*

04 GAVALAS WINERY

Grapes on Santorini are typically harvested in August, and while the grape-crushing process has been mechanised in Santorini's wineries, it's still possible for visitors to see (and take part in) the old-fashioned way – barefoot – in some small, family-run ones such as Gavalas Winery during the annual harvest

celebrations. There are nine wines to choose from here, including the excellent dry whites Assyrtiko, Aidani and Katsano, and the dry reds Mavrotragano and Xenoloo. Nibbles are provided as you sit beneath a canopy of vines. *Megalohori, Santorini; www.gavalaswines.gr*

05 SANTORINI BREWING COMPANY

Quaff the island's other homegrown beverage, the popular Donkey beers, at this local island brewery. Sample the Yellow Donkey (hoppy golden ale), Red Donkey (amber ale), Crazy Donkey (IPA), White Donkey (wheat with a touch of orange peel), Blue Donkey (blonde saison) and Lazy Ass lager. All are unfiltered,

unpasteurised and extremely easy on the palate. In August, look out for the seasonal Slow Donkey, matured in oak barrels from Argyros Estate after it's used them to ferment its Vinsanto dessert wine.
Messaria–Kamari Rd, Santorini; www.santorinibrewingcompany.gr; closed Sun

06 TEREZA

The countryside of Tinos is a glorious mix of broad terraced hillsides, mountaintops crowned with crags, unspoilt villages, fine beaches and fascinating architecture that includes picturesque dovecotes, a legacy of the Venetians. There's a strong artistic tradition on Tinos, especially for marble sculpting because of its famous quarries, but it's also known for its cuisine. Tereza in the

village of Myrsini is a unique place for a special meal. As you approach through the cobbled streets you come to a simple minimarket with just a smattering of tables at its doors. Here, you can have the meal of a lifetime, featuring locally produced specialities fresh from the oven: roasted goat, okra, *pastitsio* (Greek lasagna) – this is traditional island cooking at its finest.
Myrsini, Tinos

07 O NTINOS

This taverna, set on a sunny terrace overlooking the broad scoop of Giannaki Bay, offers superlative home-cooked island specialities. Its offerings include a particularly rich selection of *mezedhes* such as mackerel in oil with basil and fennel, or aubergine with spicy Tinian cheese. Complimentary fish

soup and homemade ice-cream often bookend the meal.
Ormos Giannaki, Tinos; www.facebook.com/ontinos.tinos; closed Oct-May

08 NISSOS CYCLADES MICROBREWERY

As you circle back toward the main town, wrap up with a crisp brew at Nissos Cyclades Microbrewery. One of the early entries into the Cycladic island craft beer game, Nissos has flourished, developing six beers covering everything from lager to porter. Take a tour of the microbrewery for an explanation of their brewing methods, and if you're feeling peckish, choose the food pairing that matches beers with local Tinian charcuterie.
Tinos-Ormou Agios Ioannis, Tinos; www.nissos.beer

WHERE TO STAY
TINOS HABITART
Seven houses
incorporate local stone
and marble and come
with kitchens, living
spaces and outdoor
areas (most with
private pool). For an
authentic slice of
Tinos, book the
dovecote that has
been irresistibly
transformed into a
three-bedroom villa.
www.tinos-habitart.gr

AROMA SUITES
Overlooking Santorini's
caldera at the quieter
southern end of Fira,
this boutique hotel has
charming service and
six rooms and suites
built into the cliff
face. Traditional
interiors are paired with
monochrome decor,
smooth stone bathrooms
and dreamy sea-view
balconies.
www.aromasuites.com

WHAT TO DO
SANTORINI'S BEACHES
What's a Greek island
tour without hitting the
beaches? Santorini's
volcanic geology makes

the beaches diverse.
Take the full spectrum
tour, from Black (Mesa
Pigadia) Beach backed
by bluffs and a single
taverna, to Red (Kokkini)
Beach, rimmed by rust-
and-fire coloured cliffs.
End at White (Aspri)
Beach, one of Santorini's
prettiest, only accessible
by boat.

**CHURCH OF THE
ANNUNCIATION**
Tinos is famous for
this Greek Orthodox
pilgrimage site, with its
icon, Our Lady of Tinos,
said to have healing
powers. The icon was
uncovered in 1823 in the
ruins of a chapel beneath
the current church, after
a nun, now St Pelagia,

received visions from the
Virgin to help her find it.

CELEBRATIONS
**FEAST OF THE
DORMITION OF THE
MOTHER OF GOD**
On 15 August Tinos'
main town of Hora gets
overwhelmed with
pilgrims and visitors for
the Virgin Mary's feast day.

GET THERE
Thessaloniki's Makedonia
Airport is connected to
many major European
cities. Alternatively, ride
into Thessaloniki on one
of Greece's few rail lines,
from Athens, Larissa, or
even Kalabaka – the stop for
monastic Meteora.

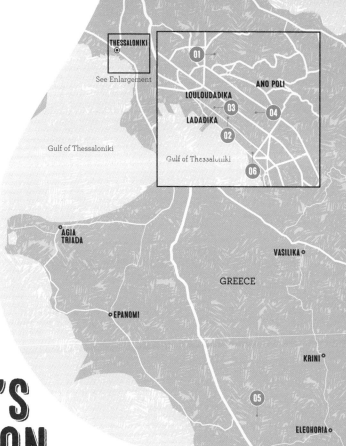

[Greece]

THESSALONIKI'S FOOD EVOLUTION

Greece's spirited second city became the country's first Unesco City of Gastronomy in 2021, thanks to its cosmopolitan culinary development through the ages.

Thessaloniki has been known by many names — Salonica, Salonique, even SKG — but the Macedonian metropolis prefers its modern epithet, Saloniki. The northern capital's multitude of names stems from its historically cosmopolitan character, each wave of immigration bringing tasty new additions to an already-packed recipe repertoire.

On the Via Egnatia trade route between Rome and Asia, ancient Thessaloniki's kitchens eagerly assimilated travelling spices such as pepper and cinnamon. The city became second only to Constantinople in the Byzantine world, before the Ottomans took over in 1430. It was the latter who encouraged migration to Thessaloniki from across its Levantine empire, introducing the city to the concept of *mezze*.

Each culture, religion and people to pass through — from Slavic shepherds to Sephardi Jews — have

put down plates on Thessaloniki's table, but perhaps the biggest influence was the arrival of hundreds of thousands of ethnic Greek refugees from modern-day Turkey (specifically the Pontic Black Sea Coast and Aegean port of Smyrna, now Izmir) during the 1920s collapse of the Ottoman Empire. Dolmades, pastries and many taverna staples that now dominate menus can be traced back to this Asia Minor exodus.

In 2021 Thessaloniki was designated Greece's first City of Gastronomy by Unesco, reflecting its culinary importance. Today, the city is also a gateway to other world cuisines, with Latin American, African and Asian restaurants joining the tavernas in its compact, chic city centre. It's an exciting time to bounce between the markets, restaurants, bakeries, cafes, bars and wineries of Thessaloniki as the city becomes more assured of its gastronomic importance.

01 Food stalls
on Thessaloniki's
waterfront

02 Colourful streets in
the cobbled Old Town

03 Freshly baked
bougatsa

04 Marianna of
Marianna's Vineleaves

01 BOUGATSA BANTIS

Thessaloniki's breakfast of choice is *bougatsa* (a slab of thick semolina custard between rippling layers of filo). It can be found on most street corners, but Bantis is one of a few bakeries to still make its own pastry thanks to third-generation *bougatsa* master Philippos Bantis.

Thessalonians and tourists alike come to Bantis for this slice of heaven every morning. Explore a mixed menu, from classics to left-field variants such as Mexican BBQ. "It's a kind of magic. Simple ingredients – flour, oil, water – make all these things", smiles Philippos.

The Sunday menu features Philippos' favourite, the 'authentiki': unadulterated filo delight, with golden-brown flakes doused in butter from nearby Drama and sprinkled with crystallised sugar. Be sure to come before church finishes at 11am to beat the Sunday rush.
Panagias Faneromenis 33;
https://bougatsa-bantis.
business.site

02 AGORA MODIANO

Modiano Market, which reopened in 2022 after six years of renovation, is a crash course in Thessaloniki's multicultural munchies. Built by Sephardi Jewish architect Eli Modiano on the site of an old synagogue, the all-new *agora* retains its art deco interior. On the ground floor, around 75 kiosks peddle everything from spicy *soutzoukakia* (Smyrna meatballs) to mountain tea from Crete.

Make a beeline for Olicatessen, a honey, olive oil and organic store operated by engineer-turned-eco entrepreneur Alex Stefanidis. Take part in a tasting and become a Halkidiki extra virgin connoisseur: Stefanidis teaches proper hand warming, smelling and sipping (read: slurping) etiquette.

On the market's mezzanine there's also a franchise of Estrella, the Thessaloniki brunch bar that reached peak Instagram when it blended semolina custard with croissants to create 'bougatsan'.
Vasileos Irakleiou 30;
www.agoramodiano.com

03 YPSILON

Greek lore has it that *frappé* – the unofficial national beverage – was invented by experimentation in Thessaloniki in 1957, so it's only right that visitors should try it in the city. Ypsilon is a minimalist cafe housed inside a high-ceilinged neoclassical paper factory – one of the few buildings to survive the 1917 Great Thessaloniki Fire.

Grab a foamy, on-the-rocks glass of the city's happiest accident and soak up the local coffee culture inside. By day Ypsilon is also a co-working space, with occasional exhibitions and documentary screenings; by night it becomes a split-level DJ venue.
Edessis 5; www.facebook.com/ ypsilonproject

04 MOÚRGA

Meaning 'dregs' in Greek, the name of this passion-packed *psarotaverna* (fish restaurant) belies the care taken with every dish. Moúrga has an open kitchen overlooked by bar stools, so you can witness the chefs making precise cuts of fish such as dentex, grouper and mullet. The selection changes daily depending on what the local fishers catch, with diners given a hand-scrawled menu.

Moúrga's collaborative relationship with its suppliers extends to the wine list: ask about the Ktima Ligas. The waiters will proudly tell you that this unfiltered white from nearby Pella is mostly exported to France, but Moúrga gets its own special allocation.

Be sure to book at least a couple of days ahead, as it's popular and there are never enough tables.
Christopoulou 12; www.instagram. com/mourga2016

05 MARIANNA'S VINELEAVES

Vineyards aren't just for wine; this family enterprise uses every part of the grape plant to make anything but. Its flagship product is *dolmadakia* - small vine leaves, preserved in salt and lemon, wrapped around dill-filled teaspoons of al dente rice to make buttery umami parcels – a recipe from the owner Marianna's Armenian mother's cookbook.

While Marianna's sons Sakis and Pangalos make you feel at home with lively chatter, pull up a chair at

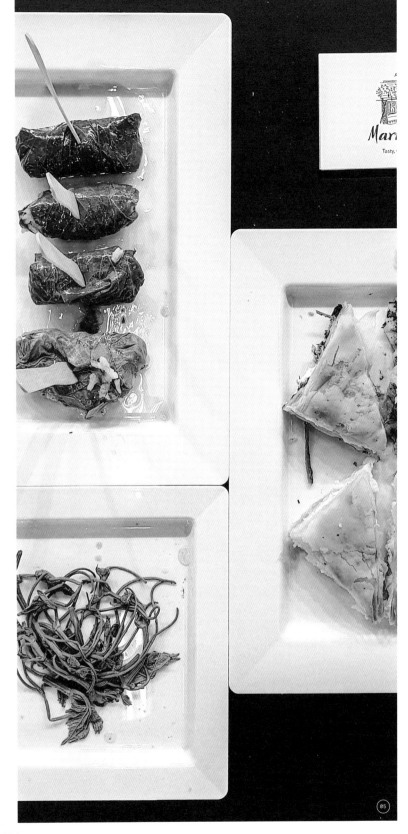

05 Buttery *dolmadakia* at Marianna's Vineleaves

06 Thessaloniki's landmark 16th-century White Tower

the lace-embroidered table to try the rest of Marianna's homegrown offerings. Scrumptious sultanas, grape extract, spoon sweets and pickled vine stems all get gobbled up with sips of the family's fine oak-barrel aged grape brandy, Abelon. *Nea Gonia 630 80; www.ntol madakia.com; closed weekends*

06 DORE ZYTHOS

Most terrace cafes on Stratiou Tsirogianni offer uninterrupted views of Thessaloniki's 16th-century White Tower, but Dore Zythos is the one to pick. Its menu truly reflects the combined culinary wealth of the city's communities. Inside, the mosaic-tiled saloon cooks up Cretan *dakos* (barley rusks topped with juicy tomato, feta and black olives), and creates dishes using Byzantine pomegranate sauce, *mastic* (aromatic plant resin) from Chios, Italian orzo, and even Persian *halva* (a syrupy paste made with rosewater and cardamom). The standout is *bouyourdi*, an Ottoman roasted feta dip with hot peppers. "It means everything mixed together," says manager Dionisis Katranitsas. *Stratiou Tsirogianni 9; www.zithos.gr*

WHERE TO STAY

HOTEL ONOMA

Personality is the name of the game at this uber-modern hotel by Thessaloniki's train station, which aims to make your stay as personalised as possible. Guests control everything from check-in to curtains, and the panoramic pool terrace is home to a bar where bartenders will create cocktails based on your name. There's also a restaurant, Good Mood Food, serving western comfort food with Thessaloniki twists. *www.onomahotel.com*

WHAT TO DO

THE WHITE TOWER

Rebuilt in the 16th century during the reign of Ottoman Sultan Suleiman the Magnificent, the White Tower is an architectural symbol of Thessaloniki. Over the centuries it has served as a prison, garrison, fort and sea defence, but it now houses a fascinating museum. Each floor uncovers a theme of

Thessaloniki's past since its founding in 315 BCE. The sixth floor is all about flavours, and touch screens set into tables play videos showing how the region's best-loved meals are made. Visitors can also ascend a spiral staircase to the tower's roof for the best bird's-eye view of the city, stretching across Halkidiki and the

Thermaic Gulf over to Mt Olympus. *www.lpth.gr*

CELEBRATIONS

THESSALONIKI FILM FESTIVAL

Every November, the warehouses and piers of Thessaloniki's port become a cinephile's fantasy. Indie Balkan filmmakers rub shoulders with Hollywood big

hitters (previous headliners have included John Malkovich and Francis Ford Coppola) to dish out gongs and talk all things filmmaking. Missed it? The Documentary Festival comes around in March, outdoor cinemas abound in summer, and the eccentric Cinema Museum is open all year. *www.filmfestival.gr*

GET THERE
The easiest way to reach Alentejo from the capital Lisbon is to get one of the frequent daily trains to Évora (1½ hrs) and then hire a car, as driving is the only real option for exploring the region.

ALENTEJO

ARRAIOLOS
03
VENDAS NOVAS
MONTEMOR-O-NOVO
04 ÉVORA
05

SETÚBAL

ALCÁCER DO SAL

ATLANTIC OCEAN
Lagoa de Santo André
ALENTEJO

BEJA

SINES

Rio Sado

VILA NOVA DE MILFONTES
02
CASTRO VERDE

OURIQUE

ODEMIRA
SÃO TEOTÓNIO
01

[Portugal]

HISTORY & HEARTY DISHES IN ALENTEJO

Between the Algarve and Lisbon, this rustic swathe of Portugal is locally beloved for its food and wine, yet often escapes the attention of tourists.

Speak to practically any Portuguese person and they'll tell you that Alentejo is synonymous with good food in their country. Yet beyond Portugal, this sprawling region is still something of a culinary secret. Home to some of Europe's most vivid scenery – red cork trees, olive orchards, fields of sunflowers, pine-covered forest floors and near-deserted sandy beaches – Alentejo's beauty, and its flavours, will remain etched on your memory long after a visit.

Roughly the size of Belgium, Alentejo is Portugal's most sparsely populated area and has been influenced by its Greek, Arab and Roman visitors over the years. Today its modern dishes are a fusion of traditional cultures, rich in red meat, sausages and *porco preto* (black pork), bread, creamy cheese, fish, clams and dishes that consist of simple, fresh ingredients, infused with garlic and laced with herbs such as parsley and coriander. Catholicism has also had a hand in shaping the region's food: many

desserts from the historical capital Évora were invented by Clarissian nuns. Giggle-inducing names for these egg-based, sweet treats such as 'Nun's Belly' and 'Heaven's Kiss' are a nod to their religious history and many pastries are still made using centuries-old recipes.

When it comes to wine, oenophiles will have a field day. Alentejo is in close competition with its more famous northern neighbour the Douro. Visitors can expect equally good quality here, with well-balanced whites and rich, full-bodied reds. Alentejo receives three times more rain than the rest of the country, making it the perfect climate for grape production. And the region's flavourful grapes have attracted a new generation of winemakers, who are applying new technologies and earning acclaim for zingy *vinho verde*, organic grapes and sustainable farming.

With a rich history, evocative landscapes, and great food and wine, Alentejo deserves more of the love that Lisbon and Porto are getting from visitors.

01 CRAVEIRAL FARMTABLE

Encompassing 22 acres of organic farmland, Craveiral is the brainchild of a Lisbon lawyer who escaped city life to transform a swathe of Alentejo land into an elegant countryside escape in 2010.

The nucleus of the site's agricultural operation is its farm-to-table, open-air restaurant. Here, the innovative seasonal menu sings of the restaurant's surroundings; 70% of the ingredients come from the onsite vegetable garden and orchard of Craveiral Farmhouse, while the remaining 30% is drawn from producers in the Odemira region.

The food at Craveiral is fresh, hearty and wholesome, blending old and new flavours. A highlight is the locally sourced *porco preto* (black pork found across the Iberian Peninsula), served with a glass of red and cooked on a sizzling open fire beside your table.

Diners also have the option to stay at one of Craveiral's 38 luxury villas, equipped with cork baths. Guests are encouraged to pick fruit and veg from the garden and get treated to daily breakfasts with eggs from the farm's chickens and copious helpings of farm-fresh fruit, tomatoes and honey.
Estrada Municipal 501, Km 4, São Teotónio; www.craveiral.pt

02 TASCA DO CELSO

For excellent, authentic Alentejan cooking, head to this rustic, family-run restaurant 10 minutes from Milfontes beach. There's a laid-back at-home feel, with utensils and tools hanging from the walls, and an open, airy kitchen leading into a shop that sells spreads and wine.

Sitting close to the point where the Mira River sluices into the Atlantic, seafood takes centre stage at Tasca do Celso. Specialities include shrimp sautéed in garlic, clams cooked in coriander and grilled monkfish or sea bass, but there are also meat options such as veal with roasted tomatoes or black pork salad.

Staff are attentive and knowledgeable and there's a wine list running to more than 30 pages. If visiting in summer, it's best to book ahead for dinner or you can chance

your luck at walk-in for lunch.
Rua dos Aviadores 34, Vila Nova
de Milfontes; https://tascacelso.
eatbu.com; closed Mon

03 HERDADE DE COELHEIROS

Some 30 minutes from Évora,
this vast family estate has been
producing wines since 1991. Full of
bright greens in summer and purple
grapes during harvesting season,
Coelheiros specialises in organic
reds and whites. France and Brazil
are its main export markets, but
its popularity is now growing
elsewhere too.

Take a tour of the vineyard,
which lasts two to three hours and
includes a walk through the estate's
cork and olive trees, where you

might even spot wild deer. You'll
get to taste the grapes and learn
about the harvesting and wine
ageing process. Wine sampling is,
of course, part of the tour: try the
light, citrusy whites, which lean
heavily on the local Arinto grape;
and rich, woody award-winning
reds, which blend grapes such
as Cabernet Sauvignon with local
varieties including Touriga Nacional
and Alicante Bouschet.
Herdade de Coelheiros, Igrejinha,
Arraiolos; www.coelheiros.pt;
closed weekends

04 DOM JOAQUIM RESTAURANT

To finish your Alentejo food tour,
head deep into the medieval
alleyways of the pretty regional

capital, Évora. After a stroll within
the city's 14th-century walls,
Dom Joaquim feels like the
perfect retreat. This family-run,
Michelin-starred restaurant
offers Portuguese dishes cooked
to perfection.

You'll find many of Alentejo's
classics here, such as roasted
octopus, grilled sea bass and codfish
cakes, but it's the meat and game
dishes, using locally sourced cuts
from animals raised on Alentejo's
plains and in its cork oak forests,
that really grab the attention.

Try the melt-in-the-mouth half
partridge marinated in a cherry
sauce, and the pork crackling –
best served with a hearty black
bean or rice stew. Wines are
another feature, with bottles

06 The pretty medieval centre of Évora

07 Pumpkin-filled pastry at Pastelaria Conventual Pão de Rala

08 The infinity pool at Quinta da Comporta

protruding from practically every wall in the restaurant – staff are well-versed on which bottles will perfectly pair with your meal.
Rua dos Penedos 6, Évora; http://restaurantedomjoaquim.pt; closed Mon

05 PASTELARIA CONVENTUAL PÃO DE RALA

Many of Évora's desserts were invented by Clarissian nuns, and this famed local bakery is one of the most lauded places to try their recipes. Lined with traditional blue tiles, the bakery is steeped in local history. Try the almond and egg-based *queijinho do céu* ('little cheese from heaven') and the *pão de rala* (a flourless, lemon-flavoured bread cake with almonds), or the amusingly titled 'Nun's Belly', which combines sugar, eggs, butter and bread.

There's even a bacon-inspired sweet treat, indicative of the region's obsession with all things pork. A spherical, jam-filled, flour-based tart with a salty aftertaste, it's called *pastel de toucinho* (pastry of bacon) but there's actually no longer any meat in these - the name has just stuck.

Pull up a chair at one of the tiny wooden tables indoors, order a *cafe pingado* (shot of espresso with a dash of milk) and watch the city of Évora roll by as you tuck into your sweet treats.
Rua de Cicioso 47, Évora; https://m.facebook.com/profile. php?id=169787683079463

WHERE TO STAY

QUINTA DA COMPORTA

For some serious R&R head to this former rice farm, which has been transformed into a complex of 73 luxury rooms and four white-washed villas. Take a dip in the solar-heated infinity pool overlooking rolling rice terraces, or grab a bike and cycle down to the nearby beach. The glass-fronted restaurant at Quinta da Comporta also offers incredible views of the fields.
*https://pt.quintada
comporta.com*

ALBERGARIA DO CALVÁRIO

Unpretentiously elegant, discreetly attentive and comfortable, this beautiful guesthouse is housed inside a 16th-century olive oil mill in Évora. The breakfasts are outstanding, with locally sourced seasonal fruits, homemade cakes and egg dishes. Gorgeous lounge areas are decked out with a tasteful melange of antique and modern furniture,

and there's a pleasant garden patio area. It's in a delightful part of town, near Porta Velha da Lagoa and the aqueduct. The excellent staff also give good insider tips for exploring Alentejo.
https://adcevora.com

WHAT TO DO

RESERVA NATURAL DAS LAGOAS DE SANTO ANDRÉ E DA SANCHA

Alentejo has some of Portugal's most gorgeous and quietest wild places, and this nature reserve is one of the best. It consists of the Lagoa de

Santo André, (the largest lagoon on the Alentejo coastline) and the smaller Lagoa da Sancha. Visitors can canoe the reserve or drink in the spectacular mountain views while hiking among its grassy dunes and wetlands. Birdwatching is particularly good here in late summer and early autumn. If you're lucky, you might even spot a dolphin or two at the Sado's mouth.
*https://natural.pt/
protected-areas/
reserva-natural-lagoas-
santo-andre-sancha*

CELEBRATIONS

NATIONAL CULINARY FESTIVAL

Alentejo is Portugal's gastronomic soul, so it follows that the National Culinary Festival is held here. It's been hosted by the Alentejo town of Santarém since 1981 and usually runs for around 10 days in October. Visitors get the opportunity to sample dishes from each of the 18 different regions in Portugal, as well as from the Azores and Madeira.
*www.festivalnacionalde
gastronomia.pt*

GET THERE
International routes
serve Porto's airport,
around 40 minutes by
metro from the city
centre. Rail services
connect Porto with the
main towns along the
inland Douro River.

PORTO & THE DOURO: A PERFECT PAIRING

Vintage Port cellars and Bourdain-worthy sandwiches make Porto a gourmet delight – the perfect prelude to wine-tasting among Unesco-listed Douro vines.

It's hard to imagine that a city where the locals are known as *tripeiros* (tripe eaters) and a sauce-soaked sandwich is seen as a defining dish could be a gastronomic destination. Yet, somehow, Porto's plates and tipples provide a refreshingly relaxed culinary experience. Much of this is a testament to the city's strong-spirited community and passionate business owners, who have helped this northern city develop a unique and somewhat understated cuisine. From storied, historical recipes to a new generation of forward-thinking coffee roasters and brewmasters, Portugal's second city can never be called complacent.

Among the colourful houses that climb up the steep streets from the riverbank, tiny traditional *tascas* serve signature dishes, such as *bacalhau à Gomes de Sá* – Porto's take on the nation's beloved codfish. Beyond the classics, contemporary brunch hot spots and artisanal beer shops are enhancing the city's food and drink appeal further.

Across the river, the historic Port cellars of Vila Nova de Gaia house barrel upon barrel of Portugal's world-renowned fortified wine, which arrives here after a meandering journey along the Douro River. Upstream, the scenic and steeply terraced vineyards of the Douro – many family-run – boast the title of the oldest demarcated wine region in the world (regulated and defined since 1756), and the near 2000-year-old vines of the Alto Douro are so celebrated that they have earned Unesco-listed status.

01 A COZINHA DO MARTINHO

Tripas à moda do Porto is a dish that defines the city's spirit, and while on paper it may sound dubious, A Cozinha do Martinho serves up one of the best takes. In fact, it was here that Anthony Bourdain sampled the signature stew while filming *Parts Unknown*.

Cooked with white beans and a variety of meat (stomach, intestines – the lot), the origins of the dish date back to the Age of Discovery, Portugal's seafaring colonising period. As the legend tells, the city was asked by Prince Henry the Navigator to give up all its cured meat to feed Portugal's sailors –a sacrifice that left Porto's residents with nothing but guts and poor-quality cuts. Scraping the

barrel, the city's cooks crafted this now renowned recipe.
Rua Costa Cabral 2598-2606, Porto; closed Mon

02 A REGALEIRA

This Porto institution opened its doors in 1934, with António Passos dishing out traditional recipes to well-heeled diners. Later, in an attempt to broaden the restaurant's appeal, new affordable dishes were born – including the *francesinha*, which would become one of Portugal's most famous sandwiches.

The birth of the *francesinha* followed a 1950s encounter in France with the bartender Daniel David da Silva, who returned with Passos to work in Portugal. It was

Silva who developed this croque monsieur-inspired dish. Heavier than its French counterpart, the Porto version is a stacked affair of bread, cheese, sausage, pork leg, and a rich beer, tomato and spiced sauce.

The restaurant closed its doors in 2018, only to eventually re-open a few doors down from its original location. Luckily, the original *francesinha* recipe remains unchanged.
Rua do Bonjardim 83, Porto; https://en-gb.facebook.com/ ARegaleira; closed Mon

03 FÁBRICA NORTADA

Like many of Porto's craft breweries, Fábrica Nortada's story started in 2015 with a couple of

friends, Tiago Talone and Pedro Mota, seeking to create something different to the two lagers – Super Bock and Sagres – that have dominated Portugal's beer scene for decades.

In 2018, their dream was realised with the opening of a contemporary brewpub in Porto's Bolhão neighbourhood. Clean lines and modern decor complement the fermentation tank-lined walls, with IPAs, stouts and Weiss Bier, among others, poured from the bronze-tapped bar. Factory tours, including guided tastings, can be booked in advance for an up-close look at brewing methods.
Rua de Sá da Bandeira 210, Porto; https://cervejanortada.pt; closed Sun & Mon

04 THE PINK PALACE, WOW

When WOW (World of Wine) arrived in Gaia, across from Porto's historic Ribeira neighbourhood, the city's landscape was changed forever, with some small port lodges lost to the construction. The vast cultural district (or, to some, theme park) opened to much fanfare in 2020, housing multiple museums, restaurants and a wine school.

The Pink Palace, entirely dedicated to rosé wine, is perhaps the most exuberant of the seven experiences. Visitors get five tasting samples paired with colourful interactive areas, ranging from a room dominated by a pink ball-pit to an 'upside down' picnic space. It's more about enjoying the photoshoots and fun than

spittoons and tasting notes.
Rua do Choupelo 39, Vila Nova de Gaia; https://wow.pt

05 TAYLOR'S PORT CELLAR

While the region's famed fortified Port wine is produced further down the Douro, the riverfront city of Vila Nova de Gaia (facing Porto) has become the industry hub – meaning an afternoon of tastings and learning doesn't require a designated driver. Ancient Port cellars crowd the sloped hill atop a labyrinth of underground aged barrels.

Taylor's 300-year-old Port cellar is one of Gaia's oldest, and with an informative self-guided 60-minute audio tour in multiple languages, one of the easiest to visit without

05

05 Dishes at DOC are a feast for the senses

06 Porto's opulent Palácio da Bolsa

inspiration from his own (clearly exceptional) memories.

The splendour of the climbing vineyard backdrop is best appreciated during lunch from the boardwalk dining terrace suspended over the river. *Cais da Folgosa, Estrada Nacional 222, Folgosa; www. docrestaurante.pt; closed Tue & Wed lunch*

08 QUINTA DO CRASTO

Leonor and Jorge Roquette's family have operated the Quinta do Crasto wine estate for over a century, following in the footsteps of Leonor's father and grandfather, who produced DOC Ports and Douro wines.

However, these scenic vines date back further, with documents proving production since 1615 – long before the 1756 pillar defining the demarcated region. Contemporary and classic techniques are harmonised, from the modern barrel stacking system to traditional *lagares* (stone vats) used to tread the Port grapes by foot.

Guided tours and tastings (reservation required) cover the jaw-dropping vineyards and cellars, concluding with some samplings. Choose from the latest released harvests, old vine *reservas* or a range of excellent Ports. *Gouvinhas, Sabrosa; https://quintadocrasto.pt*

a reservation. Tastings of two Ports are included in the tour; make a reservation if you want to try more samplings and different vintages. *Rua do Choupelo 250, Vila Nova de Gaia; www.taylor.pt*

06 A PRESUNTECA DE LAMEGO

Detouring slightly inland from the Douro, Lamego is a popular sightseeing stop to visit the 18th-century Sanctuary of Nossa Senhora dos Remédios, famed for its 686-step baroque staircase. But the city has a few other treasures – most notably *presunto de Lamego*, a salted, smoked and cured ham revered across Portugal.

On the grassy terrace of A Presunteca de Lamego, *tábuas* (tasting boards) of this delectable pork treat flow freely, as does the local and prestigious *espumante* (sparkling wine), another of Lamego's celebrated products since the 16th century. *N2, Lamego; www.facebook.com/ apresunteca.apresunteca*

07 RESTAURANTE DOC

Housed in a glass-fronted building on the bank of the Douro in Folgosa, DOC, by two Michelin-star chef Rui Paula, is a reservation worth making. Although the striking setting is extraordinary, the renowned chef still wants flavour to come first. Focusing on fresh seasonal ingredients to craft modern, sensorial tasting menus, Paula's philosophy is that "the memory of the taste of food must be respected", aligning with the fact he takes most of his

WHERE TO STAY

THE YEATMAN HOTEL
Situated on Gaia's
riverbank hill, among
historical Port lodges, The
Yeatman's spectacular
vistas across Porto's
jumble of colourful
houses – especially from
the infinity pool – are
reason enough to book a
room.Add in a wine cellar,
spa and two Michelin-Star
restaurant, and you've got
a proper luxury stay for
gourmet travellers.
*www.the-yeatman-
hotel.com*

QUINTA DA PACHECA
If sleeping among
16th-century vines isn't
enough, at Quinta Da
Pacheca you can stay
inside a wine barrel. Set
on the Douro's left bank
in the village of Cambres,
the wooden-clad barrel-
style bedrooms even
have circular windows to
frame the panorama.
*www.quintada
pacheca.com*

WHAT TO DO

PALÁCIO DA BOLSA
A guided tour of Porto's
most opulent building,
dating from the mid-

1850s, will dazzle –
especially inside the
Salão Árabe, where
gold-coated Islamic-style
stucco walls dominate.
www.palaciodabolsa.com

DOURO RIVER CRUISE
Slow down and soak in
the scenic terraced views
and tiny hamlets from
the waters on board a
day or lunch river cruise
down the Douro.
www.rotadodouro.pt

**PARQUE
ARQUEOLÓGICO DO
VALE DO CÔA**
Discover the history
of the Alto Douro long
before vintners were
residents on a guided
tour of these open-air
Paleolithic engravings.
www.arte-coa.pt

CELEBRATIONS

DOURO GRAPE HARVEST
In September (dates
vary year to year), the
terraces of the Douro
come alive as vintners,
workers and volunteers
clip, collect and crush
the annual harvest.
It's an exciting time
to visit, as you can often
upgrade tastings in
quintas to include the
whole experience
– sometimes even
joining story-sharing
locals in the age-old
tradition of grape-
stomping.

GET THERE

As a handy alternative to flying, Ibiza has good ferry links to Valencia, Dénia and Barcelona on mainland Spain. To explore the island you'll need your own wheels, though the local bus system is convenient for hopping between Ibiza Town and other big towns.

MEDITERRANEAN
SEA

IBIZA

PORTINATX

CALA SANT
VICENT

SANT MIQUEL
DE BALANSAT

SANT JOAN
DE LABRITJA

05

SANTA AGNES
DE CORONA

SANT MATEU
D'ALBARCA

06

04

SANT LLORENÇ
DE BALÀFIA

CALA
LLENYA

SANTA
GERTRUDIS
DE FRUITERA

SANT ANTONI
DE PORTMANY

07

IBIZA

03

SANTA EULÀRIA
DES RIU

CALA LLONGA

01

02

IBIZA
TOWN

08

ES CUBELLS

SANT FRANCESC
DE S'ESTANY

[Spain]

FARM TO FORK IBIZA

Savour a different side to the Balearics' White Isle, bouncing between lively village markets, traditional ibicenco *kitchens and boho-chic farm-to-table restaurants.*

Flung out in the Mediterranean Sea, off Spain's east coast, this party-loving Balearic island is home to a deeply soulful world of gastronomy, in which flavours from all over the globe collide and small-scale local producers are celebrated. Since the arrival of the Phoenicians more than 2000 years ago, salt has been harvested and wine has been made on this bewitching, sun-washed island – just the beginning of a long, rich food and drink heritage that revolves around ancient flavours and ingredients.

It's this unique combination of Balearic culinary traditions, including spectacular seafood creations and irresistible *arrossos* (rice dishes), and international influences that makes Ibiza's food scene such a tantalising adventure. Golden olive oils, fresh fish and seafood, delectably rich charcuterie, glistening artisanal salt and smooth local cheeses count among the island's prized bounty.

Ibizan wines are gaining traction too. Traditionally, wines here were rustic drops made simply for home consumption, but today's intimate, family-owned bodegas are innovating with production methods and putting the IGP (Indicación Geográfica Protegida) *Vino de la Tierra de Ibiza* firmly on the map.

To accompany these island wines, a wave of farm-to-table restaurants is upping the ante with wonderfully creative cookery. Evocative *agroturismes* are fuelling meals with their own on-site gardens, while an ever-growing number of farming projects are putting an organic ethos front and centre.

All over the island, buzzing farmers markets bring only the freshest produce to local streets, much of it organically grown. One of the best happens to the sound of live music in northern Sant Joan de Labritja every Sunday morning – the perfect embodiment of Ibiza's enormous gastronomic attraction.

01 MERCAT NOU

All things food in Ibiza start with the local market, and the modern Mercat Nou (New Market) is Ibiza Town's fresh-produce hub, a 10-minute stroll northwest of historical Dalt Vila. Mountains of tomatoes, dangling bunches of carrots, rows of prickly pineapples, shelves of goat cheeses and counters stacked with the freshest fruits of the sea tempt local shoppers, with most ingredients sourced right here on the island. If you're picking up a picnic for the beach, this is the spot.

Over in the shadow of Dalt Vila's 16th-century ramparts, don't miss the neoclassical Mercat Vell (Old Market), another beloved spot for everything from Ibiza-made olive oil to just-baked bread and artisanal honey.
Carrer de Canàries, Ibiza Town;
closed afternoons & Sun

02 CA N'ALFREDO

The endless, subtle Mediterranean flavours of traditional *ibicenco* cooking shine at Ca n'Alfredo, a long-established local favourite in the thick of Ibiza Town. Originally founded in 1934, it has been run by the respected Riera family since the 1940s. A lively lunch here might start with an olive-oil-drizzled *ensalada pagesa* (country-style salad topped with cod) and a few slivers of wafer-thin spinach-and-pine-nut coca bread, followed by Catalan-style *canelons* (stuffed pasta tubes), oven-baked snapper or rabbit with snails and mushrooms. The sizzling rice dishes are a signature, including seafood paella and *arròs negre* (squid-ink rice), and all wines come from bodegas across the island.
Passeig de Vara de Rey 16,
Ibiza Town; www.canalfredo.com;
closed Mon

03 CAN MUSON

Just west of the buzzy coastal community of Santa Eulària, this calming all-organic farm is a deep-dive into the island's traditional rural roots and rich agricultural heritage. Take a guided tour to meet local goats and donkeys, stock up on farm-fresh goodies at the shop, or settle in among the orange trees

for a glass of Ibiza-made wine, a glorious local-produce breakfast or a Km0 salad bursting with homegrown ingredients.

You can also join hands-on workshops to learn the secrets behind *pa pagès* (rustic artisanal bread), *flaó* (a typical cheesecake), goat cheese and other classic Ibiza creations.
Carretera de Santa Eulària Km 11, Santa Eulària des Riu; www.ibizacanmuson.com; closed evenings

04 LA PALOMA

With its romantic *finca*-style setting, lantern-lit gardens and live-music evenings, it's no surprise that mellow La Paloma ranks among Ibiza's most popular rural restaurants, drawing devotees to tiny Sant Llorenç from all over the island. Tuscan chef Prasuna Coppini's creative, always-changing menu is an Italian-Middle Eastern feast of fresh, organic island produce and other Spain-sourced ingredients. Zingy pesto pasta, homemade falafel and smoked aubergine with feta might grace the tree-shaded tables; the bread is home-baked each day; and creative salads revolve around ingredients plucked straight from the on-site garden. During cooler months, dine by the fire in the stylishly rustic interior.
Sant Llorenç; www.palomaibiza. com; cafe open lunch year-round, restaurant open evenings only & closed Jan & Feb

05 THE GIRI CAFÉ

In the delightfully low-key northern village of Sant Joan, this locally loved jewel of a Mediterranean restaurant evokes all that's wonderful about the rise of Ibiza's farm-to-table movement, with its sunny back garden, boho-chic design and handful of seductive hotel rooms.

"We carefully curate our evolving menus to reflect the changing seasons, cherry-picking the finest organic, pesticide-free ingredients from local markets and farmers – or by growing them in our own vegetable garden," says owner Rosa Pil Hildebrandt. "Try the fish of the day with roasted aubergine, chermoula and pomegranate, or the all-time

06 An organic feast at Aubergine

07 Ibiza Town's Unesco-listed Dalt Vila spirals uphill to a cathedral

favourite avocado cheesecake."
Plaça d'Espanya 5, Sant Joan de Labritja; www.thegiri.com; closed Nov-Feb

06 AUBERGINE

A whitewashed country *finca*, sage-green furniture and meandering terraces wrapped in hot-pink bougainvillea set the scene for fabulous farm-to-table cooking at Aubergine, just south of Sant Miquel in the island's rugged north. Most of the ingredients used in the kitchen come from the organic-vegetable garden of luxe *agroturisme* Atzaró, its sister business. The restaurant delivers imaginative, season-fired dishes such as pumpkin-and-feta salads, red-prawn tabbouleh and zesty house-made hummus, along with rainbow-coloured fresh juices and smoothies.
Carretera de Sant Miquel Km 9.9; www.aubergineibiza.com

07 BODEGAS CAN RICH

Founded in 1990, just outside Sant Antoni, family-owned Can Rich is a prize-winning winery with a strong sustainable ethos, where 20 rolling hectares yield elegant whites, reds, rosés and sparkling wines.

"In Ibizan wines you can feel the salty influence of the Mediterranean and also the island's herbs," says owner and winemaker Stella González Tuells. "Our wines are all organic-certified and part of the IGP Vino de la Tierra de Ibiza, which focuses on Km0 products and reducing carbon footprints. For us, the land is life."

The winery's intimate tours and tasting sessions are by appointment – you'll get to sit out in the Mediterranean sun while sampling a raft of *ibicenco* wines paired with rosemary-rimmed goat cheese, *pa pagès* and Can Rich's own olive oil.
Camí de Sa Vorera; www.bodegascanrich.com

08 ES BOLDADÓ

One of the Balearics' most magical dining settings awaits at this classic seafood address, tucked into the cliffside in protected Cala d'Hort on the southwest tip of Ibiza. The mystical islet of Es Vedrà looms offshore, with the Mediterranean shimmering all around in shades of turquoise and cobalt.

But it's not just about the views – with over 30 years of culinary history, Es Boldadó also wows with its traditional, ultra-fresh *ibicenco* recipes, such as *bullit de peix* (savoury fish stew) followed by *arròs a banda* (rice cooked in fish stock), and perhaps a spread of local island cheeses. Complete your meal with a *café Caleta* (aromatic coffee with spices, citrus and brandy). If you're lucky, you might also get a complimentary glass of limoncello to send you on your way.
Cala d'Hort; www.esboldadoibiza. com; closed evenings

WHERE TO STAY

CAN MARTÍ

This luxuriously restored 400-year-old *finca* near Sant Joan offers a peaceful retreat with a sustainable focus (solar power, organic gardens, permaculture), a natural lava-rock pool and a handful of elegant, light-flooded, wood-beamed rooms.
www.canmarti.com

LOS ENAMORADOS

A dreamy vision of Ibizan design, overlooking the fishing boats in northern Portinatx, nine-room Los Enamorados also hosts a hugely popular restaurant where locally sourced seafood and organic island ingredients take centre stage.
www.losenamorados ibiza.com

WHAT TO DO

IBIZA OUTDOORS

Get out into the wild on a thrilling, expert-guided hike around southern Ibiza's salt flats, the remote northern bay of Es Portitxol, the spine-tingling cliffs

overlooking Es Vedrà, and more. Founder Toby Clarke is also behind Ibiza Food Tours, which runs gastronomic walks to meet local chefs and taste island specialities in Ibiza Town.
www.ibizaoutdoors.com

DALT VILA

Ibiza Town's enchanting, Unesco-listed historical core was founded by the Phoenicians in the

7th century BCE. Pop into the 14th-century Catalan gothic cathedral, clamber up the imposing 16th-century ramparts and dive into the Museu d'Art Contemporani d'Eivissa.

CAMINO VERDE

Learn all about nutritional and medicinal autochthonous plants on a foraging walk through one of the island's hidden

natural corners.
www.camino-verde-ibiza.com

CELEBRATIONS

The remote northern village of Sant Mateu d'Albarca, in Ibiza's grape-growing region, hosts the lively Festa del Vi Pagès each December, celebrating traditional homemade wines and showing off typical *ball pagès* dancing.

GET THERE
Of Galicia's three airports
– Vigo, A Coruña and
Santiago de Compostela
– the latter is best
connected. Autobuses
Alsa (www.alsa.es) travel
between major cities and
some smaller towns,
but hiring a car offers
more freedom.

01

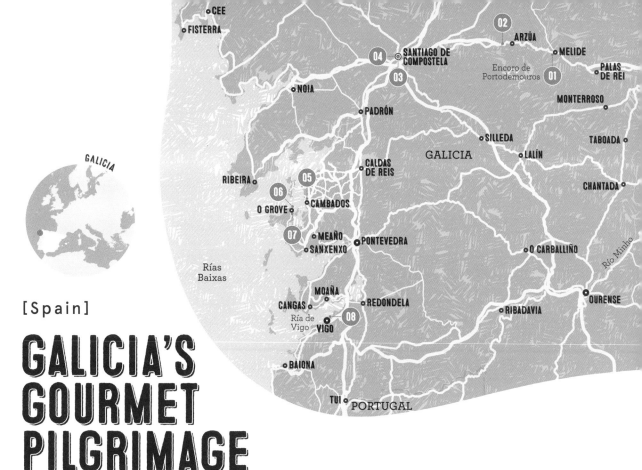

The map shows locations across Galicia including: CEE, FISTERRA, ARZÚA, MELIDE, SANTIAGO DE COMPOSTELA, PALAS DE REI, Encoro de Portodemouros, MONTERROSO, NOIA, PADRÓN, SILLEDA, TABOADA, GALICIA, LALÍN, CHANTADA, RIBEIRA, CALDAS DE REIS, O GROVE, CAMBADOS, MEAÑO, O CARBALLIÑO, Ríos Baixas, SANXENXO, PONTEVEDRA, Río Miño, MOAÑA, CANGAS, REDONDELA, OURENSE, Ría de Vigo, VIGO, RIBADAVIA, BAIONA, TUI, PORTUGAL. Numbered markers: 01, 02, 03, 04, 05, 06, 07, 08.

[Spain]

GALICIA'S GOURMET PILGRIMAGE

Set out on a culinary journey through Spain's green northwest corner, trying only-in-Galicia dishes, a saintly tart and some of the country's best wine and seafood.

Though nowhere near as famous as the Michelin star-studded Basque Country, this northwestern region of Spain has been quietly obsessive about food for generations. With good reason – this is where you'll find some of the best seafood in the country. Everything from mussels to monkfish is plucked from the wave-lashed shores of the Costa da Morte and whisked onto your plate with almost indecent haste. It's also home to some of the country's most niche culinary offerings, including a delicious but somewhat unappealingly named octopus dish, *pulpo*, and a breast-shaped cheese.

The city that puts Galicia on the map is Santiago de Compostela, where pilgrims pursuing the *Camino de Santiago* (the Way of St James) eventually all land up. Others flock here for an epiphany of a different kind – as the region's capital, it's an excellent place to try produce from all over the area, its thriving restaurant scene buoyed in part by religious tourism. Outside this holy city, you'll find Galicia is a relatively under-the-radar destination with a unique, Celtic-infused culture; its landscape smattered with the *castros* (fortified villages) its modern inhabitants' forebears left behind.

All these influences come together at the Galician dining table. Though there's no shortage of good options on that score, this is a destination where the best food is often the simplest – dishes that allow the peerless produce of this green and fertile land to shine. Galicia is cooler and wetter than regions further south, but the Albariño grape thrives here, producing some outstanding wines. Their popularity abroad has soared in recent years, but you'll find they taste even better drunk in situ. Raise your glass with a toast of *Saúde!*; Galician for 'good health'.

① PULPERIA EZEQUIEL

The literal translation of *pulperia* is 'octopussery', but a fabulously Bond girl-esque name isn't the only special thing about this simple canteen in Melide. The crossroads for two Camino pilgrimage routes, the tiny town is around 100km (61 miles) inland from the coast – but it's nevertheless the best place to try the region's signature dish, *polbo á feira* (boiled octopus with garlic and paprika). Nowhere near as challenging as it sounds, the cephalopod is tenderised by cooking and served on wooden plates with sides of boiled potatoes, bread and good red wine.

Cantón de San Roque 48, Melide; www.pulperiaezequiel.com

② A GRANXA DE TATO

A delightful pitstop on the drive into Santiago de Compostela, this rural grocery store-cum-cafe exclusively serves dishes made with local and seasonal products. Take lunch either in its wood-heavy dining room or in the lovely garden. Menu highlights might include chorizo with turnip tops, or a hot sandwich filled with Arzúa Ulloa cheese and tangy quince paste.

You'll almost always find proprietor Jose Veses on duty. "Galicians deeply value traditional foods," he says. There are plenty of those on sale, but this is also a good place for visitors to stock up on more contemporary culinary souvenirs, including community-made craft beers and kombucha.

Lugar A Peroxa; www.agranxa detato.com

③ MOSTEIRO DE SAN PAIO DE ANTEALTARES

With a St James cross dusted on its top in icing sugar, Santiago's namesake tart is perhaps Spain's holiest confection, synonymous with the many pilgrims who arrive in the city each year. So where better to purchase a Tarta de Santiago than a nunnery?

Founded in 1499, the order's motto is 'pray and work', and since the 18th century much of the sisters' labour has been devoted to baking peerless biscuits and cakes. To ensure the nuns aren't seen these artisanal products are sold

01 Santiago de Compostela's cathedral, end point for pilgrims

02 Galicia's signature dish, *polbo á feira*

03 A plate of padrón peppers

04 Green and fertile hills on Galicia's coast

through a revolving window, which only adds to the fun.
Calle de San Paio de Antealtares 23, Santiago de Compostela; www.monasteriosanpelayo.org

04 MERCADO DE ABASTOS

Santiago's 1940s-era food market is as much a visual experience as a culinary one, with indoor and outdoor stalls loaded with the finest produce from around the region. It's a prime spot for purchasing the area's most voluptuous dairy product, *tetilla* – an iconic Galician cheese that's been produced in the region for more than 1000 years.

The name, which translates as 'nipple', comes from the fact that the cheese's conical shape is reminiscent of a breast. Once you've tried a few samples, head for aisle number five. Here, chefs make use of the market's abundance to prepare dishes such as *filloas* (Galician crêpes) and fine seafood.
Rua Ameás, Santiago de Compostela; www.mercado deabastosdesantiago.com; closed Sun

05 BODEGA PALACIO DE FEFIÑANES

Cambados is the capital of the Albariño wine region and right at its heart is the Praza de Fefiñáns, a broad square built in the 1500s that looks like a *Game of Thrones* set. Almost as old is its namesake winery, which has been cultivating grapes since the 17th century and now offers guided tours by appointment. It's an exceptionally pretty spot: the grounds dotted with vine-strewn pergolas and myriad archways trailing ivy and colourful flowers, the barrel-filled cellars moodily atmospheric. The bodega makes four very different wines – taste them all on site, then fill the car with your favourite.
Praza de Fefiñáns, Cambados; www.fefinanes.com; closed Sun

06 CRUCEROS DO ULLA

A series of coastal inlets dotted with sandy beaches and pretty fishing villages, the Rías Baixas are one of the under-visited regions of Galicia's few holiday hotspots. But as well as possessing dazzling landscapes, this area is rich in

05

aquaculture – specifically, mussel production. You can take in both on these small-boat tours through the Ría de Arousa, which depart from the port of O Grove to explore the unique, raft-like *batea* mussel farms plus picturesque spots where oysters and scallops are cultivated.

As a finale to the trip, which lasts a little over an hour, you'll be served a plate of steaming mussels and a glass of local wine.
Avenida de Beiramar, O Grove; www.crucerosdoulla.com

07 D'BERTO

Galicia's wave-lashed coast supplies some of the country's best seafood and the pick of the haul

seems to end up at this relatively modest restaurant. Loved by superstar Spanish chefs including José Pizarro and Nieves Barragán Mohacho, it's been going strong for more than three decades.

Situated in the fishing village of O Grove, its low-key dining room is decorated with wine bottles and local artworks – but the dishes are the real stars of the show, from goose barnacles to grilled lobster. "Our magic lies in buying the best and biggest fish and shellfish, and treating the product with love and affection," says restaurant owner Berto Domínguez.
Avenida Teniente Domínguez 84, O Grove; www.dberto.com

08 CALLE DE LAS OSTRAS

Though officially the home of Vigo's fishmongers, this short stretch in the Old Town is better known as the city's 'oyster street'. Rock up between 10.30am and 3.30pm and you'll find it packed with people slinging back bivalves freshly shucked by the street vendors, who buy them straight off the boats.

The street is also lined with restaurants – buy a drink at one and they're happy for you to pull up a pew with your takeaway. Locals swear by oysters and a glass of Albariño as a fail-safe hangover cure, best consumed at breakfast.
Rúa da Pescadería, Vigo

WHERE TO STAY

SAN FRANCISCO HOTEL MONUMENTO

Occupying an 18th-century Franciscan monastery on the edge of Santiago's Old Town, this stylish hotel bears no trace of the deprivations endured by its former order (and now has an indoor pool). However, the brothers' legacy lives on in the restaurant, which specialises in 'convent cuisine'. Menus feature traditional recipes served in religious communities across Spain, prepared with all-natural ingredients.
www.sanfrancisco hm.com

PENSION VINOTECA RIBEIRA DE FEFIÑÁNS

Also a restaurant and specialist wine store, the proprietor of this good-value Cambados guesthouse is a font of oenological knowledge – ask José Aragunde to recommend a bottle from his 500-strong cellar and savour it on the sea-facing terrace.
www.ribeiradefefinans. com/la-pension

WHAT TO DO

You only have to walk the last 100km (61 miles) of the Camino de Santiago to qualify as a bona fide pilgrim. Tenedor Tours do tailormade routes through northern Spain, handpicking hotels and planning hiking routes to suit ability. They also offer guided food tours of Galicia; a great option for anyone lacking confidence in their Spanish.
www.tenedortours.com

CELEBRATIONS

SANTIAGO (É) TAPAS

Each autumn, Galicia's capital hosts a giant, city-wide tapas competition – and you get to help judge. All you have to do is pick up an official guide to vote, which will also give details of deals at participating restaurants across Santiago de Compostela.
www.santiagoe tapas.gal

FESTA DO ALBARIÑO

Wine and music are natural bedfellows, and this 10-day celebration of both takes place annually in Cambados, the seafaring capital of the Albariño region, surrounded by wineries. Rock up late July/early August to sample Spanish pop alongside the crisp signature drop.
www.fiestadel albariño.com

06

GET THERE
Bilbao is the main entry
point to the Basque
Country and is connected
to many European cities
by frequent flights.
Another alternative is
to fly to Biarritz in the
French Basque Country,
which is only 20 minutes
from San Sebastián.

[Spain]

IN CELEBRATION OF BASQUE BRILLIANCE

The food-obsessed locals of Spain's Basque Country are natural born chefs, forever competing to take their culinary stardom to new heights.

What is it that makes the food of Spain's Basque Country so good? The climate is an obvious one. Ample sunshine and a lot of rainfall (often at the same time!) encourages things to grow with rare enthusiasm. You only have to drop an apple core here for it to turn into a tree glistening in shiny red apples. And then there's the varied landscapes. From a storm wracked, fish-filled Atlantic Ocean to mountain pastures grazed by fat cows and sheep, the Basque Country has a geography suited to growing and producing almost anything. But, perhaps above all, there's the Basque people's obsessive love of food.

This is a land of members-only gastronomic societies. A region where people labour up mountain slopes to buy ewe's milk cheese straight from shepherds, or wait at dawn for the return of fishing boats so they can bag the freshest catch. Alongside this food obsession is an in-born artistic streak and a keen sense of pride that leaves Basque chefs engaged in constant competition to outdo one another with the creativity of their cooking. Nowhere else in the world could come up with cod-flavoured ice-cream.

The result is an astounding collection of world-class restaurants and – perhaps the Basques' defining contribution to the world culinary scene – the *pintxo*. Calling this culinary marvel the Basque version of a *tapa* does it a great disservice. Small, varied and intensely unexpected, a *pintxo* is, in fact, the essence of the Basque Country condensed into one bite. So, practise your *topa!* (Basque for cheers) and dive in.

01 LA RIBERA MARKET

A culinary tour of Bilbao should start at the source: this art deco market is where any chef worth their salt and pepper buys most of their ingredients. It covers some 10,000 sq metres (107,639 sq ft) near the riverfront and is described by the *Guinness Book of Records* as the biggest covered produce market in the world, which seems appropriate for a food-obsessed city like Bilbao.

Inside you'll find around 180 businesses all grouped together according to the produce they sell. Almost all of it is grown, raised or caught within the Basque Country and, thanks to the food court, you can taste some of these ingredients as fresh as they come.
Erribera Kalea s/n, Bilbao

02 GURE TOKI

Gure Toki has been a Bilbao *pintxo* institution for almost as long as *pintxos* have existed. You could almost say it was a driving force in the movement that pitted bar against bar to come up with ever more ornate culinary creations. It's on the atmospheric Plaza Nueva in Bilbao's old quarter. Make sure you order the house special of scallop with potatoes.
Plaza Nueva 12, Bilbao;
www.guretoki.com

03 HELADERÍA NOSSI-BE

The Nossi-Be ice-cream parlour has a history going back over a century. At first it was just the classics such as vanilla, strawberry and chocolate. But, this being the Basque Country, Nossi-Be's ice-cream eventually ended up becoming as creative as every other edible morsel here.

Inspired by classic Basque and Cantabrian dishes, the Heladería Nossi-Be invented the concept of squid ink ice-cream, which is served complete with a squid. Other unusual savoury combinations await visitors, too – there's a cod fish ice-cream, a mushroom ice-cream, and so the list goes on.

Some of them are definitely an acquired taste, but nobody can deny that they're not original. And they do still have plain old vanilla – here it's served with Bourbon.
Nafarroa Kalea 1, Bilbao;
www.heladeria-bilbao.com

⓸ ELKANO

Growing up in a small fishing village on the shores of the often stormy, wave battered, Basque coast, Pedro Arregui knew about fishing and fish. And he knew about cooking fish, so one thing led to another and Pedro started grilling fish to sell from outside his mother's grocery shop.

One day, a fisherman brought him a fish that was too big to grill in the classic way so he simply roasted it whole without removing the skin. Such a simple act. Yet such a revolution. From that moment on the stage was set and – now under the guidance of Pedro's son, Aitor - Elkano has become one of the planets most acclaimed fish restaurants. And it's all done using that same simple, but game changing cooking technique.
Herrerieta Kalea 2, Getaria; closed Tue

⓹ BERGARA BAR

It was San Sebastián that made the Basque Country a place of legend among world foodies. And, with one of the highest per capita Michelin Star rates in the world and a *pintxos* scene that is considered the best in Spain, that's hardly a surprise. Most of the action focuses on the *Casco Vieja* (Old Town), which is virtually wall to wall *pintxos* bars. But, with so many tourists now flooding this part of town most locals prefer to pop a *pintxo* in their mouth in one of the bars elsewhere in the city. Bergara Bar, in the surf beach neighbourhood of Gros, is a classic local hangout with tasty morsels piled up along the bar top and more (normally the hot, made to order ones) chalked up on a black board. The house special is anchovy tortilla or spider crab mousse.
General Artetxe 8, San Sebastián; www.pinchosbergara.es

⓺ ASADOR ETXEBARRI

Tucked into the lush green foothills of the Basque interior, this stunning Michelin-starred restaurant is widely considered the best place in the world to eat flame grilled meats.

The secret to chef Victor Arguinzoniz's success is the best quality Basque meat; the careful selection of wood to burn (vine

Ø5 Salt pans at Valle
Salado de Añana

Ø6 Marqués de Riscal
winery and hotel,
designed by Frank Gehry

trunks, ancient olives, holm oak – each lends a different taste); and an innovative, fully adjustable grill system he designed himself. *San Juan Plaza 1, Axpe; www. asadoretxebarri.com; lunch only, closed August & late Dec to mid-Jan*

07 TOLOÑO

Although San Sebastián wears the *pintxo* crown, the inland Basque capital of Vitoria-Gasteiz – a stately town with a medieval core – is also worthy of any gourmand's attention and unjustifiably often gets overlooked. Toloño Bar is the most awarded *pintxo* bar in Vitoria,

serving classic and creative *pintxos* in a contemporary bar. Its risotto with mushrooms is a local favourite. *San Frantzisko Aldapa 7, Vitoria-Gasteiz; www.tolonobar.com*

08 VALLE SALADO DE AÑANA

"What have the Romans ever done for us?", When the actor John Cleese famously asked this question in Monty Python's *Life of Brian*, he hadn't thought of the Valle Salado de Añana and salt. The Romans knew the salt coming out of the Basque Country's Valle Salado de Añana, some 30km (19 miles) west of Vitoria-Gasteiz,

was not your average salt and they harvested it with enthusiasm. It's an industry that continues to this day, with many of Spain's best chefs sourcing their salt here.

Tours of the salt pans are easy to arrange and fasctinating: some 4km (2.5 miles) of wooden aqueducts transport high-saline spring water from 200-million-year-old underground salt deposits to a series of terraces where it's harvested. After the tour, visitors can buy and taste the salt, including gourmet ones flavoured with wine or olive oil. *Real Kalea 32, Gesaltza Añana; www.vallesalado.com*

WHERE TO STAY
BASQUE BOUTIQUE
Combine an arty style with affordable rates and a plum position in the heart of Bilbao's Old Town and you get Basque Boutique; a fabulously one-of-a-kind place with exposed red brick, gnarled wood beams and individual eye-catching details.
www.basqueboutique.es

HOTEL MARQUÉS DE RISCAL
This spectacularly designed luxury hotel is the work of Frank Gehry (he of Guggenheim museum fame) – a flouncy rainbow wave of titanium that stands in utter contrast to the old wine village behind. Close to the border of La Rioja, it's part of a vast wine estate that can be toured.
www.marquesde riscal.com

WHAT TO DO
PYRENEAN FOOTHILL VILLAGES
The real heart and soul of the Basque Country is to be found in the countryside. Head to the prim villages of the Pyrenean foothills, such as Roncal, to truly experience Basque culture – and some unforgettable food.

GUGGENHEIM BILBAO
This Bilbao art gallery is one of modern architectures most iconic buildings and shouldn't be missed. There are rotating exhibitions as well as a stellar permanent collection.
www.guggenheim-bilbao.eus

CELEBRATIONS
TRANSHUMANCE
This twice-yearly event occurs when shepherds lead their livestock up to summer alpine pastures in about June and then when they descend again in late September. In certain areas, the movement of livestock is accompanied by village markets and fairs with a strong food element. Ask at tourist offices in mountain areas for exact dates.

06

GET THERE
Jerez and El Puerto de
Santa María are easily
reached by train from
Cádiz, Seville and beyond.
Sanlúcar has good bus
services, with Damas and
Monbus. If flying, Jerez
and Seville airports are
most convenient.

BONANZA

08

07 SANLÚCAR DE
          BARRAMEDA

Gulf of
Cádiz

06

CHIPIONA

CÁDIZ

CÁDIZ

02

01   03
JEREZ DE LA
FRONTERA

ROTA

[Spain]

ATLANTIC
OCEAN

EL PUERTO
DE SANTA
MARÍA

05 Río Guadalete

04

Bay of
Cádiz

INSIDE THE SHERRY TRIANGLE

With its Atlantic-influenced food scene, centuries-old markets and bold wines, Cádiz's Sherry Triangle has become one of Spain's greatest culinary adventures.

This soulful pocket of Cádiz province – a 140-sq-km (54-sq-mile) expanse between Jerez de la Frontera, Sanlúcar de Barrameda and El Puerto de Santa María – has been producing wines since the Phoenicians arrived around 1100 BCE.

The chalky, mineral-rich *albariza* soils yield a wealth of *palomino* grapes, which, after fermentation, are aged for at least three years in spectacular cathedral-like bodegas using the ingenous *criadera* and *solera* system in American-oak barrels. Jerez-Xérès-Sherry was the first ever Denominación de Origen (DO) to be created in Spain, back in 1933. Today, sherries (locally called *vinos de Jerez*) are just as much part of daily life here as a *jamón* tapa.

Andalucía's fresh bounty, meanwhile, fuels an irresistible regional gastronomy renowned across Spain for both its fuss-free originality and its pioneering creativity. Artisanal cheeses from Grazalema, Conil-grown fruits, *retinto* beef, delicate spices (inherited from Moorish times), *jamón* from Huelva and the famous wild *almadraba* tuna (caught using a sustainable millennia-old technique) are just a few of the ingredients you'll savour – whether at a fine-dining address, a family-run fish restaurant or a crammed urban tapas bar.

The epicentre of the Sherry Triangle is the flamenco-loving city of Jerez de la Frontera, whose unstoppable food scene revolves around earthy tapas hangouts, flamenco-filled *tabancos* (sherry bars) and, in recent years, the arrival of cutting-edge kitchens such as LÚ Cocina y Alma (an experimental French-flavoured delight from Juan Luis Fernández) and Mantúa (an ambitious ode to Cádiz's flavours by Israel Ramos), both of which now hold Michelin stars.

01 BODEGAS TRADICIÓN

There's nowhere better to dive into the Sherry Triangle's flavours than Jerez's timeworn bodegas, with their vine-shaded courtyards, arched ceilings and sky-reaching *crianza* (ageing) halls. Tradición was created in 1998 by a trio of respected wine-making families (Domecq, Rivero and López de Carrizosa), and ranks among the region's most respected and intriguing wine-world names.

"We are the only bodega in Jerez devoted exclusively to very old wines (VOS and VORS) and brandy," says second-generation president Helena Rivero. "These are completely natural wines, whose flavours, aromas and colours are produced only by ageing and the watchful eye of our expert winemakers." Entry to the bodega is by appointment. Visitors also get treated to a look at Tradición's astonishing private art collection, with pieces by Goya, Velázquez and Zurbarán hidden among the ancient barrels.

Calle Cordobeses 3, Jerez;
www.bodegastradicion.es

02 TABANCO PLATEROS

Until a decade ago, Jerez's traditional *tabancos* (sherry bars) were in serious danger of dying out. Now, these irresistible, unpretentious temples to flamenco, sherry and Cádiz-style tapas have been reborn, celebrating their 20th-century roots while also pushing forward fresh foodie ideas.

Opened by Luz Saldaña and Jaime Jiménez in 2011, Tabanco Plateros was the first to kick off this renaissance. On any day of the week, its narrow, light-flooded bar (a reimagined fashion boutique) overflows with people sipping *fino* straight from the barrel and snacking on payoyo cheese, *chicharrones* (fried pork belly) and other divine *gaditano* (from Cádiz) tapas.

The team often hosts sherry tastings, too. Other unmissable *tabancos* include Las Banderillas (loved for its meaty tapas) and El Pasaje (with twice-daily flamenco performances).

Calle Algarve 35, Jerez;
www.facebook.com/tabanco.
plateros; closed Sun lunchtime

01 Wine harvesters shouldering *palomino* grapes

02 Helena Rivero, Bodegas Tradición

03 Cádiz' Sherry Triangle has been producing wines since Phoenician times

04 Michelin-starred Aponiente pushes boundaries with its creative dishes

05 La Carboná restaurant is housed inside a 19th-century wine cellar

⓸ LA CARBONÁ

Within a revitalised 19th-century wine cellar, La Carboná is a wonderfully imaginative celebration of *jerezano* cuisine by top local chef Javier Muñoz, often called *El Chef del Sherry* (The Sherry Chef). "At La Carboná we drink and eat wines," says Muñoz. "Our cooking is based on respect for fresh, quality local produce from our *tierra* (land)." This might mean red *almadraba* tuna (often described as the world's best), olive oils and cheeses from the Cádiz mountains, or Sanlúcar's king prawns.

"We also take advantage of the vine's other gifts – for example, using the *velo de flor* [a layer of yeast] for home-baked bread each day. And our dedicated sherry menu has over 300 local wines," says Muñoz. All of which means the fabulous sherry-pairing menu is the way to go.
Calle San Francisco de Paula 2, Jerez; www.lacarbona.com; closed Tue

⓸ BODEGAS GUTIÉRREZ COLOSÍA

A switched-on family team heads up this intimate, innovative winery in El Puerto de Santa María, the lively southernmost stop on the Sherry Triangle. Gutiérrez Colosía only began selling its wines in the 1990s, but its roots go back to 1838.

On a small-group guided tour (no drop-ins; recommended after-dark itineraries in summer), you'll travel through the world of *fino, amontillado, oloroso, palo cortado* and *Pedro Ximénez* sherries beneath soaring wood-beamed ceilings and sweeping arches. Afterwards, visit the bodega's creative sherry-and-tapas bar, Bespoke, just a few steps away.
Avenida Bajamar 40, El Puerto de Santa María; www.gutierrez colosia.com

⓹ APONIENTE

Andalucía's only three-Michelin-star restaurant is the brainchild of Jerez-born chef Ángel León, who is credited with elevating local seafood to a boundary-pushing art form. From the moment you stroll into the stylishly converted 17th-century tidal mill, this vision of sustainable culinary creativity is pure sensory overload.

Signature dishes from *El Chef del Mar* (The Chef of the Sea) include plankton tarte tatin and Atlantic tuna belly. If you're set on a particular date, book several weeks ahead. Or try Aponiente's informal sister restaurant La Taberna del Chef del Mar as an alternative – it's run by León's wife, Marta Girón. *Calle Francisco Cossi Ochoa, El Puerto de Santa María; www. aponiente.com; closed Dec-Feb*

06 MERCADO DE ABASTOS DE SANLÚCAR

Sanlúcar de Barrameda is an ancient town at the mouth of the Guadalquivir River, now known for its dazzling yet down-to-earth food scene and an Atlantic breeze that brings a salt-tanged edge to the local variety of sherry, *manzanilla*. Get a taste of where it all begins at the meticulously restored 18th-century fresh-produce market, on the edge of the historical Barrio Alto. Plump tomatoes, zesty Seville oranges,

artisanal Grazalema cheeses, Huelva strawberries, fragrant parsley and fresh Andalucian seafood beckon from the stalls, which swing into action around 8am. If you want to tour the market with an expert, join one of the excellent guided food-and-sherry tours with Sanlúcar Smile (www.sanlucarsmile.com), which include a *mercado* stop.

The market is just off the main Plaza del Cabildo, where Sanlúcar's most celebrated tapas bars await; don't miss *tortillitas de camarones* (shrimp fritters) at Casa Balbino or *papas aliñás* (vinegar-dressed potato salad with tuna) at Barbiana. *Calle Bretones, Sanlúcar de Barrameda; closed afternoons & Sun*

07 BODEGAS HIDALGO-LA GITANA

Founded in 1792, this evocative bodega still produces the 'La Gitana' *manzanilla* that first made its name. Now run by the eighth generation of the same family, it's a beautiful place to explore on an

expert-guided tour, sipping sherries as you wander past barrels stacked three-rows high. In summer, there are inspired after-dark tours, and sunset tasting sessions among the vines outside Sanlúcar. The elegant in-house restaurant EntreBotas, set on a bougainvillea-fringed patio, is worth a visit in its own right: *manzanilla*-dressed prawns and grilled *almadraba* tuna are among chef José Luis Tallafigo's signatures. *Calle Banda de la Playa, El Puerto de Santa María; www. bodegashidalgolagitana.com; closed Sun*

08 BAJO DE GUÍA

Just across the Guadalquivir River from Parque Nacional de Doñana, this 19th-century *sanluqueño* fishing neighbourhood has grown into a beloved gastronomic boulevard packed with fish-and-seafood restaurants, all with sunny terraces overlooking the beach.

Family-run kitchens going back decades cook up Sanlúcar classics such as *arroz caldoso* (soupy seafood rice) and grilled local langoustines, along with deliciously fresh fish. You can't really go wrong, but standouts include Casa Bigote (try the salt-baked fish of the day), Poma (for its langoustines and rices) and Avante Claro (superb fish-for-sharing with Sanlúcar potatoes). *Bajo de Guía*

WHERE TO STAY
HOTEL BODEGA TÍO PEPE
Jerez's seductive sherry hotel is tucked into a 150-year-old building within the renowned bodega González-Byass, with a twinkling rooftop pool. Vintage furnishings fill the 27 boutique-feel rooms, and days kick off with home-cooked *gaditano* breakfasts in the hotel's bougainvillea-filled gardens.
www.tiopepe.com

LA ALCOBA DEL AGUA
Set across two creatively converted townhouses in central Sanlúcar, La Alcoba combines stylish white-and-red design with a welcoming vibe, an Andalucian patio and a salt-water lap pool.
www.laalcobadel agua.com

WHAT TO DO
PARQUE NACIONAL DE DOÑANA
One of Europe's wildest spaces, this 601-sq-km (232-sq-mile) national park protects the endangered Iberian lynx,

as well as wild boar, deer, shimmering wetlands and 400 bird species. Sanlúcar-based Visitas Doñana runs guided 2½-hour 4x4 excursions.
www.visitasdonana.com

ANNIE B'S SPANISH KITCHEN
For a hands-on gastronomic jaunt, join Scottish chef and sherry expert Annie Manson for a tapas tour, a wine-tasting excursion, or a

cooking course in her adopted home of Vejer de la Frontera, south of Jerez.
www.anniebspain.com

ALCÁZAR DE JEREZ
A rare relic of Andalucía's Almohad era, Jerez's rambling fortress has Alhambra-flavoured gardens, sky-lit Moorish baths, a 12th-century mosque and a beautiful rose-walled baroque palace.

CELEBRATIONS
Spring gets going with Sanlúcar's Feria de la Manzanilla and El Puerto's Fiestas del Vino Fino, while Jerez honours all things wine with its September Fiestas de la Vendimia, a two-week harvest party with traditional grape-treading. Held each February/March, the Festival de Jerez is the world's premier flamenco celebration.

GET THERE
Tenerife has two airports. The biggest is Tenerife South, served by major airlines as well as budget operators. Renting a car makes it easier to reach off-the-radar places, but buses connect the big towns and resorts; inexpensive shuttles make airport transfers a breeze.

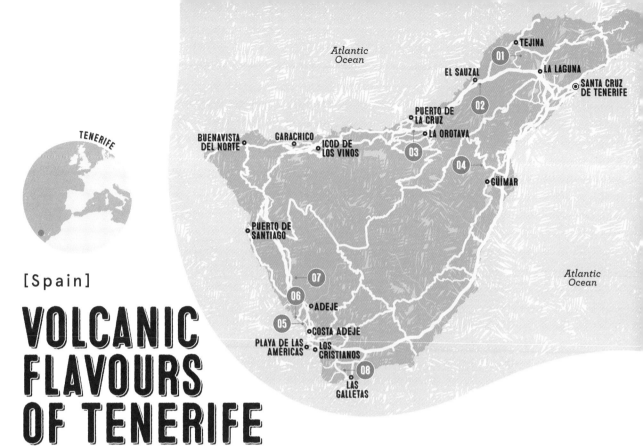

Atlantic
Ocean

TENERIFE

01 TEJINA

EL SAUZAL

LA LAGUNA

SANTA CRUZ
DE TENERIFE

02

PUERTO DE
LA CRUZ

LA OROTAVA

BUENAVISTA
DEL NORTE

GARACHICO

ICOD DE
LOS VINOS

03

04

GÜÍMAR

PUERTO DE
SANTIAGO

Atlantic
Ocean

07

06 ADEJE

05

COSTA ADEJE

PLAYA DE LAS
AMÉRICAS

LOS
CRISTIANOS

08

LAS
GALLETAS

[Spain]

VOLCANIC FLAVOURS OF TENERIFE

Defined by its fiery geology and closer to Africa than Spain, Tenerife is riding new gourmet waves as it embraces its culinary roots with creativity and flair.

If you still think of Tenerife as a fly-and-flop destination for winter sun, cheap booze and all-day English breakfasts – amigo, things have changed. Tenerife might not immediately spring to mind when you start searching for gourmet breaks but, trust us, this island is going places in the kitchen.

In recent years, the food scene here has been quietly smouldering like Mt Teide, the 3715m (12,188ft) volcano that presides over the island. And it's now ready to erupt, with each year bringing a glitter of new Michelin stars. Chefs are getting imaginative with locally farmed and fished produce, their menus singing gustily of island and season, mountain and sea.

The specialities here are boat-fresh seafood and wines from volcanic vines. Tenerife's subtropical microclimate is perfect for growing fruits you'll rarely find elsewhere in Europe – bananas, mangoes, papayas, guavas, even coffee. Spice? You'll find it

in *mojo*, a feisty and highly addictive sauce made with bell peppers, garlic and cumin, coriander (in the green version) or chillies (the red version). This never tastes better than when dolloped on *papas arrugadas*, the wrinkly potatoes Tinerfeños, as locals are known, are so crazy about.

While top-of-their-game chefs are raising the bar by riffing modern on Canarian produce in elaborate tasting menus, there is still much to be said for the island's humble *guachinches* – one-pan pop-up restaurants that open for three months a year, where simple *comida casera* (home cooking) is paired with generous quantities of house wine.

Starting in the rugged north, this trail takes you through the island's volcano-topped, mountain-buckled heart to the surf-smashed south coast, giving you a taste of everything that makes Tenerife's cuisine so utterly unique.

01 Hiking volcano paths
in Teide National Park

02 New-wave
guachinche cuisine at
La Bola de Jorge Bosch

03 Terraced vines at
Bodegas Monje

02

01 LA BOLA DE JORGE BOSCH

"My favourite dish on the menu
is my mother's *rancho*, a soup of
thick noodles, meat and chickpeas.
Each and every bite takes me back
to my childhood," says chef-owner
Jorge Bosch Barrera, who has
elevated the *guachinche* to new
gourmet heights at this old-school
restaurant in northeastern Tenerife.

Revealing a profound love of
place and playing up ingredients
from the family farm, the menu is
a feast of clean, bright, modern
Canarian flavours: fish *churros*
dunked in mango mayo, fresh
tuna tartare with Canarian avocado,
and smoked goat cheese with
mojo and *gofio* (roasted grain)
crumble. Food is served here
with warmth and generosity, either
in the rustic interior or palm-
fringed garden.
*Calle El Lomo 18, Tegueste; https://
chefjorgebosch.com; closed Mon
& Tue*

02 BODEGAS MONJE

"The *terroir* in Tenerife is unique
because of the volcanic soil –
within 600m [1968ft] of the winery,
I can make 16 different varieties of
wine," says director, wine-maker
and oenologist Felipe Monje at
his family bodega, 15km (9 miles)
southwest of Tegueste.

The view from the terrace is
astonishing: vineyards stagger
down lava-rippled slopes, a
cloud-wreathed Teide pops up
on the horizon and beyond the
Atlantic spreads out like a blue silk
sheet. The Monje family have been
harvesting, pruning, fermenting
and bottling here since 1750.
Here you get a proper sense of the
wine-making process from start
to finish, with guided tours of the
vines and must-scented, oak-
barrel-lined cellars.

Make a day of it by hooking onto
a *mojo* workshop before lunch
in the restaurant or a picnic in
the vines. Monje's signature reds
(made with the Listán negro grape)
burst with aromas of truffle and
blackberry. Upgrade your tasting
to try the winery's one-of-a-
kind *crianza* wines, aged in an
underwater winery in the Atlantic.
*Calle Cruz de Leandro 36, El
Sauzal; https://bodegasmonje.
com; restaurant closed Mon*

03 ORIGEN CAFÉ

You might well wonder what's so special about a shopping centre cafe, but it is worth seeking out this indie one on the outskirts of La Orotava. Staff bubble over with enthusiasm for good java and – most crucially – will prepare you a delicious cup made with beans from nearby Finca Sanssouci, home to the world's northernmost coffee.

Given that Tenerife coffee is produced only in tiny batches and never leaves these shores, this is a rare chance to try the island's sun-dried, naturally fermented coffee, which is well-rounded, smooth and sweetly fragrant. Ordinarily associated with more tropical climes, coffee has grown on Tenerife since 1788, when King Carlos III of Spain introduced the first plants to the island.
Centro Comercial La Villa, La Orotava; https://origencafe.es; closed Sun

04 BODEGAS FERRERA

"I talk to my vineyards and though they don't reply, I know they understand me," says winemaker Carmen Gloria Ferrera. In the cool Güímar Valley, a twisty hour's drive south through the mountains. Tomás Ferrera founded the winery in the 1940s, raising the dry-stone walls, ploughing the land by mule and tenderly hand-planting each vine.

Now the bodega is winging its way into the 21st century with organic wines that taste intensely of Tenerife. Try the straw-gold, dry white Listán blanco, with aromas of apricot and banana, and the deep Syrah red, full of ripe red fruit and with a touch of vanilla. For the full-on experience, sign up for a sunset lava walk, followed by dinner with wine pairing and stargazing.
Calle Norte 44, Arafo; https://bodegasferrera.es; closed Sun

05 NUB

Heading into ritzy Costa Adeje, Michelin-starred NUB at hotel Bahía del Duque is the vision of Chilean-Italian couple Fernanda Fuentes-Cárdenas and Andrea Bernardi, who found their spiritual home in Tenerife. Served in an art-slung, rustic-chic space looking out over the palm fronds to sea, the food reflects their distinct roots and

cheese-making process and see the feeding and milking of their herd of 1000 goats. The icing on the cake is getting to taste the dairy's exceptional goat cheeses, from fresh varieties as light as a cloud to more pungent semi-cured ones smoked, studded with figs, sprinkled with paprika or macerated in wine. They make terrific gifts.
Tijoco Bajo; www.quesos montesdeoca.com

references the astounding bounty of produce found on the island. Dishes appear deceptively simple – goat cheese and truffle fritters, red prawn on toasted brioche, corn crème brûlée with aged onion-and-herb ceviche, for example – but they are all flawlessly executed and presented with an artist's eye.
Avenida de Bruselas, Costa Adeje; https://english.nubrestaurante. com; closed Sun & Mon

06 EL RINCÓN DE JUAN CARLOS

A stone-skim north, there's another Michelin star at this slickly contemporary restaurant on the fifth floor of the Royal Hideaway Corales Beach resort. It's headed up by Canarian chef Juan Carlos Padrón, whose passion for cooking evolved from a childhood spent in his father's kitchen. In a white, coolly minimalist restaurant, with glass walls framing every colour

shift in sea and sky, Padrón delivers inimitable flavours full of nuance with finesse.

The tasting menu adds sophistication to primary ingredients in dishes such as corn mille-feuille with toasted buttercream and black garlic, sea lettuce patty with cod, and blackberry sorbet with smoked yoghurt, beetroot and Sichuan pepper cream. Allow three hours for the experience.
Avenida Virgen de Guadalupe 21, Adeje; https://web. elrincondejuancarlos.com; closed Sun & Mon

07 QUESERÍA MONTESDEOCA

So you think you know goat cheese? Prepare for your palate to be surprised by the unique varieties at this award-winning dairy, a quick hop north. For the inside scoop, take a guided tour of the farm to learn more about the

08 FINCA LAS MARGARITAS

Canarian bananas are rarely found overseas today, but once they were a major export – and indeed it is this fruit trade that gave London's Canary Wharf its name in the 1930s. Smaller and sweeter than a regular banana, the *plátano de Canarias* ripens for six months rather than the usual three, giving it a more intense flavour.

You'll learn all this and much more at this finca, where you can take a self-guided tour at 10am, 11am or noon, through the fronds of row after row of banana trees. Tours conclude with a tasting of banana wines, jams, sweets and liqueurs in the plantation shop.
Las Galletas; https:// lasmargaritasbananaexperience. com; closed Sun

WHERE TO STAY
BANANA PARADISE
Overlooking banana
fronds and the dark
half-moon of El Bollullo
beach, Banana Paradise
in La Orotava has
tranquil holiday cottage
accommodation,
with a hot tub and
barbecue area.
*http://banana-paradise.
canary-islands-
hotels.com*

**BODEGAS
FERRERA FINCA**
Spend a starry night
among the vines at
Bodegas Ferrera's eco-
friendly finca. It sits on
a hill at almost 1000
metres (3281ft) above
sea level – you can
imagine the views.
*https://finca-ecologica-
ferrera.amenitiz.io*

WHAT TO DO
**PARQUE NACIONAL
DEL TEIDE**
Dive headfirst into
Tenerife's wilderness on
a romp through volcanic
Parque Nacional del
Teide, with its striking
lava formations, craters
and rust-red canyons.
The big hike is a climb

to Pico del Teide (elev
3715m/12,188ft), Spain's
highest peak, which has
out-of-this-world views
of La Gomera, La Palma
and El Hierro shimmering
across the Atlantic. By
night, the park dazzles
with stargazing potential,
with the Milky Way and
many constellations
visible with the naked eye.

CELEBRATIONS
CARNIVAL
In February, island capital
Santa Cruz goes wild with
glitzy costumes, Latino
beats, parades and a
feast of street food, from
giant paellas to Canarian
ropa vieja ('old clothes'),
a hearty beef stew with
garbanzo beans and
tomatoes.

FIESTA DE SAN ANDRÉS
The wine-producing
north celebrates
with this fiesta on
29 November. It's an
opportunity to try
new wines, along with
roasted chestnuts and
island specialities such
as sweet potatoes,
cherne (grouper) and
gofio bread.

GET THERE
International flights
arrive at İstanbul Airport
on the European shore,
or Sabiha Gökçen Airport
on the Asian shore.
Modern airport buses
transport passengers
to Taksim, from where
public transport options
service most parts of
the city.

EBCİN SPICE CENTER
CURRY

EBCİN SPICE CENTER
STAR ANISE

EBCİN SPICE CENTER
MIXED PEPPERCORN

EBCİN SPICE CENTER
DRIED VEGATABLE

EBCİN SPICE CENTER
CARDOMOM

İSTANBUL

The map shows locations with numbered markers:

KURTULUŞ — 08
ORTAKÖY
YILDIZ
BEŞIKTAŞ
TAKSIM
Bosphorus Strait
05 — 06 KABATAŞ
BEYOĞLU
FINDIKLI
07
ÜSKÜDAR
KARAKÖY
Galata Bridge
01 — 02
EMINÖNÜ
HAREM
Grand Bazaar
SULTANAHMET
HAYDARPAŞA
KADIKÖY — 03
04

[Turkey]

İSTANBUL'S CULINARY CROSSROADS

Beyond the kebab shops, visitors to Turkey's dynamic culture capital will find an innovative dining scene championing regional specialities and local wine.

The national capital in all but name, İstanbul is Turkey's largest city and greatest treasure. The sum of its wildly disparate parts – it has been ruled by pagan despots, Christian emperors, Muslim sultans and revolutionary nationalists – this is a city like no other, one with a rich multicultural culture and a comfortable acceptance of its unique location at the geographical point where Europe meets Asia.

Thanks to its past, İstanbul is crammed with evocative buildings from the Roman, Byzantine and Ottoman periods. But the city's cuisine is also high on the list of attractions. İstanbul's food draws on the rich and diverse bounty of the surrounding seas and agricultural lands, as well as the varied culinary influences that have been brought to the city by waves of regional and European migration over the centuries.

It's these influences that make eating and drinking here such an exhilarating exercise. There are fish dishes

and *pide* (Turkish pizza) from the Black Sea region, pungent grilled liver dishes from Thrace, herb-laden *mezes* from the Aegean coast, succulent and spicy kebaps from central Anatolia and baklava studded with plump pistachios from Gaziantep near the Syrian border. These dishes are just a few of the regional specialities that you will encounter here, served from street stalls, in no-frills eateries and at fine-dining destinations. Talented chefs are celebrating seasonality and putting their individual and often quirky twists on classic dishes from around the country.

Şarap (wine) is also a drawcard. The city's proximity to Thrace and Marmara means that vintages from the growing number of lauded boutique wineries in those regions are fixtures on many wine lists, often joined by equally impressive Aegean wines. But the nation's signature drink is *rakı* (an aniseed-flavoured spirit) – all excellent matches for İstanbul's truly great cuisine.

01 SPICE BAZAAR (MISIR ÇARŞISI)

Merchants, traders and customers have been flocking to this atmospheric bazaar since its construction in the 17th century and the building retains much of its original Ottoman-era splendour. A wealth of local produce is on offer: Cankurtaran Gida at number 33 is known for its amber-hued honey from the east of Turkey, its pungent pastrami from Cappadocia and its cheeses from every corner of the country; Malatya Pazarı at number 44 for its delectable dried apricots from the eastern city of the same name: and Arıfoğlu at number 31 for its saffron, herbs, oils and freshly roasted spices. Directly opposite the bazaar's eastern gate, on Hasırcılar Caddesi, is the wonderfully aromatic historic coffee roastery Kurukahveci Mehmet Efendi.
Eminönü Meydanı

02 ALİ MUHİDDİN HACI BEKİR

Be it studded with nuts, fragrant with rosewater or tangy with lemon, the sugar-dusted sweet treat known here as *lokum* and elsewhere as Turkish delight is a national treasure. It's also a wonderful souvenir to take home. When Hacı Bekir Effendi established his first store selling *lokum* on this site near the Spice Bazaar in 1777, he soon gained a coterie of loyal customers including Sultan Mahmud II, who appointed him chief confectioner to the Ottoman court. Customers make their choice from the wide variety of flavours on offer, but the classics are *fıstıklı* (pistachio), *bademlı* (almond), *cevizli* (walnut), *nanelı* (lemon) and *güllü* (rosewater). You can also order a *karışık* (mixed) assortment.
Hamidiye Caddesi 33, Eminönü; www.hacibekir.com

03 KADIKÖY PRODUCE MARKET (KADIKÖY PAZARI)

There are a number of good reasons to venture out of central İstanbul and head across the Sea of Marmara to the Asian suburb of Kadıköy, not least being the scenic ferry ride from Eminönü

01 İstanbul's bazaars are famous for their fragrant spices

02 Street snacks are an İstanbul trademark

03 Kadıköy's fresh produce market is the city's best

04 Turkish delight, flavoured with rose water, is a national treasure

05 Hagia Sophia mosque at sunrise

or Karaköy. On arrival, Kadıköy's second enticement – its famed fresh produce market – is conveniently located just across from the ferry dock, in the streets around Yağlıkçı Ismail Sokak. Known for the stalls selling fresh fish, fruit and vegetables, this is a wonderful place to see the breadth and quality of Turkey's home-grown produce as well as the glistening seasonal catches that come from its waters.

Fast-food stands sell tasty street food including freshly baked *simits* (sesame-studded bread rings), *midye dolma* (stuffed mussels) and *lahmacun* (a tasty oven-baked flatbread topped with tomato paste, spiced minced meat and fresh herbs).

04 ÇIYA SOFRASI

At the heart of Kadıköy Produce Market, Çiya Sofrası is one of İstanbul's most beloved foodie haunts. This frills-free *sofrası* (dining table) was established in 1998 by owner-chef Musa Dağdeviren to showcase regional recipes from Anatolia and the Eastern Mediterranean. "Slowly but surely, the seeds we sow for the revival of Turkish culinary traditions are growing," he says. Despite having become something of a celebrity courtesy of his appearance on Netflix's *Chef's Table*, he can often be spotted at the front counter, where soups, pilafs, salads and daily specials are displayed.
Güneşlibahçe Sokak 43, Kadıköy; www.ciya.com.tr

05 HAYVORE

Off the main thoroughfare of İstiklal Caddesi, Hayvore is a notable example of the traditional Turkish restaurant type known as a *lokanta*. Geared towards local workers, *lokantas* serve affordable, ready-made food warmed in bains-marie.

Specialising in dishes from the Black Sea region, Hayvore offers treats such as *muhlama* and *kuymak* (thick cheese fondues) for breakfast and *hamsili pilav* (oven-baked rice encased in fresh anchovies) at lunch. The chefs are also known for their tasty *mücver* (courgette/zucchini fritters topped with yoghurt) and decadent *laz böreği* (flaky dessert pastry with custard and hazelnuts).
Turnacıbaşı Sokak 4, Beyoğlu; www.hayvore.com.tr

06 Neolokal serves up contemporary riffs on Anatolian dishes

07 Sensory overload at the Grand Bazaar

06 ZÜBEYİR OCAKBAŞI

You may have eaten a kebap before, but you are unlikely to have eaten one as succulent and tasty as those served at Zübeyir. The kebaps are expertly grilled on a copper-hooded *ocakbaşı* (charcoal grill), which dominates the rustic downstairs dining room at this decades-old city institution. Choose one of the chicken, lamb or beef dishes, considered some of the best in the city.
Bekar Sokak 28, Beyoğlu; https://zubeyirocakbasi.com.tr

07 NEOLOKAL

Chef Maksut Aşkar is one of a growing number of İstanbul-based chefs seeking to document, refine and celebrate the traditional dishes of the Anatolia region. The menu at his fine-dining restaurant Neolokal features contemporary riffs on village and regional dishes and the results are as good to gaze upon as they are to eat.

Many of the ingredients used are listed on the Slow Food Foundation's Ark of Taste, so diners are introduced to treats such as aged kaşar cheese from northeastern Turkey, mulberry molasses from Eğin in Erzincan and *haviar* (dried egg sacks of the grey mullet) produced in Dalyan on the southwestern coast.

The extensive wine list is equally enticing, focusing on vintages from boutique wineries in Thrace, Marmara and the Aegean.
SALT Galata, Bankalar Caddesi 11, Beyoğlu; www.neolokal.com; closed Sun & Mon

08 KURTULUŞ COOKING CLASS

İstanbul's neighbourhoods are as diverse as they are multitudinous. Rich repositories of ethnic and religious traditions, they underpin the city's exhilarating cultural diversity. Kurtuluş, north of Beyoğlu, has traditionally been home to members of the Greek and Armenian communities and its reputation as a centre for great food is well deserved. These cooking classes, led by former restaurateur and local resident Aysin, start in Kurtuluş' main shopping strip, where participants shop for ingredients, before heading to Aysin's home kitchen to learn how to cook six traditional Turkish dishes that are enjoyed over lunch.
https://culinarybackstreets.com

WHERE TO STAY
MARMARA PERA
In the heart of Beyoğlu's boisterous eating and entertainment action, this hotel offers comfortable rooms and serves an excellent breakfast in its ground-floor buffet. However, the greatest inducement to staying here is the glamorous rooftop bar with spectacular views. Also here is Mikla, the only restaurant in the city to feature on the San Pellegrino list of the world's best restaurants. www.themarmarahotels.com/en/hotels/pera

WHAT TO DO
GRAND BAZAAR (KAPALI ÇARŞI)
An essential stop on every visitor's itinerary, this labyrinthine Ottoman-era marketplace in the old city is home to atmospheric *bedestens* (warehouses), hidden *hans* (inns) and a network of vaulted laneways lined with stalls selling tempting wares including carpets and rugs, jewellery, bathwares, homewares and textiles. There

are also many simple restaurants and fast-food stands secreted within and around the walls of the bazaar – a good way to discover these is to take the 'Backstreets of the Bazaar Quarter' tour operated by Culinary Backstreets (see Kurtuluş cooking class, stop 8).

CELEBRATIONS
RAMAZAN (RAMADAN)
During this Islamic holy month, observant Muslims eschew food and drink from dawn to dusk before breaking their fast at a meal known as *iftar*, which is often enjoyed with family, friends and neighbours at communal tables in specially erected tents throughout the city. While these gatherings are only for Muslims observing the rules of Ramazan, many restaurants and cafes in the city offer special Ramazan meals that can be ordered by all customers.

INDEX

First Edition
Published in May 2023 by Lonely Planet Global Limited
CRN 54153
www.lonelyplanet.com
ISBN 978 1 8386 9991 8
© Lonely Planet 2022
Printed in Malaysia
10 9 8 7 6 5 4 3 2 1

Managing Director Piers Pickard
Associate Publisher Robin Barton
Commissioning Editor Lorna Parkes
Editor Clifton Wilkinson
Art Direction Jo Dovey
Indexer Bridget Blair
Cartographer Rachel Imeson
Image Research Heike Bohnstengel
Print Production Nigel Longuet

Authors: Isabel Albiston (Northern Ireland), Eleanor Aldridge (France), Alexis Averbuck (Greece), Alice Barnes-Brown (Greece), Joe Bindloss (Finland, Sweden, UK), Cristian Bonetto (Italy), John Brunton (Belgium, France, Italy), Stuart Butler (Spain), Amanda Canning (Croatia), Daniel James Clark (Portugal), Richard Franks (UK), Ethan Gelber (France), Georgina Lawton (Portugal), Virginia Maxwell (Turkey), Anna Melville-James (Denmark), Isabella Noble (Spain), Mary Novakovich (France), Lorna Parkes (Lithuania, Switzerland), Kevin Raub (Italy), Brendan Sainsbury (Italy), Laura Sanders (Estonia), Daniel Stables (UK), Nathan James Thomas (Albania, Poland), Orla Thomas (Spain), Kerry Walker (Austria, France, Germany, Norway, Spain, UK), Nicola Williams (France)

Cover images: Daniel Alford | Lonely Planet; Sarah Coghill | Lonely Planet; Susan Wright | Lonely Planet; Lena Granefelt | Lonely Planet; Helen Cathcart | Lonely Planet; Adrienne Pitts | Lonely Planet; Pete Seaward | Lonely Planet

Lonely Planet Global Limited

Digital Depot, Roe Lane (off Thomas St), Digital Hub, Dublin 8, D08 TCV4 IRELAND

STAY IN TOUCH lonelyplanet.com/contact

Although the authors and Lonely Planet have taken all reasonable care in preparing this book, we make no warranty about the accuracy or completeness of its content and, to the maximum extent permitted, disclaim all liability from its use.

Paper in this book is certified against the Forest Stewardship Council™ standards. FSC™ promotes environmentally responsible, socially beneficial and economically viable management of the world's forests.